Praise for *The Church in the Public*

"In this fresh take on public and political theology, Ilsup Ahn offers a proposal for the formation of a church that is historically aware, present in the current moment, and committed to alleviating suffering 'in a cruel and indifferent age.' Insisting that a church that seeks to be relevant and transformative must reckon with the histories and impact of colonialism and neoliberalism, Ahn pushes the boundaries of the church's sense of its presence and mission in the public. By proposing a church invested in building the coalitions necessary to dismantle oppressive structures, Ahn's efforts renew the Great Commission as both eschatological hope and present agenda for the essential work of justice-making in the world today. This volume invites the reader to deep theological considerations of what it means to be (and create) a public church, while also providing a blueprint for relationship building toward effective and transformational public action."

—María Teresa Dávila, visiting associate professor of practice, Merrimack College

"Ahn's book is a clarion call for churches to carry out their mission by engaging in rhizomatic politics for the least among us. Challenging traditional notions of church and state, it offers fresh insights for political organizing to combat cynicism, inertia, and pessimism. A prophetic text for our critical time!"

—Kwok Pui-lan, Dean's Professor in Systematic Theology, Candler School of Theology, Emory University

The Church in the Public

THE CHURCH IN THE PUBLIC

A POLITICS OF ENGAGEMENT FOR A CRUEL AND INDIFFERENT AGE

ILSUP AHN

Fortress Press
Minneapolis

THE CHURCH IN THE PUBLIC

A Politics of Engagement for a Cruel and Indifferent Age

Cover image: iStock/rolfst
Cover design: John M. Lucas

Print ISBN: 978-1-5064-6796-2
eBook ISBN: 978-1-5064-6797-9

To Jaeyeon

CONTENTS

ACKNOWLEDGMENTS

Since the early 2010s, I have wanted to write this book, *The Church in the Public*, although I had no clear picture of what it would be like. I knew, though, that it would be about what it means for a church to become the church it is called to be in today's world. During this time, slowly yet surely, I came to a sense that there is a hole in the big picture of the Western church in the contemporary world, and this has to do with its hesitance about, ignorance about, or inability to address what social thinkers call structural and systemic injustice in this world. As I engaged more in scholarly research in the field of Christian social ethics, especially immigration justice, financial ethics, ecological ethics, and other structural and systemic issues, this hole became larger and starker to me. In some sense, my feelings of this hole were not new; even back in the days when I was a high schooler, I grew up in the church hearing frequent sermons from the pulpit in which the pastor deplored the holes of social change that were not addressed by the church. This book is thus a deferred act to tackle this hole from earlier in my life.

Doubtlessly, without the direct and indirect help from others, I would not have been able to finish this book. I wrote it during the Covid-19 pandemic, which inadvertently unveiled various aspects of the deep-seated and age-old structural injustices of our world. And yet during this time, I had the luxury of sabbatical leave and was able to write this book. For this reason, while I express my gratitude to North Park University, which granted me a half-year sabbatical, I cannot begin this book without acknowledging my unsettled debt to many "frontline workers," whose sacrifice enabled me to sustain and write this book during a precarious time.

This book would not have been possible without the hearty support from my colleagues in the Brandel Library of North Park University. I requested countless numbers of interlibrary loan materials, and they helped me by providing all the needed sources through their tireless work. I would like to offer my deepest appreciation to my editor at Fortress Press, Ryan Hemmer, who kindly walked through all the processes with me from the beginning stage to the final publication. I also give my heartfelt gratitude to my book's project manager, Elvis Ramirez, who helped me tremendously in the final stages of revising and editing. I must gratefully recognize my personal debt to four church leaders who graciously responded to my request to interview them. Their stories were indispensable for this project. I had a series of interviews with them via Zoom in the spring of 2021. These four church leaders are Rev. Dr. Liz Theoharis, the cochair of the Poor People's Campaign and the director of the Kairos Center for Religions, Rights, and Social Justice at Union Theological Seminary in New York City; Rev. Dr. Michael Nabors, the senior pastor of Second Baptist Church in Evanston, Illinois, and the president of the Evanston/Northshore National Association for the Advancement of Colored People; Rev. John Fife, the former senior pastor of Southside Presbyterian Church in Tucson, Arizona, and a founding leader of the Sanctuary Movement; and Rev. Kaji Douša, the senior pastor of Park Avenue Christian Church and the chair of the New Sanctuary Coalition in New York City.

Finally, and above all, I would like to offer my deepest gratitude to my parents, Byungwon Ahn and Nanggeun Suh. Their everyday prayers and constant emotional and spiritual support have always been strong lifelines for me. It is impossible to disremember my debt of gratitude to my spouse, Jaeyeon Lucy Chung, and my two sons, Daniel and Joshua. I had many good conversations and discussions with Jaeyeon regarding the various ideas this book tries to convey to the public. The title of this book, *The Church in the Public*, was her suggestion after a long yet exceedingly enjoyable talk in our backyard on a hot summer day. I am grateful to dedicate this book to my lifelong companion, Jaeyeon.

INTRODUCTION

When the state fails to provide justice to its citizens as they are victimized by structural injustice and systemic violence, what should the church do? What if the state becomes an agent of that victimization rather than its cure? Such questions are not implausible, even in democratic societies. In fact, no governing authority has ever fully resolved structural injustice and systemic violence in its society. Neither has the church. But what is structural injustice? What is systemic violence? While academics and activists often use such terms, only rarely are they defined. Let me offer here a brief definition of what they mean. Structural injustice is a distinctive type of injustice caused by unfair rules, skewed cultural norms, and historical legacies, which typically entail an accumulative and perennial negative impact on victimized social groups of typically racial, political, or cultural minorities. Systemic violence is intrinsically interlinked with structural injustice because the victims of structural injustice experience their social sufferings in conjunction with systemized oppression, discrimination, and domination, which cannot be effectively tackled without changing the structural and systemic aspects of society.

What possible relationship is there between structural injustice and the church? The influential French social philosopher, historian, and literary critic René Girard says, "We are not Christian enough." But what does this mean? Not Christian enough for what? What must we do to become Christian enough? According to Girard, although Christianity has uncovered the core structure of what he calls mimetic violence (e.g., a scapegoat mechanism) and provided an antidote to it, it is failing now at preventing the world from falling into an apocalyptic situation. He writes, "Christianity is the only religion that has foreseen its own failure. This prescience is known as the apocalypse." Girard adamantly argues that at the center of this historical trajectory of the apocalypse lies the problem of violence: "Indeed, it is in the apocalyptic texts that the word of God is most forceful, repudiating mistakes that are entirely the fault of humans, who are less and less inclined to acknowledge the mechanisms of their violence."[1]

When Girard writes that "we are not Christian enough," he also implicates the church. If we are not Christian enough, then our church is not churchly enough as well. It is not clear, however, what the church should do if it wants to be churchly enough. Girard does not tell us what it means to be Christian enough. If "Christianity truly demystifies religion because it points out the error on which archaic religion is based: the effectiveness of the divinized scapegoat," then one can certainly ask, Why can't Christianity demystify the problem of violence? His answer to this critical question is that although Christianity unearths the falsity of the scapegoat mechanism, it stops short of resolving the problem of the mimetic rivalry itself. He thus writes, "*When sacrifice disappears, all that remains is mimetic rivalry, and it escalates to extremes.*"[2]

Why does the church stop short of resolving the problem of the mimetic rivalry itself? Why does it fail to address the problems of structural injustice and systemic violence that are intrinsically linked to the extremities of escalating mimetic rivalry? We can answer this question from different angles, but I would focus here on an ecclesial reason: the church's self-exile or self-retreat from the realm of the public to that of the private and the local. What is the result of this self-exile or self-retreat? The church effectively disappears from the public realm. It has been effectively reduced to a geographical or locational entity. The invisible wall between the church and the state, between the ecclesial space and the political world, between private faith and public conviction is still in place. The most troublesome result of the localization of

---

1. René Girard, *Battling to the End: Conversations with Benoît Chantre*, trans. Mary Baker (East Lansing: Michigan State University Press, 2010), x.
2. Girard, 198 (italics in the original).

the ecclesial space and the privatization of Christian faith is the church's neutral and apathetic attitude toward various issues of the rising structural injustice and systemic violence. The localized church has accordingly lost its public voice and status due to its self-exile and self-retreat. Of course, there were some historical exceptions (e.g., the Black church's active leadership during the civil rights movement and the Sanctuary Movement during the 1980s) in which we could find a beacon of hope amid darkness. This book is devoted to amplifying this hope.

In this book, I argue that the reconstruction and reformation of the Western church are not possible without the church's rediscovery of itself as a public church. One of the key aspects of the public church is that its congregants not only know how to engage and deploy its alternative politics but also practice it with other public or nongovernmental organizations to resist and dismantle structural injustice and systemic violence. I call the church's alternative politics "rhizomatic politics." In biology, a rhizome (gingerroot, for example) is "a root-like, underground stem, growing horizontally on or just under the surface of the ground, and capable of producing shoots and roots from its nodes."[3] Let me provide a brief reason, however, as to why I attempt to appropriate the image of a rhizome in developing an alternative model for the church's politics.

First, a rhizome is invisible from the surface of the ground because it exists underground. Metaphorically speaking, while the tree trunk above the surface signifies the visible, official, or formal politics of the state, the rhizomatic movement indicates nonparliamentary yet dynamic underground politics beyond the visible world of state politics. The church historian David D. Daniels III writes, "Under slogans including 'Souls to the Polls,' 'AME Voter Alert,' and 'COGIC Counts,' Black denominations and national bodies such as the Conference of National Black Churches have partnered with civil rights organizations including the NAACP [National Association for the Advancement of Colored People] in a concerted effort to increase

---

3. K. Lee Lerner and Brenda Wilmoth Lerner, eds., *The Gale Encyclopedia of Science*, 5th ed. (Farmington Hills, MI: Gale, 2014), 3765–66, https://link.gale.com/apps/doc/CX3727802082/GVRL.modified?u=npc_wallgren&sid=GVRL.modified&xid=e18323a1.

voter turnout among African Americans."[4] The Black church's voting rights movement exemplifies the underground characteristic of a rhizome.

Second, rhizomes grow horizontally. As subterranean plant organisms that send out roots and shoots from their nodes, rhizomes develop from axillary buds and grow horizontally. The botanical imagery of the horizontal growth of rhizomes offers us a critical-analogical perspective regarding how the church's rhizomatic politics would be planted, nurtured, and extended without necessarily causing social unrest and uprising. What is more, given that rhizomes can spread into separate areas that might be demarcated by walls, fences, or barricades beneath the ground's surface, the church's rhizomatic politics may be formulated in such a way that not only reaches out to the broader constituents of the public but also includes any civic or nongovernmental organizations, crossing over whatever boundaries or demarcations lie between them. For instance, the Sanctuary Movement of the 1980s became a national movement when the Southside Presbyterian Church in Arizona decided to come out to the public by inviting other churches and organizations to join their movement. Over five hundred churches across the country joined at its peak, and soon after, universities, cities, counties, and even states joined by declaring their official sanctuary status for undocumented migrants.

Third, rhizomes regenerate. While rhizomes grow horizontally as they send out roots, they also maintain their capability to allow new shoots to grow upward. The regenerative aspect of rhizomes provides us with a hopeful and transformative image of the church's rhizomatic politics. As an alternative to the state's biopolitics or power politics, the church's rhizomatic politics aims at transforming unjust and dehumanizing social systems and structures, such as the growing wealth gap between the haves and the have-nots. In many cases, since this social and structural transformation requires changing public policies, the church's rhizomatic politics is geared toward those policy changes. The Poor People's Campaign, which Rev. Dr. Martin Luther King Jr. originally planted and is now organized by Rev. Dr. William Barber II

---

4. David D. Daniels III, "The Black Church Has Been Getting 'Souls to the Polls' for More Than 60 Years," *Conversation*, October 30, 2020, https://theconversation.com/the-black-church-has-been-getting-souls-to-the-polls-for-more-than-60-years-145996.

and Rev. Dr. Liz Theoharis, illustrates what such a transformative vision of the church's rhizomatic politics is like. It notes, "From Alaska to Arkansas, the Bronx to the border, people are coming together to confront the interlocking evils of systemic racism, poverty, ecological devastation, militarism and the war economy, and the distorted moral narrative of religious nationalism. We understand that as a nation we are at a critical juncture—that we need a movement that will shift the moral narrative, impact policies and elections at every level of government, and build lasting power for poor and impacted people."[5] If we would see more clearly the structural nature of poverty that is closely interlocked with the neoliberal economy, we would also see better why the world needs the church's rhizomatic politics to alleviate the socioeconomic discrepancies.

The idea of rhizomatic politics is crucial because it substantiates the notion of the "public church." I formulate the idea of the church's rhizomatic politics as an ecclesial answer to the state's failure to provide justice to its constituents, especially those who are victimized by various types of structural injustice and systemic violence. But the church's rhizomatic politics should not be mistaken for the politics of Christendom. Although I formulate the idea of its rhizomatic politics in disagreement with its reactionary recourse to self-exile or self-retreat in a post-Christendom era, I do not endorse a return to Christendom. Its main mission is to care for the "least of these" (Matt 25:45), and the idea of its rhizomatic politics is to keep and maintain that care. I contend that for it to practice rhizomatic politics, it should rediscover and reposition itself *in* the public rather than staying *outside* of it or transcending *above* it.

The early church of the apostolic age was planted and began to grow in a time in which the governing authorities not only failed to provide justice to their constituents, especially those who were at the bottom of society, but also became the agents of structural injustice and systemic violence. Jesus's crucifixion is the unmistakable proof of it. According to the Christian historian Gerald L. Sittser, modeling itself after Jesus's unique identity and mission, the

5. "About the Poor People's Campaign: A National Call for Moral Revival," Poor People's Campaign, accessed February 25, 2022, https://www.poorpeoplescampaign.org/about/.

early church devised what was then known as the Third Way, a phrase that first appeared in a second-century letter to a Roman official named Diognetus. The essence of the Third Way lies in how Christians related to culture. As Sittser describes it, "Christians engaged the culture without excessive compromise and remained separate from the culture without excessive isolation. Christians figured out how to be both faithful and winsome."[6]

The most significant change brought about by the early church and the Third Way of Christian living was the introduction, formation, and dissemination of a new way of building relationships among people based on justice.[7] "They lived differently in the world," Sittser writes. "Christians were known as the people who cared for the 'least of these,' challenging Rome's patronage system and culture of honor and shame. They lived this faith out with enough consistency and success to attract Rome's attention, which is why Rome identified the Christian movement as the Third Way."[8] By spreading this new way of building relationships based on justice, Christians became "a nation within a nation, a new *oikoumene* or universal commonwealth that spanned the known world, crossing traditional cultural barriers."[9] The early church was neither a private organization nor an agency of the governing authorities. It related to the public by continually attempting to build and extend new relationships based on justice.

The Western church and the global church as well must rediscover and reground their place in the public. The church should become a public church to truly identify itself as a body of Christ. For too long, the Western church has uncritically adopted the dualistic "church and state" paradigm as if it is the only way to talk about political theology. Whether one argues for its separation or integration, the dualistic paradigm of the church and the state has been taken for granted. I hold that this dominant paradigm is in fact a Constantinian framework that was established after the apostolic age—that is, after Christianity

---

6. Gerald L. Sittser, *Resilient Faith: How the Early Christian "Third Way" Changed the World* (Grand Rapids, MI: Brazos, 2019), 16.

7. The idea of building relationships based on justice is best conceptualized by Paul's words in Gal 3:28: "There is no longer Jew or Greek, there is no longer slave or free, there is no longer male and female; for all of you are one in Christ Jesus."

8. Sittser, *Resilient Faith*, 176.

9. Sittser, 176.

became a religion. This means that even though one may oppose the church's Constantinianism, it still inherits a Constantinian framework. It should revive and recover its original yet forgotten model—the apostolic model—as it strives to reestablish itself as a public church. Unlike the Constantinian paradigm, the apostolic paradigm stresses the church's place in *the public* rather than in *the religious* to promote justice.

From its beginning, Jesus's redemptive ministry was consistently characterized as a public ministry. Because of his public presence, testimonies, and performances, he was criticized and even attacked by religious people. If his ministry was carried out outside the public, he would have never been labeled "a glutton and a drunkard, a friend of tax collectors and sinners" (Luke 7:34). Following Jesus, the early church established itself as a public movement rather than a religious or political one. Acts 5:42 tells us that "every day in the temple and at home they did not cease to teach and proclaim Jesus as the Messiah." By grounding itself in the public, the early church not only influenced and impacted people with its presence, proclamation, and performances but also grew horizontally, spreading into other areas across Asia Minor.

The church's rhizomatic politics is devised as an equivalent to the Third Way of the early church to substantiate the idea of the public church in our world. Just as God's justice was proclaimed, promoted, and expanded through the Third Way, the church's rhizomatic politics is committed to the continual proclamation, promotion, and expansion of the reign of God's justice by dismantling the structural injustice and systemic violence in our world. Like the underground rhizome, the early church grew horizontally, crossing all the social lines and political demarcations while bringing social transformation in a way to enhance justice and solidarity among people despite the fact that they were social, religious, and political underdogs. In sum, we discover the original archetype of the public church in the early church of the apostolic age.

Let me briefly describe how each chapter has been constructed in accordance with the overall theme of this book. I argue in the first chapter that for the Western church to reconstruct or reform itself in a way to address structural injustice and systemic violence, it should begin by reckoning its historical sin of colonial complicity. The Western church has long been complacent about this grave history even though it has been deeply involved with the expansion of Western colonialism and imperialism. Despite the historical reality, however, the Western church and its leaders and scholars have not shown that they are taking this historical sin seriously. In the first chapter, I investigate how the Western church got into the historical sin of colonial complicity and what needs to be done for the church to reckon with its past. Without such a reckoning, the Western church will never effectively or authentically address the structural injustice and systemic violence of our world.

In the second chapter, I explore the scope and nature of structural injustice by focusing on the perilous ideology of neoliberalism. The worrisome realities of structural injustice are now detected everywhere—not only in the global economy but also in our educational system, our cultural world, and even our religious institutions. In analyzing various types of structural injustice, I also examine how the rise of structural injustice relates to secularization. The purpose of this critical examination is to show the limits of state politics. Although modern secularism was established with the political promise that it would end religious violence, secular politics in fact has shown that it cannot resolve its own systemic violence. By uncovering the limitation of state politics, I argue that the church should engage in its alternative politics to address the structural injustice of this world. In doing so, I engage in a critical and constructive dialogue with such thinkers as Charles Taylor and William T. Cavanaugh. In sum, the church must develop its distinctive politics to address structural injustice and systemic violence that cannot be fully addressed by state politics. I also develop an argument that it should substitute nomadic thinking for its agelong thinking habit—territorial thinking.

The third chapter is devoted to laying out the biblical foundation for the church's rhizomatic politics. I outline the content of nomos, which becomes the biblical-theological basis that substantiates the church's nomadic thinking vis-à-vis structural injustice and systemic violence. In doing so, I focus on answering three questions: What are the biblical foundations that substantiate the nomos of the church's rhizomatic politics? What are the contemporary theological discourses that could provide us with key theological insights to develop a more holistic ecclesial ethics and politics? What are the key theological tenets of the church's rhizomatic politics? Answering these questions,

I develop an argument that the biblical concepts of righteousness (*dikaiosyne*), covenant, and the kingdom of God substantiate the nomos for the church's alternative politics against various forms of structural injustice.

In the fourth chapter, I develop a new conceptual paradigm for the church's political-theological engagement to address the structural injustice of our world. In so doing, I critically appropriate Gilles Deleuze and Félix Guattari's seminal notion of a rhizome. I also introduce a new perspectival paradigm to replace the traditional "church and state" framework. The new paradigm is established when we shift our political-theological focus from the church and state relation to that of the church versus structural injustice. From the latter perspective, the church could either stand with the state to resist structural injustice or stand against the state to dismantle structural injustice. From this perspective, the church's primary political-theological task is then identified to resist and confront structural injustice in solidarity with its victims.

In the fifth chapter, I introduce the concept of a rhizome organizer as an ideal type, which refers to those church leaders who are leading rhizomatic politics. In doing so, I include in-depth interviews with four church leaders whom I identify as rhizome organizers. These church leaders include Rev. Dr. Liz Theoharis, the cochair of the Poor People's Campaign and the director of the Kairos Center for Religions, Rights, and Social Justice at Union Theological Seminary in New York City; Rev. Dr. Michael Nabors, the senior pastor of Second Baptist Church in Evanston, Illinois, and the president of the Evanston/Northshore NAACP; Rev. John Fife, the former senior pastor of Southside Presbyterian Church in Tucson, Arizona, and a founding leader of the Sanctuary Movement; and Rev. Kaji Douša, the senior pastor of Park Avenue Christian Church and the chair of the New Sanctuary Coalition in New York City. I argue in this chapter that all church leaders are called to become rhizome organizers, and thus they should be ready to respond to the call when they hear it.

In the last chapter, I argue that the church should welcome working with other civic or nongovernmental organizations to resist or dismantle structural injustice and systemic violence. I also investigate the work of community organizing as an essential part of the church's rhizomatic politics. In so doing,

I compare Saul D. Alinsky's secular method and Rev. Dr. William Barber II's Christian community organizing. The goal of this comparison is not for evaluation but for integration with the purpose of developing a more holistic approach to community organizing. I conclude the chapter by laying out a theological foundation for the church's community organizing. The church's rhizomatic politics is what substantiates the idea of the public church, and the historical origin of the public church is traced back to the early church of the apostolic age. For a church to become the church as it is called to be, it must reestablish itself as a public church by practicing rhizomatic politics.

1

RECKONING AND BEING RECKONED

INTRODUCTION

While visiting Bolivia in July 2015, Pope Francis offered a direct apology for the complicity of the Roman Catholic Church in the oppression of Latin America during the colonial period.[1] In his speech, Francis noted that Latin American church leaders in the past had acknowledged that "grave sins were committed against the native peoples of America in the name of God." He went further, saying, "I humbly ask forgiveness, not only for the offenses of the church herself, but also for crimes committed against the native peoples during the so-called conquest of America."[2] Francis's public apology for the church's historical sin of colonial complicity was not the first one offered by the Catholic

---

1. Jim Yadeley and William Neuman, "In Bolivia, Pope Francis Apologizes for Church's 'Grave Sins,'" *New York Times*, July 9, 2015, https://www.nytimes.com/2015/07/10/world/americas/pope-francis-bolivia-catholic-church-apology.html.
2. Paola Flores et al., "Pope Apologizes for 'Serious Sins' during Colonization of Americas," *Associated Press*, July 10, 2015, https://nationalpost.com/news/world/pope-apologizes-for-serious-sins-during-colonization-of-americas#:~:text=from%20our%20team.-,Pope%20apologizes%20for%20'serious%20sins'%20during%20colonization,of%20Americas%20Back%20to%20video&text=John%20Paul%20II%2C%20for%20his,visit%20to%20the%20Dominican%20Republic.

Church. When Pope John Paul II visited the Dominican Republic in 1992, he had already apologized to the continent's Indigenous people for the "pain and suffering" caused during the five hundred years of the church's presence in the Americas.[3] John Paul II's apology, however, was not as specific as Francis's. Although Francis's public apology for the Catholic Church's grave sins might be considered an important historical step toward the reconciliation between the descendants of the former colonizers and the colonized, he stopped short of providing specific solutions to some of the critical social-structural problems of our world that have radically disrupted many people's lives (especially those of the poor and the disenfranchised) as well as Mother Earth. He said, "Don't expect a recipe from this pope. . . . Neither the pope nor the church has a monopoly on the interpretation of social reality or the proposal of solutions to contemporary issues. I dare say no recipe exists."[4] Although Francis's down-to-earth yet worrisome confession that the church has no detailed prescription could be considered as the church's truthful acknowledgment, it has left many people who were victimized by the historical legacies of Western colonialism with no remedy to their ongoing social suffering and historical trauma.

Sincere and earnest as it may be, the church's gesture of apology cannot substitute for its long-overdue work of reckoning—the reckoning with its historical sin of colonial complicity. The church's truthful and resolute reckoning is particularly important for twenty-first-century political theology, whose main responsibility is to promote justice in this world. We should note that although the term *reckoning* has to do with mathematics and accounting, its biblical use refers to God, who reckons based on human faith, as we can see in the case of Abraham (Gen 15:6, "And he believed the Lord; and the Lord reckoned it to him as righteousness"). The church's reckoning with its historical sin means that it must bring itself before God to be reckoned by God's righteousness. The church's communal effort to reckon with its own sin, however, is not merely for judgment and condemnation. It is for redemption. The church's work of reckoning with its own historical sin flows from Jesus's proclamation in Matthew 4:17: "Repent, for the kingdom of heaven

---

3. Flores et al.
4. Yadeley and Neuman, "Pope Francis Apologizes."

has come near." If one truly repents, she, then, no longer stays on the previous course; instead, she changes course toward a new direction. Likewise, if the church would truthfully repent from its own sin, it cannot but bring about fundamental change both to its theology and in its liturgy, mission, and structure.

What does it mean specifically for the Western church to reckon with its historical sin of colonial complicity? How might the church respond to this call? The church's work of reckoning must begin with uncovering and telling the stories of a countless number of people who were victimized by the structural injustice and systemic violence of European colonialism, including those who live with its legacy today. The church must listen to the voices of these victimized people while intently remembering their sufferings. This should be then followed by the communal act of mourning, which should be necessarily accompanied by a deep and surgical introspection into the core of the church's ecclesial structure, history, theology, liturgy, and beliefs. The works of the church's critical introspection and analysis ought to entail a transformative practice that will reshape its mission and vision. No single church or leader can carry out the work of reckoning alone. It should certainly take the whole church and its entire leadership to get this great task completed. In this chapter, I attempt to lay the groundwork for the church's reckoning with its historical sin of colonial complicity by examining the historical, ecclesial, and theological backdrop against which the church, unfortunately, emerged as an accomplice to European colonialism.

THE CHURCH AND THE HISTORICAL SIN OF COLONIAL COMPLICITY

The need for the church's historical reckoning with the sin of colonial complicity in the twenty-first century follows from the lack of its theological reckoning during the twentieth century. Instead of prioritizing the historical reckoning with European colonialism and the church's complicitous entanglement with it, major twentieth-century Western theologians, like Karl Barth, Paul Tillich, and Reinhold Niebuhr, began their theological

reflections with the questions that animated nineteenth-century Protestant liberalism.[5] Until new theological voices emerged from former
colonies—such as Latin America (liberation theology), North America
(Black theology), and Asia (Asian liberation theologies)—beginning in the
1960s, the long legacy of European colonialism was seldom taken up by
Western theologians and ecclesial leaders as a central issue in political theology. Meanwhile, Carl Schmitt's 1922 text, *Political Theology*, effectively
prevented European colonial states from reckoning with their colonial sins
and crimes. Such secularized theological concepts as "state sovereignty"
became completely exempted from any moral and critical scrutiny.

Some may ask, Is not European colonialism a matter of the past? Was
it not over in the previous century? Why invoke the ghosts of the past when
we have already moved into a different historical situation? Such questions
are groundless. Querying the legitimacy of the church's reckoning with its
historical sin is like questioning the legitimacy of American society's historical
reckoning with slavery. The church's reckoning is necessary for us to fulfill any
task of political theology in the postcolonial twenty-first century.

The Western church's reckoning work should be differentiated from that
done by the churches of the former colonies under the broader banner of liberation theology. For instance, Latin American theologians, such as Gustavo
Gutiérrez, Leonardo Boff, Juan Luis Segundo, and Jon Sobrino, have made a
significant impact on the global church and society by popularizing the phrase
preferential option for the poor. Liberation theology has been further diversified in
other parts of the world and has given rise to Black theology, feminist theol-
ogy, womanist theology, Dalit theology, minjung theology, Palestinian liberation theology, queer theology, and others. But we must differentiate between
liberation theology's engagements with the legacy of colonialism and the type

---

5. Although they neither wrote treatises against nor began their theological works by attempting to reckon with European colonialism, their theologies certainly imply that they were
against its practices. Barth, for instance, points out the contradictions between the Euro-
pean Enlightenment and Christian thought and European colonialism and slavery. In his
Ethics of 1928, he addresses the contradictions by saying, "My share in the sin against
Africa or Asia for the last hundred or fifty years may be very remote or indirect but would
Europe be what it is, and would I be what I am, if that expansion had never happened?"
Karl Barth, *Ethics* (Edinburgh: T&T Clark, 1981), 164.

of historical reckoning demanded of the Western church today. While the reckoning work by the churches of the former colonies is for the people colonialism victimized and traumatized, the reckoning work required today of the Western church is its repentance of its role as a colonial victimizer and traumatizer. These two types of reckoning, however, are not separated from each other. The reckoning work by the churches of the former colonies also calls for a corresponding response on the part of the Western church.

There are two reasons we must reckon with the Western church's historical sin of colonial complicity. First, there is an undeniable historical linkage between the European church of the colonial period and the Western church today. The contemporary Western church did not come into being out of nowhere; it evolved out of the previous colonial context with a unique historical, theological, and ecclesial legacy formed by the colonial European church's experiences and beliefs, which were transmitted to the next generation in the form of the church's historical consciousness. Without a critical and rigorous reckoning with the colonial European church's historical sin, the Western church today may never overcome its colonial-historical consciousness that has already shaped its theological formation, ecclesial culture, and missional goals. As we will see in the following chapter, one of the problematic aspects of the Western church's inherited colonial-historical consciousness is its inability to face such issues as structural injustice, systemic violence, and social suffering.

Second, the dominant structural injustices of our world today—such as systemic racism, the neoliberal economy, and environmental destruction—can be genealogically traced to the structural injustice and systemic violence of European colonialism. The transatlantic slave trade, the enormous accumulation of capitalist wealth, and the global exploitation of natural resources were all part of European colonialism, and we are still struggling with its toxic legacies. Since the goal of political theology is to promote justice and peace in this world, without directly confronting the historical legacies of colonial injustice, violence, and suffering, it is nearly impossible for us to do any form of political theology today.

What did the Protestant churches and the Catholic Church do during the colonial period? What is the nature of the relationship between religion and imperialism during that time? We need to define the conceptual difference between imperialism and colonialism. According to Edward W. Said, imperialism is "the practice, the theory, and the attitudes of a dominating metropolitan center ruling a distant territory; colonialism, which is almost always a consequence of imperialism, is the implanting of settlements on distant territory."[6] Regarding himself as an anti-imperialist, Said holds that Christianity was essential to European imperialism. In a lecture delivered in Ireland in 1988, he said, "At the heart of European culture during the many decades of imperial expansion lay what could be called an undeterred and unrelenting Eurocentrism. This accumulated experiences, territories, peoples, histories; it studied them, classified them, verified them; but above all, it subordinated them to the culture and indeed the very idea of white Christian Europe."[7] In his 1978 *Orientalism*, Said also claims that during the colonial period, the European church served the "interests" of European colonialism, which he identifies as "the expansion of Europe."[8] According to him, the main apparatuses for tending these interests were various mission organizations from Europe—from the Society for Promoting Christian Knowledge (1698) to the British and Foreign Bible Society (1804).

Said's postcolonial critique of the European church is echoed by theologians such as Willie James Jennings. In his book *The Christian Imagination: Theology and the Origins of Race*, Jennings argues that "it would be a mistake to see the church and its ecclesiastics as entering the secular workings of the state in the New World, or to posit ecclesial presence as a second stage in the temporal ordering of the New World." Jennings emphasizes that the European church was from the beginning a partner in the state effort to colonize the New World: "No, the church entered with the conquistadors, establishing camp in and with the conquering camps of the Spanish. The ordering of Indian worlds was born of Christian formation itself. Though the church

---

6. Edward W. Said, *Culture and Imperialism* (New York: Vintage, 1993), 8–9, quoted in Hilary M. Carey, *God's Empire: Religion and Colonialism in the British World, c. 1801–1908* (Cambridge: Cambridge University Press, 2011), 15.

7. Edward W. Said, *Nationalism, Colonialism and Literature: Yeats and Decolonization* (Minneapolis: University of Minnesota Press, 1990), 72.

8. Edward W. Said, *Orientalism* (New York: Vintage, 1979), 100.

may not have been in control, it was also not marginal."[9] For Jennings, Western Christianity has never reckoned with its historical sin in any substantive manner. He thus writes, "Sadly, Christianity and its theologians live in conceptual worlds that have not in any substantive way reckoned with the ramifications of colonialism for Christian identity or the identity of theology."[10]

The postcolonial critique of the complicitous relationship between Christianity and European imperialism is best illustrated by the so-called Doctrine of Discovery, which provided the religious, political, and legal justification for Europe's imperial expansion and subsequent colonization of the non-European world. Its origins go back to the 1430s, during which time the Spanish and Portuguese colonized the Canary Islands. In 1436, convinced by Portuguese demand, Pope Eugenius IV issued a papal bull granting Portugal exclusive control of the islands to "civilize and convert the Canary Islanders to the 'one true religion.'"[11] The "civilization cause" was later widely adopted by colonizing countries to justify their colonial expansion. As Portugal expanded its explorations farther down the west coast of Africa, it then convinced Pope Nicholas to issue another bull in 1455 to justify its seizure of the land. Soon after, Spain also sought papal approval for its colonial expedition in the New World (the discoveries of Columbus), and Pope Alexander VI issued the papal bull *Inter Caetera* (1493), which legitimized Spanish explorers' claims on land and waterways they allegedly discovered. After acquiring the church's ecclesial-institutional support, Spain and Portugal applied the Doctrine of Discovery in Africa, Asia, and the Americas.[12]

---

9. Willie James Jennings, *The Christian Imagination: Theology and the Origins of Race* (New Haven, CT: Yale University Press, 2010), 81.

10. Jennings, 291. Jennings not only criticizes Western Christianity's lack of reckoning with its own historical sin but also blasts the current pedagogical schemas that "separate missionary texts from theological texts, missiology from theology." He calls it "immoral" that the work of José de Acosta and of many theologians like him remains relegated to missionary texts, not to standard texts on the performance of theology in the New World. As Jennings correctly points out, "The immorality here lies in the loss of historical consciousness." The belated work of reckoning aims at evoking and dismantling such immorality. Jennings, 114.

11. Robert J. Miller, "The Doctrine of Discovery: The International Law of Colonialism," *Indigenous Peoples' Journal of Law, Culture & Resistance* 5, no. 1 (2019): 35–42, here 36.

12. Miller, 37.

Robert J. Miller identifies ten constituent elements that make up the Doctrine of Discovery, all of which explicitly upheld European superiority in religious, cultural, and political aspects. Although the religious conversion and civilization of Indigenous peoples are acknowledged to be the major elements of the Doctrine of Discovery, the element of *terra nullius* clearly exemplifies the doctrine's prejudice. *Terra nullius* is a Latin phrase that means a "land that is vacant or empty," and under this element, even if lands were already occupied or if they were done so in a manner disapproved of by Euro-American legal systems, then they were considered empty, vacant, and available for discovery claims. According to Miller, "Euro-Americans often considered lands that were actually owned, occupied, and being used by Indigenous Nations to be *terra nullius*."[13]

Although European imperialism and the subsequent colonization were engineered by the church's approval of the European states' imperial expansion and colonial seizure of the lands in the non-European world, the relationship between religion and politics was not simple or straightforward. As Hilary M. Carey notes, "Imperial rule is not exerted in a simple way, but is nearly always complicated by factors such as resistance from those who are being colonized and by the rivalry of other potential colonizers."[14] Indeed, there were "different kinds of colonialism" and a complex relationship between religious mission and colonial politics.[15] Different mission strategies and theological orientations existed not only between the Catholic Church and the Protestant churches but also among themselves (such as different religious orders of the Catholic Church [the Franciscans, Dominicans, Jesuits] and different denominational groups of Protestants [the Puritans, Methodists, Baptists, Presbyterians]).

Ralph Bauer writes that "not all missionaries in the Americas imposed the same, monolithic ethnographic 'grid' on Native American culture." According to Bauer, as the earliest Christian missionaries in New Spain, the Franciscans developed their distinguished mission strategies and theological orientations in competition with the missionaries of the other mendicant

---

13. Miller, 41.
14. Carey, *God's Empire*, 15.
15. Carey, 15.

orders (the Dominicans and the Augustinians): "Like no other group, the Franciscans were obsessed with the active role of the Devil in their descriptions of pre-Conquest Native American culture. . . . Like no other group, they were unequivocally committed to Spanish imperialism, condoning the violence and coercion of the Conquest as the only viable method of bringing the American natives under the saving rule of Christianity."[16] Unlike the Catholic missionaries, the English Protestant missionaries of the London Missionary Society and Wesleyan missions initially supported the independence of Indigenous governments in Polynesia. According to David Hilliard, after the 1830s—in which "the threat of Roman Catholic missionaries" began to be visible, along with the growth of European trading and planting communities—English Protestants jettisoned the idea of isolationism and began to call for the state's intervention and aid. Even in that situation, Hilliard states, "most missionaries wanted not British annexation but protection, in the form of recognition of the native government by treaty or the occasional visit of a friendly warship."[17]

The complex and multifaceted relationship between religion (Christian mission and evangelization) and politics (Europe's imperialism and colonialism) is also seen on an individual level among church leaders and theologians. Within fifty years after Pope Alexander VI's issue of the papal bull *Inter Caetera*, several notable individual church leaders emerged who "did not hesitate to oppose not only colonial abuses but the whole system of colonization prevailing at the time." Among these, Bartolomé de Las Casas (1474–1566) and Francisco de Vitoria (ca. 1492–1546) are particularly conspicuous. After witnessing the oppression of Indigenous peoples by Europeans in the Americas, Las Casas took up the cause of the natives and vigorously pushed it until his death, acquiring the title of "champion of the American Indians."[18] The Dominican theologian of Salamanca Francisco de Vitoria argues in his essay

---

16. Ralph Bauer, "Millennium's Darker Side: The Missionary Utopias of Franciscan New Spain and Puritan New England," in *Finding Colonial Americas: Essays Honoring J. A. Leo Lemay*, ed. Carla Mulford and David Shields (Cranbury, NJ: Associated University Presses, 2001), 33–49, here 35.

17. David Hilliard, "Colonialism and Christianity: The Melanesian Mission in the Solomon Islands," *Journal of Pacific History* 9 (1974): 93–116, here 94.

18. Robert Delavignette, *Christianity and Colonialism* (New York: Hawthorn, 1964), 53.

"On the American Indians" that American Indians could not be robbed on their property, either as private citizens or as princes, on the grounds that they were not true masters. He goes on further, saying, "Granting that these barbarians [American Indians] are as foolish and slow-witted as people say they are, it is still wrong to use this as grounds to deny their true dominion (*dominium*); nor can they be counted among the slaves."[19] Although Vitoria's thesis was not well accepted by those in positions of power in the sixteenth century and their successors, he remained an influential Catholic theologian on the teaching about colonization. Robert Delavignette even writes that "Vitoria's contribution to this subject can be compared to that of St. Augustine on the subject of war and non-violence."[20]

Vitoria's thought on European colonialism became a key debate issue four hundred years later in Paris in the mid-1950s. In June of 1956, at the urgent request of Archbishop of Paris Maurice Cardinal Feltin, a small coterie of distinguished French Catholic thinkers and teachers joined in a meeting to resolve a bitter public feud over church teachings on colonization.[21] Two influential French priests—Joseph Michel and Joseph-Vincent Ducattillon—debated Vitoria's writings and their application to France's colonial empire in the 1950s. According to Elizabeth A. Foster, although they both recognized Vitoria as the preeminent church authority on colonization, Michel and Ducattillon came to opposite understandings of his teachings. While Michel found an imperative to decolonize, Ducattillon rejected Michel's interpretation and instead called for a just and vigorous defense of French colonists and French imperial interests abroad.[22] The debate did not go well, and the effort to resolve the differences between Michel and Ducattillon ended in failure. According to Foster, the failure of the debate "reveals the staggering lack of sustained, learned, or critical Catholic engagement with modern imperialism and colonization, which is symptomatic of how closely

---

19. Francisco de Vitoria, *Political Writings*, ed. Anthony Pagden and Jeremy Lawrance (Cambridge: Cambridge University Press, 1991), 251.
20. Delavignette, *Christianity and Colonialism*, 54.
21. Elizabeth A. Foster, *African Catholic: Decolonization and the Transformation of the Church* (Cambridge, MA: Harvard University Press, 2019), 95.
22. Foster, 96.

Catholic evangelism and European expansion were aligned in the modern era."[23]

The debate between Michel and Ducattillon provides us with a key perspectival clue regarding what it would take for the Western church to reckon with its historical sin of colonial complicity. In his 1954 lecture on "the duty to decolonize," Michel not only denounces colonialism but also defends the right of colonized people to revolt. "Vitoria," he insists, "pointed the way to an understanding of decolonization as one of the primary obligations of a colonizer." Michel's decolonial thesis, however, is mixed with his colonial notion of "the so-called right of tutelage of more advanced countries—the right to 'teach' more 'savage' ones."[24] The idea of "tutelage" immediately reminds us of the early colonial states' (Spain and Portugal) "civilization cause," which we saw earlier. As Foster correctly points out, "Michel allowed for the possibility of an ideal, justifiable colonization governed by a civilizing mission in accordance with Christian teachings." Michel, however, was not an idealist because he acknowledges that the actual practice of colonization is sinful. He thus argues both that "the goal of colonization is decolonization" (the goal of tutelage is to help students be independent) and that colonial practice is inextricably interlinked with the sin of colonialism.[25] Michel's decolonial thesis sounds better than Ducattillon's pro-colonial position, but it is still problematic. According to Foster, "Like many of his devout countrymen, his thought was still deeply rooted in the logic of colonialism, advocating decolonization as the natural outcome of a successful 'civilizing mission' that was both European and Catholic."[26] Unfortunately, Michel's decolonial thesis was still tied to the Eurocentric civilizing mission.

Ducattillon developed his pro-colonial thesis in his "Theology of Colonization" of 1955. He holds that Michel's right of tutelage cannot really justify colonization; instead, Ducattillon argues that to justify colonization in theological terms, it is necessary to examine Vitoria's handling of *jus communicationis*, the "natural right of communication and society," which Ducattillon

---

23. Foster, 98.
24. Foster, 102, 103.
25. Foster, 103, 102.
26. Foster, 102.

calls the right of "universal circulation and universal transmigration." The Catholic claim to "universality" plays an important role in his development of his pro-colonial thesis. For instance, the primacy of a "universal human community that is anterior to and underlies all other human communities" essentially stipulates that "the earth belong[s] to all peoples and no people [have] the right to ban another people from any part of it."[27] According to this perspective, then, the "exploitation of natural resources such as gold in rivers or fish in the sea should be open to all," with the qualification that their exploitation should not affect or inflict injury on Indigenous inhabitants. In a self-contradictory manner, he claims that as long as the dignity of the Indigenous peoples is respected and nothing is unjustly taken from them, they have "no right to object to colonization." Ducattillon adds that "Vitoria's writings did not point to a 'duty to decolonize'; rather, they justified colonization and defended the maintenance of the French Empire, by force if necessary."[28]

What is the political-theological significance of Michel and Ducattillon's debate for us today? It encapsulates the colonial church's two representative theological visions of colonialism. By critically assessing their arguments, we can proceed with the work of reckoning with the colonial church's practices and political theologies, which not only justified European colonialism and colonization but also rendered the church complicitous in this historical sin. Their decolonial/pro-colonial political theologies fail to incorporate the voices of the colonized people. Although the debate between Michel and Ducattillon is ultimately about the political destiny of those people, it was conducted without having their stories and testimonies heard. Michel might have a better intention for them, but he presumes to represent their true needs and political concerns without their input. The debate also lacks in-depth theological considerations of God's perfect justice and its relevance to the practice of European colonialism. Instead, we only detect their humanitarian phenomenology of the good life (Michel) or universalist pragmatics of political rights (Ducattillon). They might help us develop a political philosophy on "relative justice," but they both stop short of providing us with a

27. Foster, 110.
28. Foster, 111.

12

critical-theological exploration of God's "true justice" or righteousness. We do not find an anti-colonial political theology in their debate.

The church must unearth the many untold stories of the colonized people, whose voices were never heard in the ecclesial space of the colonizers. It is not coincidental that during the colonial period, one of the theological-moral issues the European church rarely discussed was human suffering. As the Catholic moral theologian James F. Keenan notes, "Strange as it might seem, we cannot find in the moral manuals from the 16th to the 20th century hardly any comment on suffering. It is simply not an ethical category." Servais-Théodore Pinckaers corroborates Keenan's discovery, writing, "The manuals of moral theology have hardly anything to say about suffering."[29] The first step toward the church's reckoning with its historical sin is to recover victimized people's untold stories of suffering so that the whole church can hear them. Along with this recovering work, it must also critically reckon with its colonial theologies that were invented to support and justify European colonial expansion in the name of God. In this book, I focus on the latter task—reckoning with the colonial political theologies. It is beyond the scope of this volume to tell the stories of the colonized people. Such a task requires the efforts of researchers, historians, anthropologists, ethnologists, and others.

TWO CITIES, TWO JUSTICES, AND TWO POLITICS

What was the political theology behind European imperialism and colonialism? How did it work? And how could we reckon with it? Since the fifth century, when Augustine wrote *City of God*, the fundamental framework of the church's political theology has been the duality of the church and the state. Thomas G. Sanders succinctly captures it as follows: "Protestantism shares with Roman Catholicism and Eastern Orthodoxy three fundamental elements of all Christian political theory: *the dualism of church and state*, the sovereignty of God over church and state, and the evaluation of the state as

---

29. James F. Keenan, "Vatican II and Theological Ethics," *Theological Studies* 74, no. 1 (2013): 162–90, here 180.

both good and evil."[30] According to Augustine, this world is divided into two cities: the city of man (Babylon, or the earthly city) and the city of God (new Jerusalem, or the heavenly city). These two cities are inhabited by two different groups of citizens who are oriented by two different kinds of love. While citizens of the city of man love themselves to the exclusion of God, citizens of the city of God love God, and by loving God, they become aliens in the city of man. Augustine writes,

> We see then that the two cities were created by two kinds of love: the earthly city was created by self-love reaching the point of contempt for God, the Heavenly City by the love of God carried as far as contempt of self. In fact, the earthly city glories in itself, the Heavenly City glories in the Lord. The former looks for glory from men, the latter finds its highest glory in God, the witness of a good conscience. The earthly city lifts up its head in its own glory, the Heavenly City says to its God: "My glory; you lift up my head." In the former, the lust for domination lords it over its princes as over the nations it subjugates; in the other, both those put in authority and those subject to them serve one another in love, the rulers by their counsel, the subjects by obedience. The one city loves its own strength shown in its powerful leaders; the other says to its God, "I will love you, my Lord, my strength."[31]

Augustine's two cities (the *civitas Dei* and the *civitas terrena*) should not be understood in the simplistic way that the church refers to the heavenly city, while the state denotes the earthly city. The heavenly city and the earthly city directly correspond neither to the church nor to the state. Rather, they represent two societies that are oriented by two opposite orders of value. These antagonistic orders of value intersect with both the church and the state. This intersectional relation is not lucidly defined if we only focus on Augustine's "two kinds of love." To see more clearly the intersectional dynamics, we need to look at his idea of justice.

---

30. Thomas G. Sanders, *Protestant Concepts of Church and State: Historical Backgrounds and Approaches for the Future* (New York: Holt, Rinehart & Winston, 1964), 6 (emphasis added).
31. Saint Augustine, *City of God* (London: Penguin, 1984), bk. 16, chap. 28, p. 593.

In book 19 of *City of God*, Augustine defines justice as "assigning to each his due" or "rendering to each his due," in line with the classic Greek view and standard of Roman jurisprudence wherein justice establishes and maintains equity between parties.[32] Augustine implies that the idea of justice can be distinguished into two kinds: true justice and imperfect justice. In book 19, Augustine uses the terms *justice* and *true justice* interchangeably, but he does not specifically adopt the term *imperfect justice*. Even though this term is not Augustine's own, a close reading evinces its conceptual validity. To define the notion of true justice, Augustine holds that we must presuppose "the correct knowledge and worship of the true God" because without them, true justice is impossible.[33] As Robert Dodaro points out, Augustine conceptualizes the idea of "true justice" by "transforming Cicero's [and Scipio's] notion of right (*ius*) into true justice (*uera iustitia*)—a move that distinguishes their interpretations of *consensus iuris* [what is right] and, thereby disqualifies Rome as a commonwealth."[34] In book 2, by referring to Cicero's account of the decay of manners in the last days of the Roman commonwealth, Augustine asserts that "true justice is found only in that commonwealth whose founder and ruler is Christ; if we agree to call it a commonwealth, seeing that we cannot deny that it is the 'weal of the community.'"[35]

What, then, is the idea of imperfect justice? Imperfect justice refers to a situation where the political ruling is maintained less than perfectly due to the lack of the rule of Christ in the ordering structure. In a word, it means the state of ruling by "what is right" (*consensus iuris*) yet without the correct knowledge and worship of the true God. In this respect, one may regard imperfect justice as the political order of justice in a secular state, in which its rulers do not worship God as its sovereign Lord. It would not be too much to say that most people in a secular world only experience imperfect justice rather

---

32. Robert Dodaro, "Political and Theological Virtues in Augustine, Letter 155 to Macedonius," *Augustiniana* 54, nos. 1–4 (2004): 431–74, here 444. This classic notion of justice can be found in Plato (*Republic*), Aristotle (*Nicomachean Ethics*), Cicero (*On Invention* [*De Inventione*]), and Roman legal codes.

33. Robert Dodaro, *Christ and the Just Society in the Thought of Augustine* (Cambridge: Cambridge University Press, 2004), 11.

34. Dodaro, 11.

35. Augustine, *City of God*, bk. 2, chap. 21, p. 75.

than true justice. If we would follow the Augustinian political-theological paradigm, true justice is only possible in the true and perfect Christendom. As noted above briefly, although Augustine does not coin the term *imperfect justice* per se, he insinuates that we can conceptualize it. For instance, he acknowledges that the Ciceronian notion of "associated by a common sense of right and a community of interest" may not be a matter of "either, or" (either perfect justice or no justice). Referring to the Roman Empire, he writes, "Now it certainly was a commonwealth to *some degree*, according to *more plausible* definitions; and it was *better* ruled by the Romans of antiquity than by their later successors."[36] Affirming this point, Bruce W. Speck writes, "Augustine believed that they can do good works when one grants that those works are *imperfect* and recognizes a *relative* scale of judgment based on perfection."[37] The state of being "devoid of true justice" does not mean that there is no justice at all in Augustine's political theology.

The political implications of these two concepts of justice and especially the possible relational dynamics between the two are not fully explored yet. We still need a further investigation to have a better understanding of Augustine's political theology of justice. To do so, we need to contextualize his works, especially *City of God*. I assume that the notion of justice presented by *City of God* has to do with the particular historical event that deeply affected his theology as well as the world where he lived. As is well known, Augustine wrote this book against the backdrop of the Sack of Rome by the Visigoths in 410 CE and the subsequent accusations against Christianity for the tragic event. He argues that Christianity should not be blamed for the Sack of Rome; instead, Christianity deserves acclamation. John O'Meara writes, "In short, Christianity was the great salvation for the State; it goes, however, beyond this life below and the harmony of the State, and provides entry to eternal salvation and the heavenly and divine republic of a certain eternal

---

36. Augustine, bk. 2, chap. 21, p. 75 (emphasis added).
37. Bruce W. Speck, "Augustine's Tale of Two Cities: Teleology/Eschatology in the City of God," *Journal of Interdisciplinary Studies* 8, nos. 1–2 (1996): 105–30, here 108 (emphasis added).

people."[38] Why, then, should we consider the historical background of Augustine's *City of God*?

We should note that unlike Augustine, who wrote his book deeply immersed in his particular historical circumstance in which the secular kingdom (Rome) was attacked and sacked by what they called "barbarians," followers of Augustine during the European colonial period did not seem to take into their consideration seriously the reverse historical context in which the secular kingdom (European empires) attacked and sacked what they deemed "pagans," "heathens," or "savages" on a global scale. The significance of this historical awareness should not be trivialized at all, especially by those who are responsible for leading the church. By failing to consider this *reversed* historical backdrop critically, the Western church was not able to formulate a relevant and rightful political theology to meet the historical challenge during the colonial period. As we will see shortly, the Western church's failure to critically incorporate the overturned historical context rendered it vulnerable to theological dualism, which eventually gave birth to "territorial thinking" within the Western colonial church.

How does our consideration of the reversed historical backgrounds regarding Augustinian political theologies help us have a more critical perspective in understanding Augustine's two concepts of justice? It is important for us to remember that there are at least two motivating factors behind *City of God*: the defense of the church against its blaming for the Sack of Rome and the theological justification for the fallibility of the state (Rome). These two motivating factors are intrinsically related to the two concepts of justice. Since the church performs worship and true worship is a communal practice of "giving God what is due," perfect justice may be found in the church. Unlike the church, however, in the state—where a ruler does not serve God, failing to give God what is due—perfect justice is impossible. It is right for Dodaro to say, "Hence, justice in political society and in its leaders is always at best *partial, contingent, subject to reform* on the basis of experience and of a graced, ongoing conversion of heart."[39] Being devoid of true justice, the state

---

38. John O'Meara writes this in his introduction to *City of God*, xiv.
39. Robert Dodaro, "Justice," in *Augustine through the Ages: An Encyclopedia*, ed. Allan D. Fitzgerald et al. (Grand Rapids, MI: Eerdmans, 1999), 481–83, here 483 (emphasis added).

is always on the edge of failing to be the commonwealth, being prone to its fallibility. This is the reason Augustine appropriates Cicero, who brought a judgment on the Roman commonwealth (book II, ch. 21) for its lack of justice. In this manner, Augustine asks, "Remove justice, and what are kingdoms but gangs of criminals on a large scale?"[40]

Regarding the fallibility of the state and its associated notion of imperfect justice, there is a debate among Augustinian scholars regarding the possibility of finding social and political justice among pagans. According to Katherine Chambers, "The received reading of Book 19, as found in the work of Mary Clark, Rowan Williams, John Milbank, Oliver O'Donovan and Robert Dodaro, is that in Book 19 Augustine rejected the possibility of finding social and political justice among pagans." Chambers calls this reading of the impossibility of achieving social and political justice among pagans the "standard reading." The origin of the standard reading lies in these scholars' particular way of reading Augustine's claim in book 19, chapter 21, of *City of God*, in which Augustine writes, "Non est ulla iustitia" (There is no justice) in one who does not serve the true God. According to Chambers, these scholars regard this claim as Augustine's political-theological statement that "non-Christians would inevitably lack social and political justice."[41]

Why, then, is this standard reading problematic? Chambers reasons that it is a mistake to assume that Augustine's rhetorical question—"Where, then, is the justice of man, when he deserts the true God?"—refers to social and political justice. Chambers argues that "Augustine gave no indication that the justice that he denied was found among pagans was the justice of giving other human beings their due of social and political goods." She continues, "Rather, the fact that he followed this question by asking, 'Is this to give everyone his due?,' indicates that the justice that he denied was found among them was the justice of giving God his due."[42] Chambers shows that for Augustine, whenever anyone worships any god but the true God, true justice is simply absent.

---

40. Augustine, *City of God*, bk. 4, chap. 4, p. 139.
41. Katherine Chambers, "Augustine on Justice: A Reconsideration of *City of God*, Book 19," *Political Theology* 19, no. 5 (2018): 382–96, here 382.
42. Chambers, 388.

This scholarly debate helps us see more clearly why we must differentiate between the *fallibility* of the pagan state (or secular politics) and the *destiny* of the pagan state. If Chambers is right, *City of God* is a critique of the *fallibility* of the pagan state and its imperfect justice, not of its political *destiny*. If the political destiny of the pagan state has been already predetermined, what is the purpose of engaging in it? If a nation is doomed, what political efforts would matter? What if European imperialism and colonialism were considered the political destiny of European secular politics? What could the European church do about them? For this reason, I contend that it is a mistake for us to hold that Augustine theorizes the political destiny of the pagan state in *City of God*. Rather, I argue, what he formulates in *City of God* is a critical reflection on the fallibility of the pagan state due to its inevitable failure to give God what is due.

The standard reading, especially its interpretation regarding the idea of the political *destiny* of the pagan state, has to do with the loosely identified conceptual affinities between the idea of the "state" and that of the "city of man" outlined in *City of God*. Augustine warns us not to directly identify the state and the church with the city of man and the city of God, respectively. Just as the church should not be exactly identified as the city of God (the heavenly city, *civitas Dei*), the state should not be equated with the city of man (the earthly city, *civitas terrena*) per se. One of the key differences between these two paired notions is that while the city of man and the city of God pertain to the theological *destiny* of humanity, the state and the church refer to the *fallible* and imperfect reality of humanity and the political world. Oftentimes, though, this distinction gets blurred, and the pairs are treated interchangeably. What, then, would be entailed if people misappropriate Augustine's paired notions? The outcome can be problematic, even deadly. If people miscomprehend the fallible nature of the state as the political destiny of the state, as noted above, people would not try to do anything to change what they regard as the matters of the state. In that case, they would not even bother to think that the idea of the destiny of the state is indeed the result of the habitual and uncritical identification between the state and the city of man.

Despite this limitation, people seem more capable of understanding the conceptual differences between the church and the city of God than those of the state and the city of man. The lack of this critical differentiation between the state and the city of man leads the church to be more attentive to such religious issues as idolatry but less focused on its political responsibility to such "worldly matters" as structural injustice and systemic violence. In my view, this is one of the reasons the church has become more religious rather than apostolic or prophetic. It is a moot question if Augustine's theological interest lies more in the distinction between the church and the city of God than in that between the state and the city of man. Depending on how one answers this question, her or his political theology cannot but be affected.

How should we reckon with the legacy of the Western church's Augustinian political theology? We should note that it tends to obscure the problem of human suffering (especially social suffering) caused by the state's imperfect justice. The theological endeavor to evaluate the fallibility of state politics ironically tends to normalize social suffering. We should recall that suffering was not even an ethical category during the colonial period in Europe. Since Augustine develops his theological notion of justice by adopting the Ciceronian (and classical Greek) idea of "rendering to each his due" as a foundational framework, there is little room for addressing the problem of social suffering in his political theology of justice.

During his debate with Joseph-Vincent Ducattillon, Joseph Michel proposed the idea of "the so-called right of tutelage of more advanced countries—the right to 'teach' more 'savage' ones even though this would be inevitably bound to the sin of colonialism (meaning colonial violence and human suffering)."[43] If the key notion of justice is singularly constituted in accordance with the idea of "rendering to each his due," what would be the justifiable due for those categorized as the "uncivilized" or "savages"? There seems to be a political-theological reason the European church maintained its historical sin of colonial complicity during the colonial period. For instance, during Germany's late nineteenth- and early twentieth-century colonial expansion, "Germany's colonial interest hardly figures in the discussion of German political theology."[44] The European

---

43. Foster, *African Catholic*, 103.
44. Kwok Pui-Lan, "Postcolonial Intervention in Political Theology," *Political Theology* 17, no. 3 (May 2016): 223–25, here 223.

churches during the colonial period lacked effective theological tools and frameworks with which they could have resisted the colonial rule over otherized people.

Within the Augustinian political theology of justice, the church may find it difficult to integrate the two meanings of justice (*iustitia*): that type pertaining to political and social life and that referring to the theological and spiritual sphere (right relationship with God). This difficulty gets even more explicit if we follow the standard reading of *City of God*. For instance, Chambers argues that the standard reading draws "a causal connection between these two ways of being just," in that "it finds that he [Augustine] held that achieving justice in social and political life was impossible unless we first achieved theological virtue."[45] Here is an irony. Although Augustine originally presumes that the full realization of true justice is the "destiny" of the city of God, the standard reading transforms the theological vision of "destiny" into a "*prerequisite* for political and social justice."[46] This transformation becomes the foundation on which Augustinian scholars develop the idea of "theopolitics" at the expense of setting it apart from worldly politics. In other words, the church is estranged from the public world. The desirable integration between theological justice and political justice is rendered possible only within the boundary of the true church. This, however, means that the church's political engagement in the public space of the state cannot but be weakened or even abandoned. This is also how the church's "territorial thinking" came into existence, since *City of God* was published in the history of Western Christianity. It is my contention that the European church's historical sin of colonial complicity is deeply interlocked with the church's territorial thinking. It is imperative for the Western church to settle with its long practice of territorial thinking to reckon with its historical sin of colonial complicity. By misinterpreting Augustine's political theology of two cities (by turning the *fallibility* into the *destiny* of the state), the Western church lost the theological justification to engage in the "worldly matters" of the state. This theological failure rendered the Western church indifferent to the fallible nature of the state and the matters of imperfect justice.

---

45. Chambers, "Augustine on Justice," 383.
46. Chambers, 383 (emphasis added).

A CRITIQUE OF TERRITORIAL THINKING AND
A CALL FOR A NEW POLITICAL THEOLOGY

Above, we have critically explored the Augustinian political theology of two cities, particularly his dualism of the church and the state and the relation between true justice and imperfect justice, with the purpose of reckoning with the European church's historical sin of colonial complicity. As a result of this exploration, we have uncovered two key political-theological insights regarding the church's relationship with the state. First, the church is indispensable for the state to attain true justice, since "true justice is found only in that commonwealth whose founder and ruler is Christ."[47] Second, the existence of the church, however, is not necessary for the state to attain imperfect justice. According to Frederick W. Loetscher, although Augustine nowhere gives us a systemic presentation of his views concerning the state, he stipulates clearly that it is an earthly institution for providing justice to its citizens. Loetscher also claims, "Augustine maintains that every state, being in some sense an ethical community, must have at least this rational or natural justice that administers human affairs with some regard to equity."[48] In a similar vein, Daniel Roach also writes, "Augustine believed that some level of justice is necessary for the existence of kingdoms and nations."[49] Along with this discovery, we have also uncovered that the church must reckon with its habitual way of thinking in engaging the matters of political and social justice—that is, its territorial thinking. What, then, is territorial thinking? Why is the church's habitual thinking mechanism problematic?

In a broader sense, the notion of territorial thinking refers to a type of herd mentality that is oriented to protect the group's identity and integrity by *territorializing* the association of the group and its interests.[50] Specifically, the

---

47. Frederick W. Loetscher, "St. Augustine's Conception of the State," *Church History* 4, no. 1 (March 1935): 16–42, here 25.
48. Loetscher, 18, 27.
49. Daniel Roach, "Augustinian Perspectives on Church and State Relations in Modern America," *Faulkner Law Review* 9, no. 2 (2018): 385–409, here 393.
50. There are many forms and examples of territorial thinking. For instance, Nietzsche's notion of "herd morality" or "slave morality" is as much a form of territorial thinking as the idea of white supremacy. The process of territorialization is usually accompanied by the group's self-moralization. However, it commonly lacks in its own self-criticism.

church's territorial thinking is a result of its lack of reckoning with its long legacy of Constantinianism (a formal alliance between the church and the state) as well as the theological shortcoming to develop its critical and holistic political theology. One should note that it is not the author's contention that Augustine should be blamed for the Western church's territorial thinking. As seen above, the birth of territorial thinking is, rather, related to the church's lack of a critical-contextual perspective in reading Augustine's *City of God*, especially during the colonial and postcolonial periods. As a way of thinking, territorial thinking primarily denotes a particular yet influential hermeneutic stance, according to which the church is understood as a form of distinctive territory (the spiritual kingdom), which has its different way of ruling and different standards of justice as opposed to the state. The church's territorial thinking is characterized at least by two aspects. First, as long as the state does not intervene in the church's territorial matters, the latter keeps its typical *apolitical* stance toward what it calls secular political matters. It does not engage in these because they are not relevant to it.

Second, the church's territorial thinking tends to appropriate and apply moral dualism (spiritual value and worldly value) to culture and society. The church's moral dualism is problematic because it is formed or influenced by a society's dominant ideology and cultural norms that represent partial and skewed moral values. From a theological perspective, this is a serious problem because the church's territorial thinking tends to substitute a tribal or territorial god for the God of creation and redemption. Territorial thinking itself is devoid of the critical mechanism that helps us see where we truly are. It renders those who adopt it regressively susceptible to moral complacency, complicity, deception, and hypocrisy. It, in this respect, is neither value-neutral nor innocent. It can be harmful and even deadly to the church. Unless the church is critical of this habitual way of thinking, it can become its own victim. I contend that the European church's historical sin of colonial complicity is a monumental case of this self-incurred victimization. We must dismantle the church's territorial thinking to reckon with its historical sin of colonial complicity.

Let me illustrate how territorial thinking can lead the church to moral complacency. The apolitical stance to the state policy of slavery, for example, led many white churchgoers in the South, supported by the cultural-racial norm of white supremacy, into moral complacency to the widespread structural injustice and systemic dehumanization of Black people during the era of slavery in the United States. We are also well aware of how such a moral attitude of complacency, without being checked by regulations or shocked by events, easily develops into a complicitous behavioral pattern. During the 1930s, having been complacent to the rise of the Nazi Party, many Christians who belonged to the German state church (the Evangelical Church in Germany) became complicitous with the state-sponsored mass murder of six million Jews (the Holocaust) and others in the early 1940s. What about the link between the church's territorial thinking and its deception and hypocrisy? Many European churches during the colonial period explicitly as well as implicitly endorsed Europe's colonization of non-European nations by deceiving themselves that what they were doing was for the greater good of civilization and evangelization.

The most problematic aspect of the church's territorial thinking is that as a result of its moral complacency, complicity, deception, and hypocrisy, it became irresponsive to and irresponsible for the social sin of the state's structural injustice and systemic violence. We will further discuss structural injustice in the following chapter. Briefly defined, though, structural injustice refers to a distinctive type of injustice caused by unfair rules, skewed cultural norms, and historical oppression, which usually bring an accumulative and perennial negative impact to some social groups (e.g., racial or cultural minorities) vis-à-vis others. There is a structural reason territorial thinking causes the church to be irresponsive to and irresponsible for the structural injustice of our world. The unholy combination between the church's apolitical stance (due to territorial thinking) and the fallibility of the state (imperfect justice) typically results in the former's incapacity to face and engage in structural injustice.[51]

---

51. We should note that there are many different forms or establishments of imperfect justice, ranging from the near-perfect realization of social justice to very low-level imperfect justice, which is close to social chaos. Everything in between can be regarded as a form of imperfect justice as long as the state maintains a certain level of social order within its

How, then, could we dismantle the church's territorial thinking so as to reckon with its historical sin of colonial complicity? In two ways, we may try to set it free from its territorial thinking: first, through an effort to deterritorialize it, and second, through the theological reconstruction of Augustine's political theology of justice. What does it, then, mean to deterritorialize the church? How could we make it possible? The concerted efforts of deterritorializing the church involve its self-dismantling work to erase its own invisible borders and boundaries. This requires it to be more transformative and prophetic as well as self-reflective and self-critical. To dismantle such borders and boundaries, it ought to contextualize itself in changing the world and history while focusing on the others' stories and voices as well as listening to the call of God. The church becomes the church only when it allows those people to be heard and valued with their genuine voices and stories. Unfortunately, due to its failure to reckon with its own historical sin as well as its opting out of this world (an ecclesial self-exile and self-retreat), the voices and stories of those people were buried under ecclesial territories.

Along with this necessary work of reckoning with its historical sin of colonial complicity, the Western church should also engage in critical-theological work to reform its old territorial habits in theology. Robert Dodaro's critical analysis of Augustine's idea of justice seems illustrative. According to Dodaro, Augustine's understanding of the Pauline notion of the justice of God (*Justitia Dei*) is not holistic enough because his reading of the Pauline Epistles (particularly Romans and Galatians) is solely based on the Old Latin translation of the Greek, which cannot fully capture the original Greek meaning of the Pauline notion of *dikaiosyne* (correctly translated as either "righteousness" or "justice"). Dodaro argues that although Paul's notion of the justice of God has both references—justice by which God makes a human being just and God's own justice in judging human beings—Augustine only refers to the former as he develops the notion of God's "true justice."[52] For Dodaro, then, the holistic notion of the justice of God should include not only "the right relationship" between God and human beings but also God's own righteousness by which

---

governing territory. In my view, structural injustice may be conceived as a corollary of imperfect justice.

52. Dodaro, "Justice," 482.

human beings are judged. How does, then, this new insight into Augustine's idea of justice impact us regarding our effort to dismantle territorial thinking?

We should remind ourselves that the purpose of reckoning with the church's historical sin of colonial complicity is not to lead it backward in a regressive direction. On the contrary, it is to reform and renew the Western church so that it becomes the agent of true justice to address the structural injustice and systemic violence in an increasingly neoliberalized world. In this respect, I contend that the church should develop and practice its alternative politics, which I outline in the following chapters by calling it the church's "rhizomatic politics." Its rhizomatic politics certainly does not substitute for the formal politics of the state, but it aims at covering the area that cannot be serviced by the state only. The church's alternative political practice is committed to its reformative and prophetic vision that not only attends to the social suffering of victimized people but also addresses the state's imperfect justice. This renewed vision, then, calls for the church's engagement in the practice of deterritorial intervention. In the following chapter, I develop a new political-theological hermeneutics that will replace the church's old territorial thinking. I call it "nomadic thinking," and I develop it by critically appropriating the social philosophers Gilles Deleuze and Félix Guattari's enigmatic yet seminal ideas such as "nomads." Unlike the church's territorial thinking, which is defined by territorial division and separation, nomadic thinking dismantles such a dualistic thinking mechanism. The church's nomadic thinking does not allow any territorial borders and boundaries to define what it should do and how it should be. In sum, the church's deterritorial nomadic politics envisions addressing and dismantling structural injustices and systemic violence through its practice of deterritorial intervention.

CONCLUSION

The problems of injustice and social suffering have been with humanity from the beginning of human history. But structural injustice became more prevalent and serious as our society got more complicated, systemized, and formalized by various laws, rules, and regulations. Undoubtedly, humanity

26

experienced the worst and largest case of structural injustice during the colonial period, in which the Western church implicitly or explicitly colluded in colonial expansion instead of challenging and resisting the structural injustice of European colonialism.

If the Western church is authentically to face and engage with the rise of various types of structural injustice in the twenty-first century, it must begin by completing its long-overdue reckoning with the historical sin of colonial complicity. How long could the contemporary Western church maintain its putative neutrality and feigned innocence to this historical sin? Though belated, the church's historical reckoning with colonial complicity now gets more exigent and critical than ever because we see every day the rise of new forms of structural injustice in many parts of the world. This task cannot be done by a single church. It takes the whole church to complete it. The ecclesial task to dismantle structural injustice is not an option each church can opt in or out of. It is a required one that all Christian churches should undertake in today's world. Without a doubt, the birth and expansion of the capitalistic market during the colonial period have not only exacerbated the global state of structural injustice but also complicated the study of political theology itself. In an age of rising neoliberalism, the church should no longer remain a secluded territory for the familiar ones; it should be ready to deterritorialize itself while getting itself ready to engage in deterritorial intervention to proliferate true justice beyond its borders and boundaries. In the next chapter, I develop further the church's new political theology by addressing different forms of contemporary structural injustice.

2

TAKING STRUCTURAL
INJUSTICE SERIOUSLY

INTRODUCTION

In the previous chapter, we explored the reasons the Western church must reckon with its historical sin of colonial complicity as a fundamental political-theological project in the twenty-first century. Reckoning with historical sin requires the church to go beyond confessing its collective guilt. The purpose of its reckoning is for its own transformation into an agency of promoting and implementing true justice in a world yearning for its liberation and redemption from structural injustice, systemic violence, and social-ecological suffering. Unfortunately, even though the era of official Western colonialism has ended, its legacies are still very much alive in many parts of our world, not only in political and economic systems, but also in cultural and civic life. As we shall see shortly, with the global rise of neoliberalism since the 1980s, the problem of structural injustice has increasingly affected many people's lives (especially those socially marginalized and disenfranchised) in such a way that they cannot cope with it as individuals.

The purpose of this chapter is to address the problem of structural injustice in our world from a political-theological perspective. It seeks to answer several questions: What does it mean for the church to take seriously the problem of structural injustice from a theological perspective? Should not the state be the primary institution that has the authority to address the problem of structural injustice? What does the church have to do with the contemporary structural injustice of our world? What does the Bible say about structural injustice? What are the specific roles and responsibilities of the church in taking structural injustice seriously as its key political-theological subject matter? Before answering these questions, we need to recall that the problem of structural injustice was not the only one we discovered through historical reckoning. We also have discovered that the church's complicity with colonial structural injustice stemmed from its theological incompetency to deal with the issue. What is more, this was caused by the church's self-induced age-old hermeneutic stance: territorial thinking.

Not all forms of injustice are structural, but without discussing this specific type, the church may never have a chance to promote and implement social justice. The growing dominance and the social gripping of structural injustice are the most pressing and urgent problems of our world, and the church cannot sit still without doing anything about it lest it should commit the same historical sin that the European churches did during the colonial period. The Western church must address the problem of structural injustice to claim that it has indeed reckoned with the historical sin with sincerity and earnestness.

A critical analysis of the realities of structural injustice needs to be accompanied by an in-depth examination of the state's engagement in and response to the structural injustice in our world. We should remember that the European colonization was mostly engineered, advocated, and managed by the Western states. Can we depend on the states to resolve the various problems of structural injustice in our world? Augustine's insight on the notion of "imperfect justice" helps us realize that the ideal state of true justice is not attainable by the state, and this becomes the contextual reason the church should be ready to develop and engage its distinctive political acts by dismantling the ecclesial habits of territorial thinking. The final purpose of this chapter is to show how the church's alternative politics is not only possible but also required as an ecclesial response to the structural injustice, systemic violence, and social-ecological suffering of this world. The goal of the church's distinctive politics is, then, to practice deterritorial intervention to address them. In this chapter, as a groundwork to develop the church's distinctive politics, which I call the "rhizomatic politics," I specifically focus on formulating a new perspectival paradigm that will substitute the church's age-old territorial thinking. I call this new perspectival paradigm "nomadic thinking" by adopting the social philosophers Gilles Deleuze and Félix Guattari's enigmatic yet seminal neologisms. As a result of this constructive work, then, we have a better methodical tool to develop the church's alternative politics in an age of neoliberalism.

STRUCTURAL INJUSTICE, SYSTEMIC VIOLENCE, AND SOCIAL-ECOLOGICAL SUFFERING IN THE *CIVITAS TERRENA*

What is structural injustice? How has it played out in this world? Why should the church take it seriously? In the introduction and previous chapter, we identified structural injustice as a distinctive type of injustice caused by unfair rules, skewed cultural norms, and historical oppression, which usually bring an accumulative and perennial negative impact to some social groups (e.g., racial, political, or cultural minorities) vis-à-vis others. Let me illustrate some cases regarding how structural injustice affects ordinary people and their lives and worlds.

Olga was a mother by the time she was fifteen in Mexico, and she struggled to provide for her two children before she decided to come to California. She and her children eventually settled in a small seaside farming town in Oxnard, seventy miles north of Los Angeles. Olga found out that her son, Victor, identified as a woman. Victor became known as Victoria, or Vica, by her family. In May 2007, when Vica was twenty-three, she was stopped for a driving violation and sent to a Los Angeles immigration detention center. When she was detained, the first thing she told them was that she had AIDS and needed her medication. According to Olga and fellow detainees, Vica was repeatedly denied medication for AIDS while at the federal facility. Olga could not go to see her because she was fearful of immigration officers. When Vica called Olga, she told her how badly she and other transgender detainees were treated. They were frequently humiliated, laughed at, and mocked by Immigration and Customs Enforcement (ICE) personnel, security guards, and even nurses.

Despite her wish, Vica never got AIDS medication. Soon after, Olga received a call from Deanna, Vica's transgender friend in detention, who said that Vica was very ill. Out of fear and desperation, Olga looked for any help, even calling an attorney. She soon got a call from the Mexican consulate and received a legal permit to visit her dying daughter. When Olga got to the hospital, there was an ICE guard, and Vica was fighting for her last breath. When Olga said "Vica," she immediately opened her eyes and tried to raise her arms to hug her mom, but they fell. She was so pale and too weak to raise her arms. Vica was trying to form a kiss, but she couldn't do it either. She was not even able to move on the bed without screaming due to her lung pain. While Olga and her family were visiting Vica, the guards were at the door watching every move they made. At first, Olga didn't notice Vica was shackled. She came to realize that when Vica wanted to shift her body, tired of being in the same position, she couldn't move her foot. As Olga lifted the blanket, she saw the chain, which broke her heart. Olga and her daughter Sara could not help but cry. Vica's last words were "Mami, Mami." Olga says that her life is so different now, and the first thing she thinks about every morning is Vica's death. She tells her American interviewer that she wants to make Vica's story public in English so that the Americans know and people care.[1]

Donna Young, a primary midwife servicing Vernal, Utah, goes to bed with her pistol every night. Vernal is a boom-and-bust town of ten thousand people in the heart of the "fracked-gas gold rush" of the Uintah Basin.[2] Donna used to have eighteen to twenty-five clients a year, with a spotless reputation as a midwife, but this number has gone down to four to five. What happened? In 2013, she realized there seemed to be a shockingly high infant mortality rate for such a small town like hers (at least ten in 2013), and she raised a question to Joe Schaffer, director of the TriCounty Health Department: "Why are so

---

1. Olga's story is written in Peter Orner, ed., *Underground America: Narratives of Undocumented Lives* (San Francisco: McSweeney's, 2008), 101–13.
2. Paul Solotaroff, "What's Killing the Babies of Vernal, Utah?," *Rolling Stone*, June 22, 2015, http://www.rollingstone.com/culture/features/fracking-whats-killing-the-babies -of-vernal-utah-20150622.

many of our babies dying?" Unlike other places where detecting a grave risk to children would be applauded, Donna says that in Vernal, a town literally built by fracked oil, raising questions about the safety of the fracking industry renders anyone a traitor and a target.

Prodded by Donna, the TriCounty Health Department announced a study in 2014 to assess her concerns over the infant mortality rate, but she tells the reporter that the study was designed to fail. According to her, "Any serious inquiry would have started with Suspect One: the extraordinary levels of wintertime pollution plaguing the Basin since the vast new undertaking to frack the region's shale filled the air with toxins." Instead of investigating Vernal's air pollution (with ozone readings that rivaled the worst days of summer in New York or Los Angeles, particulate matter as bad as Mexico City, ground air fraught with carcinogenic gases like benzene), the county merely counted up infant deaths. In fact, nearly all the Uintah mothers whose babies died were pregnant during the winter of 2012–13, when the basin bound on all four sides was perfectly formed for winter inversions as twenty-below weather clamped down on the valley, sealing warmer air above it. Four months after Schaffer announced the study, he retired as the director of the health department, and six months later, the department's findings were released. Sam LeFevre, who conducted the study as an epidemiologist with the Utah State Health Department, told concerned Vernal citizens that smoking, diabetes, and prenatal neglect among the basin's residents were to be blamed as the possible causes for the deaths. Donna asks, "How many dead infants does it take before you'll accept that there's a problem?"[3]

Jason Yoder was a graduate student in organic chemistry at Illinois State University. He struggled to find a job in his field in 2007 after incurring $100,000 in student loan debt. One evening, he left his family's mobile home and was later discovered in one of the labs on campus and declared dead due to nitrogen asphyxiation. Although many expressed great sympathy for Jason and ranted against the abusive student lending system, some others quickly invoked the "personal responsibility" argument, saying, "It was his fault," "Why did he take out that amount of loans?" or "Mr. Yoder took out those

---

3. Paul Solotaroff.

loans. He had an obligation to pay them back." While his mother was preparing for his funeral, student debt collectors were still phoning her regarding his student loan debt. She told them, "You are part of the reason he took his own life," then hung up the phone.[4]

According to Cryn Johannsen, many people are at risk of following Jason's pathway due to their onerous student loan debts. She points out that suicide is the dark side of the student lending crisis, and despite all the media attention on the issue of student loans, it has been still severely underreported. She introduces some alarming stories of people who are struggling with student debt. For instance, one person says, "Yes, I thought about suicide a lot over the past few years. I take anti-depressants and I had been smoking cigarettes for months, but I did end up quitting. The big issue with that is I want to be an opera singer so [smoking] was my way of giving up. I'm trying to do what I can to get through this . . . and praying for an answer." Another says, "I think about jumping from the 27th-floor window of my office every day."[5] According to *Forbes*, student debt in the United States as of February 2021 totaled $1.7 trillion (the second-largest consumer obligation after mortgages), and there were forty-five million borrowers.[6] *U.S. News* also reports that 10.9 percent of the total student debt in the first quarter of 2019 was ninety-plus days delinquent or in default. If we apply some simple math, we can figure out that there are hundreds of billions of dollars in seriously delinquent or defaulted student loans out there, which suggests a widening swath of households are unable or unwilling to pay back their school debt.[7]

What are the commonalities of these three stories described above? We can immediately sympathize with the feeling of helplessness these individuals might have experienced. At the same time, we can also realize that all three

4. Cryn Johannsen, "The One We've Lost: The Student Loan Debt Suicides," Huffington Post, July 2, 2012, http://www.huffingtonpost.com/c-cryn-johannsen/student-loan-debt -suicides_b_1638972.html.

5. Johannsen.

6. Zack Friedman, "Student Loan Debt Statistics in 2021: A Record $1.7 Trillion," *Forbes*, February 20, 2021, https://www.forbes.com/sites/zackfriedman/2021/02/20/student -loan-debt-statistics-in-2021-a-record-17-trillion/?sh=13e40da01431.

7. Bobby Gattone, "What to Know about Delinquent Student Loans," *U.S. News*, July 31, 2019, https://www.usnews.com/education/blogs/student-loan-ranger/articles/2019-07 -31/what-to-know-about-delinquent-student-loans.

people (Vica, Donna, and Jason) have been subjected to biased structural forces—such as unjust social, cultural, legal, or financial systems—rather than merely being mistreated by unscrupulous individuals. We could identify these forces as inhumane immigration laws, cultural prejudices, corporate dominance and control, or abusive neoliberal economies of debt. We are living in a world that is increasingly affected, shaped, controlled, and even exploited by systemic or structural forces whose areas of influence can easily transcend the boundaries of ordinary people's individual or communal lives, including their private, familiar, and communal relations. Such worldwide phenomena as economic globalization, mass migration, and climate change have increasingly transformed our world to be more connected to one another while making us more vulnerable to one another's needs beyond any artificial or natural demarcations, including national boundaries. If any agencies, including the church, attempted to address and promote social justice, they would not be able to do so without addressing the problem of structural injustice.

In her influential work *Responsibility for Justice*, the late political philosopher Iris Marion Young argues that some harms and injuries "arise not from the isolatable actions of individual or institutional agents, but rather from the normal, ongoing structural processes of the society."[8] Young identifies structural injustice as unjust structural processes of society, and as such, it is often overlooked or even accepted in the forms of institutional rules and policies. This is the reason we see the same pattern of structural injustice continuously recurring despite the fact that it entails systemic violence as well as social suffering and trauma.

In the year 2020, under Covid-19 lockdowns, American society witnessed how the structural injustice of systemic racism literally killed and murdered innocent Black Americans through police brutality. In particular, the murder of George Floyd by the white Minneapolis police officer Derek Chauvin reignited the BLM (Black Lives Matter) movement across the country. But before the case of George Floyd rattled the entire nation, many similar cases were occurring throughout America. The #SayTheirNames campaign encouraged citizens and media users to not just identify victims of police

---

8. Iris Marion Young, *Responsibility for Justice* (New York: Oxford University Press, 2011), 175.

brutality but focus on their dignity by using their names. Today, the hashtag often includes the names of Black men and women killed in recent years, including Trayvon Martin, Tamir Rice, Michael Brown, Eric Garner, Philando Castile, Breonna Taylor, and many others. Part of what makes the police brutality against Black and brown people a structural injustice is the Trump administration's official response. William Barr, the then US attorney general, testified before the House Committee on Oversight and Reform on Capitol Hill in Washington, DC, on July 28, 2020, saying, "I don't agree that there's systemic racism in police departments generally, in this country."[9] Of course, Barr was not the only one who denied the problem of systemic racism. In an almost concerted way, other administrative officials, such as the then national security adviser Robert O'Brien and acting Homeland Security secretary Chad Wolf, similarly dismissed the idea of systemic racism.[10] By publicly denying its existence, instead of upholding justice, they obscured the structural injustice of systemic racism.

Along with its recursive and repetitive aspect, structural injustice is also characterized by its accumulative and incremental traits. Perhaps the most obvious case that reflects these elements of structural injustice is the growing economic disparity between the rich and the poor as well as the widespread proliferation of poverty and financial fragility in US society. In his book *Evicted: Poverty and Profit in the American City*, Matthew Desmond illustrates how the accumulative and incremental impact of the structural injustice of American poverty and financial fragility radically disrupts so many people who are already on the margins of our society. Desmond reports that "the majority of poor renting families in America spend over half of their income on housing, and at least one in four dedicates over 70 percent to paying the rent and keeping the lights on. Millions of Americans are evicted every year because

---

9. Gerry Johnson, "US Attorney General Denies Systemic Racism in Policing," Human Rights Watch, July 30, 2020, https://www.hrw.org/news/2020/07/30/us-attorney -general-denies-systemic-racism-policing#.

10. Devan Cole, "Top Trump Officials Claim There's No Systemic Racism in US Law Enforcement Agencies as Americans Flood Streets in Protest," *CNN*, June 10, 2020, https://www.cnn.com/2020/06/07/politics/systemic-racism-trump-administration -officials-barr-carson-wolf/index.html.

they can't make rent."[11] He estimates that 2.3 million evictions were filed in the United States in 2016.[12] The growing wealth gap between the rich and the poor has now reached the highest level since the 1970s. In his 2019 article, "America's Humongous Wealth Gap Is Widening Further," Pedro Nicolaci da Costa writes that "the Fed's report shows, among other things, that the poorest 50% of Americans are literally getting crushed by the weight of rising inequalities." He continues, saying, "The bottom 50% saw essentially zero net gains in wealth over those 30 years, driving their already meager share of total wealth down to just 1% from 4%," while during the same period, "the richest 10% held 70% of total household wealth, up from 60%."[13]

Besides its recursive and accumulative aspects, structural injustice has to do with systemic violence and social-ecological suffering. The Norwegian sociologist Johan Galtung develops a typology for this violence in his 1969 article, "Violence, Peace, and Peace Research." He divides the concept of violence into "personal" and "structural" types.[14] Structural violence is distinguished from personal violence in several aspects. Unlike the personal type of violence, structural violence is conceived as something that shows stability. Built already into the social structure, it exhibits the stability of the social structure itself. While in a static society, structural violence may be seen to be as natural as the air around us, in a highly dynamic society, it becomes

11. Matthew Desmond, *Evicted: Poverty and Profit in the American City* (New York: Broadway, 2016), 4.

12. Terry Gross, "First-Ever Evictions Database Shows: We're in the Middle of a Housing Crisis," NPR Fresh Air, April 12, 2018, https://www.npr.org/2018/04/12/601783346/first-ever-evictions-database-shows-were-in-the-middle-of-a-housing-crisis.

13. Pedro Nicolaci da Costa, "America's Humongous Wealth Gap Is Widening Further," *Forbes*, May 29, 2019, https://www.forbes.com/sites/pedrodacosta/2019/05/29/americas-humungous-wealth-gap-is-widening-further/#259ce03d42ee.

14. Johan Galtung later adds one more type to this typology—"cultural violence." He, however, writes that "cultural violence" follows in the footsteps of the concept of "structural violence" (Johan Galtung, "Cultural Violence," *Journal of Peace Research* 27, no. 3 [1990]: 291–305, here 303).

apparent because it stands out like an enormous rock in a creek.[15] Unlike personal violence, it "slowly" and "undramatically" kills its victims.[16]

The concept of structural violence has become a key social issue for scholars across different disciplines. For instance, Paul Farmer, an American anthropologist and physician, says that "standing on the shoulders of those who have studied slavery, racism, and other forms of institutionalized violence, a growing number of anthropologists now devote their attention to structural violence." "Structural violence," he says, "is violence exerted systematically—that is, indirectly—by everyone who belongs to a certain social order."[17] It is manifested in the form of systemic "oppression," resulting in a distinctive type of human suffering—structural or social suffering. It is, therefore, necessary for us to examine the background conditions of social, economic, political, or cultural structures that may be blamed for engendering such systemic oppression. Structural violence and oppression are morally problematic because they "stop individuals, groups, and societies from reaching their full potentials."[18] As Galtung argues, structural violence should be understood as the cause that increases "the distance between the potential and the actual," impeding its decrease.[19] In other words, structural violence is a major systemic force that keeps many people from living their full and flourishing lives.

The Lutheran Christian ethicist Cynthia D. Moe-Lobeda summarizes several features of structural violence in her book *Resisting Structural Evil*. According to her, structural violence

- is generally invisible to or ignored by those who perpetrate it and or benefit from it.

---

15. Johan Galtung, "Violence, Peace, and Peace Research," *Journal of Peace Research* 6, no. 3 (1969): 167–91, here 173.

16. Johan Galtung and Tord Höivik, "Structural and Direct Violence," *Journal of Peace Research* 8, no. 1 (1971): 72–76, here 72.

17. Paul Farmer, "An Anthropology of Structural Violence," *Current Anthropology* 45, no. 3 (June 2004): 305–25, here 307.

18. Paul Farmer, "Structural Violence and Clinical Medicine," *PLoS Medicine* 3, no. 19 (October 2006): 1686–91, here 1686.

19. Galtung, "Violence, Peace, and Peace Research," 168.

- cannot happen without the actions of individuals, yet operates independently of the goodness or wickedness of the people perpetrating it.
- is passed on from generation to generation unless challenged.
- becomes more devastating with a concentration of power in fewer hands.
- consists of interlocking rather than isolated forms of oppression. Hence one may "benefit" from structural violence along one "axis of oppression" while being victimized by it along another.
- may trap perpetrators by victimizing them in the very structural violence they perpetrate.
- entails ideologies or worldviews, institutional policies, and practices so embedded in society that they *appear* natural, normal, inevitable, or divinely mandated.[20]

According to Moe-Lobeda, the actions required to maintain structural violence are taken by ordinary people who do not seem to be responsible for the decisions that mandate those actions. She illustrates this point with two cases: first, the case of a middle-level manager at Walmart who did not make the policy that denies some employees benefits and adequate wages to maintain their health, and second, the case of a gas station employee who did not decide to pay militias to kill Ogoni people who protested Shell Oil in the Niger Delta.[21] What is sinister about structural violence is that people who perpetuate it may not even know what they are doing. Ordinary people may end up supporting structural injustice without even recognizing it.

What about, then, the relationship between systemic violence and social suffering? We need to examine how structural injustice and systemic violence are closely tied to social suffering that is impinged upon those marginalized and disenfranchised. Medical anthropologists define social suffering as "the devastating injuries that social force can inflict on human experience." These injuries typically refer to "results from what political, economic, and

---

20. Cynthia D. Moe-Lobeda, *Resisting Structural Evil: Love as Ecological-Economic Vocation* (Minneapolis: Fortress, 2013), 77.
21. Moe-Lobeda, 74.

institutional power does to people."[22] As Farmer indicates, the idea of structural violence is closely linked not only to structural injustice but also to the "social machinery of oppression."[23] Since this social machinery of oppression directly or indirectly causes many people to suffer under unjust systemic enforcement and structural processes, the idea of social suffering is formulated as a corollary of structural injustice and violence. The stories of Vica, Donna, and Jason exemplify what structural suffering is like. They illustrate viscerally how marginalized and disenfranchised people can be victimized by an unjust social structure, which leads them to social suffering. The stories (recounted in Farmer's article) of Acéphie (a girl from a small village in Haiti whose town was displaced due to the construction of a dam, which eventually led her into a series of unfortunate life events, including her own death caused by AIDS) and Chouchou (a young man from rural Haiti who was brutally tortured and killed by the army of Haiti's military dictator) illustrate the sheer magnitude of structural suffering.[24]

We have explored not only the conceptual constructions of structural injustice, systemic violence, and social suffering but also their closely interwoven relation among one another. As a result of this exploration, we have discovered that there is an indubitable commonality between European colonialism and today's postcolonial Western society—the prevalence of structural injustice, systemic violence, and social-ecological suffering. Although the era of European colonialism may have ended, its long-standing harmful legacies are alive today in different forms and styles yet holding on to the same old logic. This is the reason I argue that it is crucial for the church to reckon with its historical sin of colonial complicity. If it fails to do so, then it will most likely make the same historical misstep, replicating its colonial pattern without addressing or challenging today's structural injustice, systemic violence, and social-ecological suffering. But what if the Western church did in fact reckon with its historical sin with earnestness and urgency? What would

---

22. Arthur Kleinman, Veena Das, and Margaret M. Lock, eds., *Social Suffering* (Berkeley: University of California Press, 1997), iv.

23. Farmer, "Structural Violence and Clinical Medicine," 1686.

24. The sad stories of Acéphie and Chouchou are introduced in Paul Farmer's "On Suffering and Structural Violence: A View from Below," *Daedalus* 125, no. 1 (Winter 1996): 261–83.

result? I contend that it should develop its distinctive politics with the purpose of addressing and challenging structural injustice and systemic violence. It is incumbent upon us to invent its different model of politics in today's post-colonial world. We will shortly discuss how the church's distinctive politics is possible and how it differs from the ideal type of the state's liberal politics. Before moving forward, however, we first have to answer the following questions: What about the separation between the state and the church? Is it not the role of the state to address and solve the problems of structural injustice, systemic violence, and social-ecological suffering? Are we trying to substitute the church's ecclesial politics for the state's secular politics? One may find these questions legitimate and justifiable but will soon discover that they are mistaken because, in nature and goal, the church's ecclesial politics differ from the state's secular politics.

SECULARIZATION, COLONIZATION, AND THE LIMITS OF STATE POLITICS

How is the church's distinctive politics possible? Do we even need it? First off, we must put this question in a larger historical and sociological context to have a better sense of its meaning. What, then, is this historical and sociological context? The secularization of Western society. Although Charles Taylor's *A Secular Age* has changed the public understanding of secularization, many people still regard it as the privatization of religion in contrast to the publicization of secular spaces (the economic, political, cultural, professional, recreational realms).[25] The secularization thesis is problematic particularly

---

25. We should note that the idea of secularization has been under significant criticism by religious and nonreligious scholars. For instance, Pippa Norris and Ronald Inglehart write, "After reviewing the historical evidence of church-going in Europe, Rodney Stark concludes that secularization is a pervasive myth, based on failed prophecies and ideological polemic, unsupported by systematic data" (Pippa Norris and Ronald Inglehart, *Sacred and Secular: Religion and Politics Worldwide* [Cambridge: Cambridge University Press, 2004], 11). Peter Berger also says, "I came to the conclusion some years ago that to replace secularization theory—to explain religion in the modern world—we need the theory of pluralism. Modernity does not necessarily produce secularity. It necessarily produces pluralism, by which I mean the coexistence in the same society of different worldviews and value systems" (Gregor Thuswaldner, "A Conversation with Peter L. Berger: 'How My Views Have

concerning the development of the idea of the church's politics because it tends to neutralize, nullify, or even abolish any religious attempt to develop this idea. According to this thesis, the world is secularized, and thus the church's politics is categorically irrelevant, unwelcome, and even dangerous. The secularization thesis becomes an ideological catalyst that has further fortified the church's territorial thinking.

Regarding the secularization thesis, we should especially focus on its historical background and its motivating factor. According to Frank Lechner, after the 1648 Treaty of Westphalia ended the European wars of religion, "secularization was used to describe the transfer of territories held by the church to the control of political authorities."[26] This understanding is important because one of the historical motifs of secularization and the separation of religion from politics is to prevent further social and political violence caused by religious intolerance and fanaticism, which legitimize religious wars. As Roland Robertson points out, the "consummation of the Westphalian spirit" was "the Declaration of Independence in the nascent American Republic in 1776, with its commitment to the constitutional separation of church and state."[27]

Since, as Taylor suggests, today's secularized Western society is marked not so much by the retreat of religious belief but rather by the mutual fragilization of competing religious and nonreligious, believing and nonbelieving, options in a more pluralistic world, we cannot help but ask whether

---

Changed,'" *Cresset: A Review of Literature, the Arts, and Public Affairs* 77, no. 3 [2014]: 16–21, here 17). Concurring with Berger's pluralist thesis, Charles Taylor declares his disagreement with the "orthodox" version of secularization theory. He argues that we should understand secularism not so much as a phenomenon of the falling away of belief in God or the retreat of religion from the public sphere but as a transition from a society in which it was virtually impossible to challenge belief in God to one in which that belief is one of multiple challenged preferences. Taylor, however, acknowledges the decline of religious belief and practice in the West. He writes, "It is obvious that a decline in belief and practice has occurred, and beyond this, that the unchallengeable status that the belief enjoyed in earlier centuries has been lost. This is a major phenomenon of 'secularization'" (Charles Taylor, *A Secular Age* [Cambridge, MA: Belknap Press of Harvard University Press, 2007], 530).

26. Frank Lechner, "Secularization," in *Encyclopedia of Protestantism*, vol. 4, ed. Hans J. Hillerbrand (London: Routledge, 2004), 131–40, here 131.

27. Roland Robertson, "Religion, International Relations and Transdisciplinarity," *Protosociology: An International Journal of Interdisciplinary Research* 27 (2011): 7–20, here 13.

secularization and its consummation (the separation of church and state) have effectively done away with the problem of violence.[28] Given that this problem is often seen as a religious one, it is more than justifiable for us to raise a question: Has secularization successfully resolved the problem of violence in a secularized world?

Taylor sees this problem as a "dilemma" because the struggle against evil can itself generate evil either by religion or by "modern humanism." He thus writes,

> Nothing gave Nietzsche greater satisfaction than showing how morality or spirituality is really powered by its direct opposite; e.g., that the Christian aspiration to love is really motivated by the hatred of the weak for the strong. Whatever one thinks of this judgment on Christianity, it is clear that modern humanism is full of potential for such disconcerting reversals; from dedication to others to self-indulgent, feel-good responses, from a lofty sense of human dignity to control powered by contempt and hatred, from absolute freedom to absolute despotism, from a flaming desire to help the oppressed to an incandescent hatred for all those who stand in the way. And the higher the flight, the greater the potential fall.[29]

For Taylor, the problem of violence cannot be simply consigned to its religious form because it is something "meta-biological," and history proves that the depth of this problem goes down to our human nature. He captures it as follows: "But herein lies the difficulty. These explorations of the depth meaning of violence tend either to yield an affirmation, even glorification of it; or else to show how ineradicable it is. Put in other terms, we could say that they generally tend to show the draw to violence to be too deeply anchored to be rooted out, whether they rejoice in this respect (Nietzsche) or take it with a resigned pessimism (Freud)."[30] Regarding the secularization thesis, Taylor offers an important perspective to us: modern secularism fails to put an end

---

28. Taylor, *Secular Age*, 531.
29. Taylor, 698–99.
30. Taylor, 673.

to the problem of violence, although it claims that it has ended religious wars by separating church and state, thereby successfully converting religion and belief into private matters.

While Taylor tries to be neutral in his analysis of the relation between the secularization thesis and the problem of violence, the Catholic theologian William T. Cavanaugh explores the relation specifically from a Christian theological perspective. He demonstrates that the pervasive idea that religion is divisive, absolutist, irrational, and thus prone to violence is a way of "legitimating certain kinds of practices and delegitimating others." He begins his argument by saying, "The idea that religion causes violence is one of the most prevalent myths in Western culture." Although his perspective is theological, his stance is not apologetic. He acknowledges that "under certain circumstances, particular construals of Islam or Christianity contribute to violence."[31] Indeed, as he writes, the evidence seems incontrovertible. From blood sacrifices to holy wars, crusades, inquisitions, and pogroms, religions not only were implicated in spreading European imperialism but also have legitimated the oppression of the poor and women.[32]

Cavanaugh, however, points out that the term *religion* has been used in different times and places by different people according to their different interests. In other words, the word *religion* is socially constructed. He writes, "Religion is not simply an objective descriptor of certain kinds of practices that show up in every time and place. It is a term that constructs and is constructed by different kinds of political configurations." He claims that "there is no transhistorical and transcultural essence of religion. What counts as religion and what does not in any given context is contestable and depends on who has the power and authority to define religion at any given time and place."[33] Nationalism can be a good example. As is well known, nationalism often acts like and is sometimes called a religion, although it is not one.[34] Indeed, there are other phenomena that seem to act like religion in the secular

---

31. William T. Cavanaugh, *The Myth of Religious Violence* (New York: Oxford University Press, 2009), 59, 15, 54.
32. Cavanaugh, 15.
33. Cavanaugh, 58, 59.
34. Cavanaugh, 36.

world, such as sports fanaticism or Marxism. Who, then, invented the modern concept of religion?[35] Cavanaugh points out that the birth of the modern concept of religion coincides with the birth of the sovereign modern state in the West. He writes, "It is only with the birth of the sovereign modern state that the concept of religion as it is now generally understood was born."[36]

Why was the modern concept of religion invented? According to Cavanaugh, the main purpose of inventing it was to subordinate ecclesiastical power to civil power and eventually separate them. The modern liberal state developed an effective strategy to delimit ecclesiastical power, and this strategy was focused on creating coherent dichotomies between the private and the public, religion and politics, and the church and the state, resulting in the confinement of ecclesiastical power to the realm of private life, religion, and the church. Cavanaugh thus writes, "Over the course of the fifteenth through seventeenth centuries, religion came to be an essentially interior impulse, demarcated by sets of beliefs or propositions about reality, and essentially distinct from 'secular' pursuits such as politics, economics, and the life."[37] The secularization project that promoted the religious-secular separation, however, accompanied "the state's monopoly over internal violence and its colonial expansion."[38]

Perhaps Cavanaugh's most provocative argument in his deconstruction of the myth of religious violence is that the transfer of power from the church to the state was itself the root of wars.[39] Cavanaugh justifies his argument by critically adopting the works of a host of historians and social thinkers, including Johannes Wolfart, Charles Tilly, Gabriel Ardant, Perry Anderson,

---

35. Cavanaugh adopts the concept of invented religion from the following scholars: Tomoko Masuzawa, *The Invention of World Religions; or, How European Universalism Was Preserved in the Language of Pluralism* (Chicago: University of Chicago Press, 2005); Daniel Dubuisson, *The Western Construction of Religion: Myth, Knowledge, and Ideology*, trans. William Sayers (Baltimore: Johns Hopkins University Press, 2003); Derek Peterson and Darren Walhof, eds., *The Invention of Religion: Rethinking Belief in Politics and History* (New Brunswick, NJ: Rutgers University Press, 2002).

36. William T. Cavanaugh, *Field Hospital: The Church's Engagement with a Wounded World* (Cambridge: Eerdmans, 2016), 182.

37. Cavanaugh, 182.

38. Cavanaugh, *Myth of Religious Violence*, 59.

39. Cavanaugh, 162.

Hendrik Spruyt, Anthony Giddens, and others. Based on their works, he holds that "much of the violence of the so-called wars of religion is explained in terms of the resistance of local elites to the state-building efforts of monarchs and emperors."[40] According to Cavanaugh, then, the secularist argument that religion is to be blamed for violence is misguided because the problem of violence originates in humanity's proneness to idolatry, and idolatry is not limited to the realm of religion. He summarizes his argument by saying, "People kill for all sorts of things, things like money and flags and oil and freedom that function as gods in people's lives." The secularization thesis is problematic because it presupposes that the secular world is immune to humanity's fundamental tendency to be idolatrous. It is right for Cavanaugh to say that "the enchantment that produces violence is just as likely to appear in so-called secular form—such as the putatively secular nation-state—as it is in the so-called religions such as Christianity."[41] Indeed, Cavanaugh's profound theological understanding of humanity's proneness to idolatry is widely supported and verified by historical examples. The secularist argument turns out to be insufficient and inadequate because it fails to see that there are different kinds of fundamentalisms in the secular world, which are equivalent to religious fundamentalism in terms of germinating, abetting, and spreading all forms of violence and conflicts.

Among the different kinds of secularist fundamentalisms, market fundamentalism is particularly conspicuous. The American economist Joseph E. Stiglitz defines market fundamentalism as "the notion that unfettered markets by themselves can ensure economic prosperity and growth."[42] Roksana Bahramitash argues that despite empirical evidence about its problematic nature, market fundamentalism identified as the supremacy of the market has become "more like a religion rather than a sound principle." She goes on further, saying, "Market-oriented theory is the religion of the rich and the powerful whose preachers incidentally are among the very privileged. Fashionably dressed, they sit in the highest positions of the financial ivory tower

40. Cavanaugh, 163.
41. Cavanaugh, 190, 192.
42. Joseph E. Stiglitz, *Freefall: America, Free Markets, and the Sinking of the World Economy* (New York: W. W. Norton, 2010), xiii.

institutions of Bretton Woods (the International Monetary Fund [IMF] and the World Bank). They may not look like monks, rabbis, or mullahs, but they operate on similar mindsets."[43]

As Stiglitz points out, the financial crisis of 2007–8 was an epic failure of this quasi-religious secular ideology of market fundamentalism. The real problem of market fundamentalism, however, lies in the enormity of economic and social sufferings it has engendered to a countless number of people all over the world, from many sweatshop workers in Third World countries to numerous debtors who are struggling under onerous debts in First World countries. From the 1984 Bhopal disaster in India to the 1964–92 ecological genocide by Texas/Chevron in the Ecuadorian Amazon area, from the 1997 Asian financial crisis to Argentina's second default in 2014, the system of market fundamentalism in the secular world has significantly unsettled many innocent lives and inflicted immense systemic violence on them. Indeed, if we would attempt to document the immeasurable financial damages and social sufferings of those victimized people, we may need more than multivolume works. It is empirically and ideologically groundless to say that secularism and the separation of the secular and the religious have made our world safe from violence, especially the kind wreaked by market fundamentalism. The secular world has spawned its own kind of fundamentalism, and its consequential systemic violence and social suffering are as severe as those caused by religious fundamentalism.

We should especially focus on the global dominance of neoliberalism to address the massive and far-reaching social impact of secularist fundamentalism. According to David Harvey, "Neoliberalism is in the first instance a theory of political economic practices that proposes that human well-being can best be advanced by liberating individual entrepreneurial freedoms and skills within an institutional framework characterized by strong private property rights, free markets, and free trade."[44] It is a mistake to believe that neoliberalism only refers to the domain of the market system because as a form of social

---

43. Roksana Bahramitash, "Market Fundamentalism versus Religious Fundamentalism: Women's Employment in Iran," *Critique: Critical Middle Eastern Studies* 13, no. 1 (Spring 2004): 33–46, here 34.

44. David Harvey, *A Brief History of Neoliberalism* (Oxford: Oxford University Press, 2007), 2.

ideology, it not only reshapes people's way of life but also modifies their moral values. For instance, if deeply steeped in neoliberalism, people begin to see the matters of their everyday lives (such as education, cultural activities, and even marriage) from the perspective of a market mechanism, rendering the "commodification of everything" prevalent in all aspects of their lives and social relations. Emphasizing this all-encompassing governance of neoliberalism, the sociologist Wendy Brown writes that neoliberalism is conceived "as an order of normative reason that, when it becomes ascendant, takes shape as a governing rationality extending a specific formulation of economic values, practices, and metrics to *every dimension* of human life."[45]

Neoliberalism impacts everyone living on earth, whether they acknowledge it or not. The real problem regarding the growing dominance of neoliberalism is how it influences so many people's ordinary lives, especially those of the marginalized and disenfranchised. It does not merely impact the poor people; it, rather, creates a new class of the helpless and the powerless and keeps them in that state of exploitation. The creation and perpetuation of this new class have undoubtedly to do with the structural injustice and violence of neoliberalism. The typical establishment of neoliberal structural injustice and violence follows this track. First, the rise of neoliberal financialization makes possible the extreme concentration of wealth among a small number of people and corporate entities. Second, these people and entities gradually abduct the political and legal governance of the state via personal influences (campaign contributions) and lobbying. Third, the growing dominance of neoliberal governance not only disrupts the social fabric but also depletes the social capital, leaving people helpless, powerless, and disconnected. As this sinister social process goes down deeper, the amount of social suffering inflicted upon the helpless and the powerless gets augmented and multiplied.

Social scientists generally agree that financialization refers to the growing dominance of finance capital, which comes along with the explosion of debt and new financial instruments, such as derivatives. Financialization has entailed not only the new class of what Stiglitz calls "financial rentiers" but

---

45. Wendy Brown, *Undoing the Demos: Neoliberalism's Stealth Revolution* (Brooklyn, NY: Zone Books, 2015), 30 (emphasis added).

also the enormous wealth gap between the rich and the poor. The economist Edward N. Wolff noted in 2017 that the top 1 percent of households own more wealth than the bottom 90 percent combined.[46] The accumulated wealth does not simply sit in the financial market. Finance capital systemically disrupts and destructs the lives of many innocent people as well as Mother Nature. For example, according to the *Guardian*, in 2009, the oil company BP spent nearly $16 million on lobbying the federal government, ranking it among the twenty highest spenders on lobbying that year. The purpose was "to influence US policy and regulatory oversight." Thanks to this, in September 2009, BP was able to drill the deepest well ever at its Tiber field in the US Gulf at a depth of more than thirty-five thousand feet (farther down than Mount Everest is up), and the *Guardian* says, "Anyone in the business will tell you that drilling at such depths is incredibly risky, even with the most conscientious oversight."[47] What is even more astonishing is that in 2010, when the Deepwater Horizon disaster happened, BP spent still more millions of dollars on lobbyists to protect their interests in Congress.[48]

The case of rising student debt in the United States and its associated social suffering provides us with another glimpse of how neoliberalism systemically unsettles the social fabric of American civic life. On April 20, 2005, the then president George W. Bush signed the Bankruptcy Abuse Prevention and Consumer Protection Act of 2005 (BAPCPA) into law, and this was enabled by a decade of legislative debate and intense lobbying efforts by the banking and credit card industries. The BAPCPA rendered private

46. Edward N. Wolff, "Household Wealth Trends in the United States, 1962 to 2016: Has Middle Class Wealth Recovered?," *National Bureau of Economic Research*, November 2017, https://www.nber.org/papers/w24085.pdf.
47. Antonia Juhasz, "BP Spends Millions Lobbying as It Drills Ever Deeper and the Environment Pays," *Guardian*, May 2010, https://www.theguardian.com/business/2010/may/02/bp-deepwater-horizon-oil-spills#:~:text=BP%20spends%20millions%20lobbying%20as%20it%20drills%20ever%20deeper%20and%20the%20environment%20pays,-Antonia%20Juhasz&text=While%20the%20explosion%20of%20BP,was%20neither%20surprising%20nor%20unexpected.&text=Its%202009%20revenues%20of%20%24239,largest%20corporation%20in%20the%20country.
48. Reuters Staff, "FACTBOX-BP and Other Spill Companies Up US Lobby Spending," Reuters, July 2010, https://www.reuters.com/article/oil-spill-lobbying-companies/factbox-bp-and-other-spill-companies-up-us-lobby-spending-idUKN169756720100721.

student loans nearly nondischargeable. Since then, student loans have sky-rocketed from $345 billion in 2004 to $1.56 trillion in 2020 (more than qua-druple), during which postsecondary enrollment decreased modestly.[49] Taking advantage of this nondischargeability of student loans, finance companies aggressively expanded their loan businesses to target high school graduates.[50]

Neoliberalism now has taken over almost every sector of American civic life—from education to health care, from journalism to the correctional sys-tem. It is no secret at all that prison companies such as the GEO Group and the CCA (Corrections Corporation of America) have spent millions of dollars in lobbying. In his 2015 *Washington Post* article, "How For-Profit Prisons Have Become the Biggest Lobby No One Is Talking About," Michael Cohen writes that GEO and the CCA "have funneled more than $10 million to candidates since 1989 and have spent nearly $25 million on lobbying efforts. . . . They now rake in a combined $3.3 billion in annual revenue and the private federal prison population more than doubled between 2000 and 2010." These pri-vate prison companies house "nearly half of the nation's immigrant detainees, compared to about 25 percent a decade ago."[51] The nearly limitless expansion of neoliberalism and its systemic encroachment upon our social life have not only cost social capital but also caused mounting and widespread social suffer-ing to many people, especially those marginalized and disenfranchised.

What, then, has the secular state's politics done about this? Can we depend on the secular state to protect civil society from the colonizing intrusion of neoliberalism? Unfortunately, the US sociopolitical landscape

49. Zack Friedman, "Student Loan Debt Statistics in 2020: A Record of $1.6 Trillion," *Forbes*, February 3, 2020, https://www.forbes.com/sites/zackfriedman/2020/02/03/student-loan-debt-statistics/#1081ad27281f. According to the National Center for Education Statistics, between 2009 and 2019, the total undergraduate enrollment in degree-granting postsecondary institutions decreased by 5 percent (from 17.5 million to 16.6 million stu-dents). "Postsecondary Education: Undergraduate Enrollment," National Center for Edu-cation Statistics, May 2021, https://nces.ed.gov/programs/coe/indicator/cha.

50. Victoria Wang, "Killer Loans—College Debt Triggers Depression and Suicide," Salon, June 1, 2019, https://www.salon.com/2019/06/01/killer-loans-college-debt-triggers-depression-and-suicide_partner/.

51. Michael Cohen, "How For-Profit Prisons Have Become the Biggest Lobby No One Is Talking About," *Washington Post*, April 27, 2015, https://www.washingtonpost.com/posteverything/wp/2015/04/28/how-for-profit-prisons-have-become-the-biggest-lobby-no-one-is-talking-about/.

does not invite optimism. In her book *Democracy and Other Neoliberal Fantasies*, the sociologist Jodi Dean diagnoses the grim sociopolitical situation as follows: "We have failed to counter the neoliberalization of the economy. Even worse—we have failed to provide good reasons to support collective approaches to political, social, and economic problems. It's easier to let the market decide."[52] Neoliberals have become powerful enough even to deploy state power to further their interests. As Naomi Klein points out, when Trump announced his cabinet members in December 2016, his picks had a staggering combined net worth of $14.5 billion (not including "special adviser" Carl Icahn, who's worth more than $15 billion on his own). What is particularly troubling about Trump's selection is that to an alarming extent, Trump "has collected a team of individuals who made their personal fortunes by knowingly causing harm to some of the most vulnerable people on the planet, and to the planet itself, often in the midst of crisis."[53]

FROM TERRITORIAL THINKING TO NOMADIC THINKING

We have explored how the secularization thesis was invented, evolved, and devolved in the Western world. In this exploration, we have discovered that the promise of the secularization thesis (the elimination of religious violence) has been blemished by the secular government's inability to tackle the rise of nonreligious structural injustice and violence, especially those types spawned and funded by neoliberalism. Neoliberalism has become the rule of the game in a secular age, and as Wendy Brown argues, it "is best understood not simply as economic policy, but as a governing rationality that disseminates market values and metrics to every sphere of life and construes the human itself exclusively as *homo oeconomicus*."[54] The growing crisis of the secular state's politics becomes the social-historical backdrop against which the church's

---

52. Jodi Dean, *Democracy and Other Neoliberal Fantasies: Communicative Capitalism and Left Politics* (Durham, NC: Duke University Press, 2009), 4.
53. Naomi Klein, *No Is Not Enough: Resisting Trump's Shock Politics and Willing the World We Need* (Chicago: Haymarket, 2017), 18.
54. Brown, *Undoing the Demos*, 176.

distinctive politics is called to address structural injustice, systemic violence, and social-ecological suffering. The call to develop the church's distinctive politics should be regarded as an inevitable consequence of the Western church's critical reckoning with colonialism and secularization.

How is the church's distinctive politics conceived? In a secular age, how is its alternative politics possible? How would its politics be distinguished from the state's secular politics? The political scientist Cynthia Halpern provides us with a critical perspective in answering these questions. According to Halpern, "The tradition of political theory in the West has never addressed itself to the problem of suffering, as a political or a theoretical problem." Why did the Western tradition of political theory, then, fail to address the problem of suffering? It is partly because the Western philosophical tradition comes out of Plato and Aristotle, and these Greek thinkers divide the world into three realms: the world of nature, the world of the household (*oikos*), and the public world of political teleology (polis). She goes on further, saying, "Suffering has to do with the needs of the body, the pains of the family, the vicissitudes of the household, which is the realm of women and slaves and has nothing to do with politics."[55] As Halpern takes note, even the modern political thinkers (liberal thinkers) beginning with Thomas Hobbes demarcated a public from a private realm. Suffering is squarely put "in the private realm, along with *religion* and *faith*, property and honor, bodies, women and families," while "the public realm [is] the realm of public speech, the arena for controlling private violence and constructing the boundaries and regulation of private rights."[56]

In the West, especially since the mid-twentieth century, an ideological dismantlement of this territorial division has been manifested by various social movements, including the socialist movement, the civil rights movement, the anti-war movement, the feminist movement, and the gay rights movement. As Halpern writes, these movements "have all assaulted the primordial distinctions of traditional political theory, especially the public-private distinction and the mind-body distinction which grounds it." The rise of these historical

---

55. Cynthia Halpern, "Suffering Justified and Unjustified: The Violence of Sacred and Secular" (paper presentation, 109th annual meeting of the American Political Science Association, Chicago, IL, August 29–September 1, 2013), 1–32, here 1.

56. Halpern, 2 (emphasis added).

movements signifies an important political thesis that the problem of suffering has become "the inescapable problem of politics" in today's secular world. In this respect, Halpern argues, "Suffering made an additional debut in this century at the center of politics—the suffering bodies and souls of millions of people, caught in unimaginable violence, the killing machines of mass murder and carnage, violation, massacre, and atrocity. The suffering of the mass genocides of the past century rather blasted the public-private distinction, the mind-body distinction, the subject-object distinction out of existence, and rendered the neat rationalities of political theory terribly beside the point."[57]

The rise of these social movements dismantles the traditional demarcation of a public versus a private realm in political theory and signals that the problem of human suffering (especially social suffering) is no longer confined to the private realm. The growing inability of the modern state to regulate widespread structural injustice and violence engenders a crisis of politics in a secular world. We can thus begin to see more clearly how the church's alternative politics is not only possible but also called for. Indeed, the dominance of neoliberalism renders the church's distinctive politics imperative because its primary goal is to address the social suffering caused by structural injustice and violence.

Even nonreligious political thinkers such as Halpern challenge religious believers to do something about the problem of suffering, particularly social suffering. "Suffering," she writes, "is the most ancient question and the one that most urgently and intimately calls into question our *moral or religious beliefs* that there is justice and justification."[58] As a first step in developing a new framework for the church's distinctive politics, then, we must dismantle the age-old demarcation—"the public (the realm of politics) versus the private realm (the realm of religion and faith)." For the church to effectively address the mounting problem of social suffering generated by structural injustice and violence, it must set itself free from its ecclesial habits of territorial thinking. With territorial thinking, it cannot overcome the primordial

---

57. Halpern, 2, 3.
58. Cynthia Halpern, *Suffering, Politics, Power: A Genealogy in Modern Political Theory* (New York: State University of New York Press, 2002), 4 (emphasis added).

public-private distinction and the mind-body distinction, thereby failing to effectively address social suffering.

In place of territorial thinking, the church must develop a new habit of thought, which I call "nomadic thinking." I borrow the term *nomadic* from the social philosophers Gilles Deleuze and Félix Guattari, especially from their 1987 *A Thousand Plateaus: Capitalism and Schizophrenia*. Although Deleuze and Guattari do not systemize the notion of the "nomadic" as a political ideology, we still get a seminal perspective that applies to various arenas, including psychology, culture, and politics. I attempt to outline here the idea of nomadic thinking regarding the development of an alternative model for the church's politics by highlighting its four characteristic aspects: first, it dismantles binary logic in political theology; second, it leads people to resist the rigid identity politics of the same; third, it promotes creativity in reforming or transforming the territorial space in politics; last, it enables the establishment of the multitude and assemblages of transformative subjects.

First off, Deleuze and Guattari differentiate between migrants and nomads. They write, "The nomad is not at all the same as the migrant; for the migrant goes principally from one point to another, even if the second point is uncertain, unforeseen, or not well localized. But the nomad goes from point to point only as a consequence and as a factual necessity; in principle, points for him are relays along a trajectory." Mere movement does not define the notion of the nomad; movement, rather, characterizes the identity of the migrant. The dualistic division between migrants and citizens is overcome if one sees it from the nomadic perspective. According to Deleuze and Guattari, citizens can be nomads because what defines nomads is not movement but speed. They write, "Movement is extensive; speed is intensive."[59] Enigmatic as it may seem, the idea of speed makes sense if one aligns it with the notion of "becoming" rather than "being." (One can think of speed as an awareness of noticeable social change and political transformation.) Indeed, while speed signifies the ontology of difference, movement is still tied to the ontology of the same. Although nomads and migrants can mix in many ways or form a common aggregate,

---

59. Gilles Deleuze and Félix Guattari, *A Thousand Plateaus: Capitalism and Schizophrenia*, trans. Brian Massumi (Minneapolis: University of Minnesota Press, 1987), 380, 381.

their causes and conditions are no less distinct for that. Deleuze and Guattari describe their difference by illustrating an example: "Those who joined Mohammed at Medina had a choice between a nomadic or Bedouin pledge, and a pledge of hegira or emigration."[60] In the Bible, we also find the ideal types of nomads: Saint Paul in the New Testament and Moses in the Hebrew Bible.

The idea of the nomad becomes politically relevant when it is associated with space. Deleuze and Guattari differentiate between "sedentary space" and "nomadic space." According to them, there is a significant difference between these. While "sedentary space is striated, by walls, enclosures, and roads between enclosures, . . . nomad space is smooth, marked only by 'traits' that are effaced and displaced with the trajectory."[61] They describe the difference between these spaces and their spatial ordering by analogically comparing chess and Go. They write, "The space is not at all the same: in chess, it is a question of arranging a closed space for oneself, thus of going from one point to another, of occupying the maximum number of squares with the minimum number of pieces. In Go, it is a question of arraying oneself in an open space, of holding space, of maintaining the possibility of springing up at any point."[62] What we should see from this comparison is that in distinction from sedentary space and order, nomadic space and order introduce "another justice, another movement, another space-time."[63] One of the main reasons we should substitute nomadic thinking for territorial thinking is that the latter cannot effectively address the problems of social-ecological suffering because they have essentially to do with the closed and striated structure of sedentary space.[64] Since the church's territorial thinking pertains to the sedentary ordering, for it to effectively address the problems of social-ecological suffering, it

---

60. Deleuze and Guattari, 380.
61. Deleuze and Guattari, 381. Unlike striated space, there arises a mutually crossing interaction between the previously separated parties on a smooth space. As a result, the demarcation line between the private and the public is erased on a smooth space.
62. Deleuze and Guattari, 353.
63. Deleuze and Guattari, 353.
64. One can think of the "striated structure of the sedentary space" as a political setting in which the church and the state, the private and the public, and faith and conviction are systemically and ideologically separated from each other.

should seriously consider adopting a new perspectival framework—nomadic thinking. By critically employing this new framework, the church may finally develop a new political-theological approach with which to overcome the long-standing divisive demarcation between the private and the public, the church and the state.

The political significance of nomadic thinking becomes unmistakable when Deleuze and Guattari connect their concept of the nomad, which is known as the "war machine," and the state apparatus to smooth and striated space, respectively. A brief description of their enigmatic concepts of the "war machine" and "smooth" may be required to have a better understanding of nomadic thinking. First off, Deleuze and Guattari distinguish between their notion of the war machine identified with the nomads and the military institutions traditionally identified with the state. Although the war machine is often mistakenly identified with the military institutions of the state because of the words, Julian Reid says that it is very much a faithful extension of Michel Foucault's strategic model of power, which Deleuze and Guattari employ specifically to describe a different form of power that is "exterior to, and essentially in antagonism with, the state apparatus."[65] For Deleuze and Guattari, the fundamental tasks of the state are reversely established with those of the nomads. While the state always attempts to vanquish nomadism, the nomads are committed to deterritorializing the striated territory of the state with the purpose of the reconstitution of a smooth space.

According to Deleuze and Guattari, "The war machine is the invention of the nomads insofar as it is exterior to the state apparatus and distinct from the military institution," and this is the primary feature that characterizes the nomads in distinction from the migrants.[66] The nomads also exist differently in the world from "citizens" of a state, and this difference quintessentially takes on political significance because by inventing the war machine, the nomads disrupt striated space, undoing any inherent claim to ownership

---

65. Julian Reid, "Deleuze's War Machine: Nomadism against the State," *Millennium—Journal of International Studies* 32, no. 1 (February 2003): 57–85, here 64.
66. Deleuze and Guattari, *Thousand Plateaus*, 380.

of sedentary space.[67] Christian Beck captures this dismantling political significance of the nomad's presence as follows: "The nomad's presence strips striated space of its meaning, ideology, and cultural practices, and undoes any inherent claim to ownership of the space—this is the process of *deterritorialization*. Put simply, the nomad creates smooth space through deterritorializing the Statist striated space."[68]

Can religion and its institutions (the church) become a war machine? Deleuze and Guattari are open to that possibility. They write, "We are referring to religion as an element in a war machine and the idea of holy war as the motor of that machine. The *prophet*, as opposed to the state personality of the king and the religious personality of the priest, directs the movement by which religion becomes a war machine or passes over to the side of such a machine."[69] It is now clear that for the church to address the social-ecological suffering of the striated space of the state and the structural injustice of the sedentary order, it is to substitute nomadic thinking for territorial thinking. If it fully embraces and embodies nomadic thinking, it will be able to deploy its distinctive politics as a reconstituted religious war machine. I call this distinctive politics of nomadic thinking "rhizomatic politics," and we will further discuss its constellation in chapter 4.

Regarding the idea of nomadic thinking, there is another essential element that we should not miss. Deleuze and Guattari emphasize that the deterritorial operation of a war machine, which they call "speed" and "absolute movement," is not lawless. This is the reason they write, "Speed and absolute movement are not without their laws, but they are the laws of the *nomos*, of the smooth space that deploys it, of the war machine that populates it."[70] The concept of the nomos becomes crucial for the conceptual

---

67. Deleuze and Guattari give us some examples of how a war machine is operated. According to them, each time there is an operation of a war machine against the state— "insubordination, rioting, guerrilla warfare, or revolution as act—it can be said that a war machine has revived, that a new nomadic potential has appeared, accompanied by the reconstitution of a smooth space or a manner of being in space as though it were smooth" (*Thousand Plateaus*, 386).

68. Christian Beck, "Web of Resistance: Deleuzian Digital Space and Hacktivism," *Journal for Cultural Research* 20, no. 4 (December 2016): 334–49, here 342.

69. Deleuze and Guattari, *Thousand Plateaus*, 383.

70. Deleuze and Guattari, 386.

development of nomadic thinking. What does the nomos have to do with nomadic thinking? Eva Aldea traces the etymology of the word *nomadic*. According to her, Deleuze and Guattari deliberately unpick the etymology of the word by tracing it back to the ancient Greek *nemo*, which is the root of *nomás*, meaning "roaming, roving, and wandering (to find pastures for flocks or herds)," and thus a precursor to the modern word *nomad. Nemo*, however, is also the root of the ancient Greek *nomós*. Aldea writes, "On the one hand, nomós refers to the action of distribution or allotment, and is commonly translated as 'law' or 'custom.' In this form, the term is usually opposed to physis or nature, which is without laws or rules. On the other hand, the term nomós refers to the physical result of distribution and can be translated as pasture, but also as district or province, which Deleuze and Guattari directly oppose to the ancient Greek polis or city."[71] The uncovering of this wordplay is important for us to develop the church's nomadic thinking because by renewing and reconstituting the nomos, the church can deterritorialize the sedentary space of structural injustice by deploying its alternative politics. It, then, becomes a war machine to resist unjust ordinances of sedentary distribution and determination. In the sedentary space of structural injustice, the church's nomadic thinking enables it to stand "in opposition to the law or the *polis*, as the backcountry, a mountainside, or the vague expanse around a city."[72] In Deleuze and Guattari's terms, by standing in opposition to the structural injustice and systemic violence of the law or the polis, the nomadic church fulfills its laws of the nomos with speed and absolute movement.

We have explored different aspects of nomadic thinking by critically drawing on Deleuze and Guattari's seminal works. We have not, however, laid out how nomadic thinking can practically help the church develop its distinctive model of political engagement and operations. It will require another chapter to fully address this task, and I return to it in chapter 4, in which I outline in detail such ideas as the church's rhizomatic politics, the political movement of

---

71. Eva Aldea, "Nomads and Migrants: Deleuze, Braidotti and the European Union in 2014," openDemocracy, September 10, 2014, https://www.opendemocracy.net/en/can-europe -make-it/nomads-and-migrants-deleuze-braidotti-and-european-union-in-2014/.

72. Deleuze and Guattari, *Thousand Plateaus*, 380.

the multitude and assemblages, and others. Since the concept of the nomos (which substantiates Deleuze and Guattari's notion of "trajectory") plays an essential role in terms of distinguishing the church's alternative politics from other types of nongovernmental rhizomatic politics, such as the labor movement, the gay rights movement, and the BLM movement, I launch a biblical and theological investigation to delineate the nomos of the church's nomadic thinking in the following chapter before attempting to construct the church's rhizomatic politics after that.

CONCLUSION

I argued in this chapter that the church must develop its distinctive politics to address such overbearing problems as the structural injustice, systemic violence, and social-ecological suffering of our world. As we saw in the previous chapter, the European church largely failed to do so during the colonial period. It is the church's regrettable legacy, and we should not let it happen again in our time. At the heart of this ecclesial failure is the church's uncritical appropriation of the secularization thesis and thoughtless submission to territorial thinking. Because of this lack of critical self-reflection and internal colonization, it was not able to successfully respond to the rising global structural problems. To resolve this long-standing ecclesial problem, I develop a new perspectival framework, nomadic thinking, by critically adopting Deleuze and Guattari's enigmatic yet seminal concepts, including nomads, striated space, rhizomes, and nomos. In contrast to territorial thinking, which tends to serve the maintenance of the static order of striated space or polis, nomadic thinking helps us not only resist the sedentary order of distribution but also promote the nomadic trajectory and its absolute movement.

Although the old Western colonialism faded after World War II, we are currently facing different kinds of colonial challenges in our world today that come along with different types of structural injustice, which not only entails but also proliferates systemic violence and social-ecological suffering. In an increasingly neoliberalized world of striated space, the church should adopt this new perspectival framework to deploy its distinctive politics—its rhizomatic politics—by forming the transformative multitude and nomadic assemblages. In an age of rising neoliberalism, it is consistently called to practice its distinctive politics against the structural challenges of the sedentary space. The church in the Global North must dismantle the sedentary logic of the neoliberal world because of its territorial privilege and status.[73] In the following chapter, to renew and reconstitute the nomos of the church's nomadic thinking, I launch a deterritorial biblical and theological investigation.

---

73. The sedentary logic of the neoliberal world is best exemplified by the neoliberalist beliefs that the market is separate from society and that the state should not intervene in the market economy, in that it is best managed by the "invisible hand." This logic not only disrupts the social relations in the political community but also maims our ecological world and the environment on a global scale.

3

THE BIBLE, POLITICAL THEOLOGY, AND STRUCTURAL INJUSTICE

INTRODUCTION

In the previous two chapters, we investigated the background history of the church and the contextual reasons it should develop its alternative politics against the rising neoliberal governance and structural injustice. In Deleuze and Guattari's terms, the church is called to practice deterritorial nomadic politics to dismantle the sedentary logic of striated space.[1] To address the structural injustice and systemic violence of our social and ecological world, the Western church should first start with the work of reckoning—the reckoning of the historical sin of colonial complicity (chapter 1)—and then move on to replace its age-old territorial thinking with a new way: nomadic thinking (chapter 2). Unlike territorial thinking, which tends to serve the sustenance of the static order of striated space, nomadic thinking helps the church not only resist the sedentary order of polis but also promote nomadic justice against

---

1. Simply put, while "deterritorial" means the resistance to the logic of structural injustice and systemic violence, "nomadic" denotes the vision of territorial alteration and transformation.

territorial injustice. To practice deterritorial nomadic politics, however, the church is required to renew and reconstitute its nomos by critically examining its old territorial conventions. The purpose of this chapter is to show how the reconstruction of the original nomos for the church's deterritorial nomadic politics (i.e., its rhizomatic politics) is possible.

Before we attempt to renew and recover the nomos for the church's alternative politics, we should be reminded that the way we read the Bible and the way we think theologically matter. Just as there is a territorial way of reading the Bible, there is also a nomadic way. Indeed, hermeneutics matters, and we must be aware of its importance. In his book, *The Origins of Proslavery Christianity*, Charles F. Irons illustrates how significantly southerners' evangelical faith shaped their proslavery perspectives in antebellum Virginia. He identifies paternalism and colonization as obvious examples of strong religious influences. He writes, "Whites cited chapter and verse from both Old and New Testament descriptions of slavery in public petitions defending the institution." He also emphasizes, "Divines within the Baptist, Methodist, and Presbyterian churches in the 1790s elaborated on the central themes of paternalism in sermons and in published work, explaining that white men at the top of Virginia society owed spiritual and physical nurture to the slaves, children, and women beneath them." As he correctly points out, it is indeed a theological conundrum to understand "why the parable of the Good Samaritan fell on deaf ears for so many generations" in Christian church history.[2]

History also teaches us that bad theologies or wrongheaded biblical interpretations can be way worse or more dangerous than the absence or lack of them. Neil Elliott affirms this by illustrating how the Pauline Letters were wrongfully appropriated as "ideological weapon[s] of death" in such cases as the horrendous suppression of activist religious women in the Massachusetts Bay Colony (1637), the anti-Semitism of Nazi Germany (1941–45), and the brutal massacres of whole villages in Guatemala (1982). In particular, referring to the case of anti-Semitism in Nazi Germany, he writes, "Not only did texts like 1 Thessalonians 2 facilitate the murderous anti-Semitism of Nazi

---

2. Charles F. Irons, *The Origins of Proslavery Christianity: Whites and Black Evangelicals in Colonial and Antebellum Virginia* (Chapel Hill: University of North Carolina Press, 2008), 67, 89, ix.

Germany; Paul's voice in Romans 13:1 ('Let every person be subject to the governing authorities; for there is no authority except from God') also served to stifle Christian opposition to Nazi policies, indeed to promote enthusiasm for Hitler in ecclesiastical councils."[3]

In renewing and recovering the biblical-theological nomos for the church's deterritorial nomadic politics against the structural injustice in this world, I specifically focus on answering the following three questions in this chapter: What are the biblical foundations that substantiate the nomos of the church's deterritorial nomadic politics to dismantle structural injustice? What are the contemporary theological discourses that would provide us with key theo-logical insights or methodological inspiration with which to develop a more holistic ecclesial politics? What are the key theological tenets of the church's deterritorial nomadic politics? To answer these questions, I engage in an in-depth critical exploration of key biblical sources and major theological works in recent years. In so doing, I develop an argument that the biblical concepts of righteousness (*dikaiosyne*), covenant, and gospel substantiate the nomos for the church's alternative politics against various forms of structural injustice in this world. Its nomadic political engagement in dismantling structural injustice and violence is an indispensable and integral aspect of God's covenantal com-munity. It should be ready to deploy its alternative politics to deterritorialize the unjustly striated space of the earthly kingdom (*civitas terrena*). Indeed, its nomadic political engagement is called for when it senses that "something has gone wrong at a *structural* level."[4] N. T. Wright illustrates how its alternative politics can be deployed:

> Part of the task of the church must be to take up that sense of injustice, to bring it to speech, to help people both articulate it and, when they are ready to do so, to turn it into prayer (it's surprising, until you find yourself in that position, how many of the Psalms suddenly become relevant!). And the task then continues with the church's work with the

---

3. Neil Elliott, *Liberating Paul: The Justice of God and the Politics of the Apostle* (Maryknoll, NY: Orbis, 1994), 13.

4. N. T. Wright, *Surprised by Hope: Rethinking Heaven, the Resurrection, and the Mission of the Church* (New York: HarperCollins, 2008), 231 (emphasis added).

whole local community, to foster programs for better housing, schools, and community facilities, to encourage new job opportunities, to campaign and cajole and work with local government and councils, and, in short, to foster hope at any and every level.[5]

THE ABRAHAMIC COVENANT, PROPHETIC VOICES, AND DETERRITORIAL NOMOS

In Genesis 18, the Lord appears to Abraham by the oaks of Mamre as he sits at the entrance of his tent in the heat of the day. When Abraham sees that three men are coming toward him, he not only invites them to his place but also offers hospitality to them. When they are leaving, one of them (the Lord) says to himself, "I have chosen him, that he may charge his children and his household after him to keep the way of the Lord by doing *righteousness* and *justice*" (Gen 18:19; emphasis added). The Lord, then, let Abraham know that He will go down to Sodom and Gomorrah to "see whether they have done altogether according to the outcry that has come to [Him]" (Gen 18:20–21). This announcement is followed by Abraham's pleading regarding the impending judgment on two cities by the Lord. Abraham asks, "Shall not the Judge of all the earth do *what is just?*" (Gen 18:25; emphasis added). The conversation between Abraham and the Lord comes to an end as Abraham successfully lowers the required minimum number of righteous people to abort the divine judgment from fifty to ten.

This short yet quintessential discourse shows that "doing justice" or "acting justly" is the key element that characterizes the covenantal relationship between the Lord and Abraham (and his descendants). In other words, for Abraham and his descendants to remain in the covenantal relationship with the Lord, they must do justice to one another as well as to the Lord. Later, a more detailed notion of covenantal justice is developed in the Mosaic law, such as the law of Jubilee. According to Leviticus 25:8–12, the concept of Jubilee embraces such critical measures as debt release, slave release, interest-free loans, fallow years, and land repurchase. We should not overlook here that

---

5. Wright, 231.

these detailed regulations are focused on preventing and dismantling a social structure that may systemically perpetuate unjust, oppressive, and destructive relationships. For instance, the first two regulations—the remission of debt and the liberation of slaves—clearly demonstrate that God is against any form of structural injustice and systemic violence, which tend to put people in permanently enslaved and oppressed situations. Indeed, the law of Jubilee stipulates that as a requirement of covenantal justice, no one in God's covenantal community should be kept under such a permanent indebted or enslaved status. It also reveals that God's justice not only condemns but also remedies structural injustice and systemic violence.

We should not forget that the covenant is also part of Abraham's nomadic life. In Genesis 12:1–2, God calls Abram (Abraham), saying, "Go from your country and your kindred and your father's house to the land that I will show you. I will make of you a great nation, and I will bless you, and make your name great, so that you will be a blessing." It is not too much to say, then, that the covenant is what substantiates his entire nomadic life. According to Genesis, until his death, he could not own the land, except the burying place called Machpelah (Gen 23). Given that God made a covenant with him during his nomadic life and justice is what characterizes this covenantal relationship, we can infer that justice is the nomos for his nomadic life, and by extension, justice is the central ethos that characterizes the entire covenantal community called "a multitude of nations" (Gen 17:5).

What, then, about the prophetic literature in the Hebrew Bible? The prophetic voices of the Hebrew Bible are indispensable in further substantiating the nomos for the church's deterritorial nomadic politics. As David L. Petersen points out, although it is difficult to talk about a single prophetic theology or a sole prophetic ethical perspective, we can "discern a common core or element to prophetic literature."[6] What is this common thread? Petersen summarizes it as follows: (1) God's divine condemnation of widespread religious sins and social injustices, (2) the theological importance of Israel's

---

6. David L. Petersen, *The Prophetic Literature: An Introduction* (Louisville, KY: Westminster John Knox, 2002), 37.

covenant with God, and (3) the international relevance of God's divine plan beyond Israel's national and ethnic boundary.

The prophetic literature provides us with ample examples of God's judgment on different types of human injustice. For instance, Amos 1–2 says that the nations are indicted for committing heinous crimes, such as genocidal acts (1:6, "because they carried into exile entire communities") and violence against noncombatants (1:13, "because they have ripped open pregnant women in Gilead"). The prophetic literature also demonstrates that God's judgment on Israel specifically focuses on two major transgressions: Israel's individual and collective injustices and its religious unfaithfulness. Walter J. Houston enumerates Israel's individual and collective injustices (which he calls "social oppression") as follows: bloodshed, violence and coercion, extortion, unjust gain, loss of freedom, perversion of right, and indulgence at the expense of the poor.[7] All types of this social oppression refer to what we call structural injustice and systemic violence.

As for "bloodshed," Isaiah 5:1–7 ends with God's pronouncement "I looked for justice, and found bloodshed, for righteousness and found a bitter cry."[8] Besides this, other parts of the prophetic literature, such as Micah 3:10 ("Build Zion with blood and Jerusalem with wrong") and Jeremiah 22:17 ("Your eyes and heart are only on your dishonest gain, for shedding innocent blood"), also tell us about the social injustice of bloodshed. Among Houston's list of social oppressions in the prophetic literature, "extortion and unjust gain" are especially important because they refer to the structural injustice of economic exploitation, which has huge relevance and resonance in today's neoliberal capitalist societies. In Isaiah 3:14, we discover that the Lord's judgment on the "elders and princes of his people" is due to their economic exploitations of the people: "It is you who have devoured the vineyard; the spoil of the poor is in your houses." According to the prophetic literature, the common practice of economic exploitation is targeted at the poor and the powerless, usually through coercive measures. Houston writes, "The same practices are seen from two points of view: they are exploitative—the poor

---

7. Walter J. Houston, *Contending for Justice: Ideologies and Theologies of Social Justice in the Old Testament* (New York: T&T Clark, 2006), 88–93.

8. Houston, 88.

are deprived and their creditors or rulers enriched; and they are coercive—the victims have no choice but to yield what they have."[9] We should note that in ancient Israel, the coercive economic exploitation of the poor and unjust gain or profit (Jer 6:13; 8:10; 22:17; 51:13) are often structurally related to the social injustice of slavery, especially debt slavery, and in this respect, the second common feature of the prophetic literature—Israel's covenant with God—becomes important.

Bruce C. Birch acknowledges that there is a debate in the scholarly community over the relevance of the term *covenant* in the prophetic literature. Birch points out that in the books of the preexilic prophets, the term *covenant* (*berit*) appears only three times (Hos 6:7; 8:1; Isa 24:5) as a term for Israel's relationship to Yahweh.[10] Because of this, some scholars argue that the covenant imagery was not introduced in Israel until the Deuteronomic reform in 621 BCE, while others argue that the presence of covenant-related vocabulary (e.g., *justice* and *righteousness*) and the imagery of Exodus and desert experiences imply the covenantal relationship throughout the prophetic tradition.[11] Birch affirms that there is indeed an assumption in prophetic judgment that "relationship to God entails responsibility," and yet it was not explicitly upheld. In this regard, he writes, "When the prophets speak of justice and righteousness . . . it is hard not to note the contingency of these concerns with the covenant concept of community. It may well be that the term 'covenant' itself was not a common summation term for this matrix of community concepts until Deuteronomy, but this should not prevent us from noting the prophets' role in advocating a conception of obligation in relationship to God that is covenantal in character."[12] In a similar vein, Petersen argues that it is difficult to deny a covenant background in interpreting the prophetic literature. He notes that it is difficult to read Hosea 4:2 without hearing echoes of the Ten Commandments, which are in some ways similar to the stipulations of a covenant. He also points out that curses as found in covenant texts (Deut

---

9. Houston, 90.
10. Bruce C. Birch, *Let Justice Roll Down: The Old Testament, Ethics, and Christian Life* (Louisville, KY: Westminster John Knox, 1991), 245.
11. Birch, 245–46.
12. Birch, 246.

28) also appear in the prophetic literature (Isa 34:11–17). In addition to these, he holds that the lawsuits brought by God (Mic 6:1–8) reflect the covenantal relationship between God and Israel.[13]

But why does the realization that the prophetic literature has a covenant background matter? Above all, the prophetic judgment against social and structural injustice as well as the demand for justice and righteousness implies that addressing, challenging, and transforming the social and structural injustice are the covenantal community's collective responsibility to God. As Birch writes, there is an assumption in prophetic judgment that "relationship to God entails responsibility and that this responsibility has not been upheld" by the covenantal community. He goes on further, saying, "When the prophets speak of justice and righteousness, it is hard not to note the congruence of these concerns with the covenant concept of community."[14] According to Richard A. Horsley, what is more significant about the covenant is that the covenantal relationship between the people and Yahweh is "inseparably political-economic and (almost by definition) religious."[15] He outlines the overall structure of the covenant in three basic interrelated components: (1) the declaration of deliverance, (2) principles of social policy (exclusive loyalty to Yahweh and relations among Israelites), and (3) motivation/enforcement (renewal and recitation, witnesses against selves, and blessings and curses).[16] The political-economic-religious covenantal relationship is especially highlighted by the first component of the covenant structure—the declaration of deliverance. Horsley writes, "In delivering the Hebrews from bondage in Egypt Yahweh has established a political-economic relationship with them. In Egypt and the rest of the ancient Near East, the people were bound into servitude to their king(s), in agricultural produce that supported the ruling establishment and in forced labor to build temples, palaces, and fortresses. When Yahweh delivers the Hebrews from bondage in Egypt it is a political

13. Petersen, *Prophetic Literature*, 37.
14. Birch, *Let Justice Roll Down*, 246.
15. Richard A. Horsley, *Covenant Economics: A Biblical Vision of Justice for All* (Louisville, KY: Westminster John Knox, 2009), 23.
16. Horsley, 23. For instance, Exod 20 and Deut 5 cover these three basic components of the covenant.

liberation from subjection but also economic emancipation from such servitude."[17] The prophetic literature provides us with an important perspective that as a covenantal community before God, Israelites are collectively held accountable to engage and transform structural injustice in politics and economics.

Last but not least of the common core of the prophetic literature is the international relevance of the prophets' work. According to Petersen, "Though Jeremiah is the only prophet officially designated as 'prophet to the nations,' each of the 'major' prophetic books includes a sizable collection of sayings and oracles devoted to nations other than Israel."[18] For instance, we discover in Isaiah 13:1–23 a prophecy against Babylon and in Jeremiah 46:1–51:58 various prophetic messages to Israel's neighboring nations and peoples, including Egypt, the Philistines, Moab, Ammon, Edom, Damascus, Kedar and Hazor, and Babylon. In Ezekiel 25:1–32:32, we also discover a similar pattern of prophecy targeted against Israel's neighboring nations and peoples, such as Ammon, Moab, the Philistines, Tyre, Sidon, and Egypt. Such prophetic messages are also found in the Minor Prophets. For example, Amos begins with a short set of oracles regarding Israel's neighboring nations, and Obadiah's prophetic message is heavily focused on Edom and its relation to Judah. Other works from the Minor Prophets (Joel 2:20; Mic 4:1–2; Nah 1:1; Hab 1:5–6; Zeph 2:4–15; Hag 2:21–22; Zech 1:11; Mal 1:11) also reflect the international relevance of prophetic messages. According to Petersen, even the most domestic prophetic book, Haggai, understands Judah's weal and wealth to derive from God acting on a cosmic scale: "Speak to Zerubbabel, governor of Judah, saying, I am about to shake the heavens and the earth, and to overthrow the throne of kingdoms" (Hag 2:21–22).[19] Why, then, is it important that the prophetic literature reflects the international relevance of God's divine oracles? This relevance matters to us because the scope and efficacy of God's reign of justice transcend Israel's parochial national boundary.

We have explored the tripartite common elements of the prophetic literature to uncover the nomos for the church's deterritorial nomadic politics

---

17. Horsley, 23.
18. Petersen, *Prophetic Literature*, 38.
19. Petersen, 39.

against the structural injustice of this world. What we discover in this theological exploration is twofold: first, addressing the problem of structural injustice is what composes the core communal identity of God's covenantal community; second, God's reign of righteousness and true justice transcends Israel's parochial national boundary, reaching out to the whole world (including the cosmic world). In the following section, I extend my biblical exploration into the New Testament to further elaborate on the nomos of the church's deterritorial nomadic politics. In doing so, we particularly focus on Jesus's gospels and Paul's letters.

THE GOSPELS, PAUL'S LETTERS, AND STRUCTURAL INJUSTICE

What does the church's deterritorial nomadic politics have to do with Jesus and his gospels? Oftentimes, the church seems to forget that from his precarious birth to his horrendous crucifixion, Jesus's life was deeply entangled with various types of structural injustice. His birth in Bethlehem of Judea (Matt 1) was interrupted by King Herod, who eventually sent his troops to kill all the male children in Bethlehem and the surrounding region who were two years old or under with the purpose of killing newborn Jesus. What about his brutal death on Mount Golgotha? His violent crucifixion was the result of the concerted efforts of religious leaders, political rulers, and organized mobs. The ugly face of structural injustice and systemic violence was revealed once and for all on Mount Golgotha in the most condemnable way.

At the beginning of his public ministry, in the synagogue in Nazareth, after unrolling the scroll of the prophet Isaiah, Jesus proclaims, "Today this Scripture has been fulfilled in your hearing" (Luke 4:21). This statement is very important because it confirms that Jesus himself is the realization of Jubilee ("the year of the Lord's favor," Luke 4:19). It is widely accepted that the passage Jesus unrolls refers to the Jubilee tradition adopted by the prophet Isaiah.[20] According to John Howard Yoder, the idea of Jubilee is in fact the

---

20. The passage reads, "The Spirit of the Lord is upon me, because he has anointed me to bring good news to the poor. He has sent me to proclaim release to the captives and

central message of Jesus's teaching, and the Lord's Prayer exemplifies it ("Remit us our debts as we ourselves have also remitted them to our debt-ors"[21]). We should recall that in the Hebrew Bible, the idea of Jubilee not only signifies God's judgment upon structural injustice, which puts people in permanent enslaved and oppressed situations, but also epitomizes the key organizing spirit of the covenantal community—righteousness or true justice. We should also remember that during his ministry, Jesus not only witnesses the brutal infliction of structural injustice upon innocent people (John the Baptist) but also addresses how it affects him by telling a parable (the parable of the wicked tenants; Matt 21:33–46). In Matthew 25:31–46, he gives his last sermon by condemning the nations that carry out structural injustice without giving the "least of these" their due. Indeed, if we fail to interpret Jesus's life, words, and acts without contextualizing them against the backdrop of the structural injustice of his time, we may end up with an abridged and myopic understanding of his gospels.

This abridged and myopic view becomes a serious stumbling block to the church's social, political, and ecological engagement in various structural problems of our world. It is problematic because it ultimately results in the confinement of the ecclesial space to the private territory of individual faith with no social, political, and ecological relevance. Regarding this issue as the quintessential problem of the Western church, Richard A. Horsley writes, "On the one hand, to keep it from interfering in the imperial industrial and capitalist reconstruction of the world and, on the other hand, to retain it as the remaining heart in a heartless world or spirituality to nurture sick souls, religion in the West was reduced to individual faith and marginalized activi-ties on Sabbath days."[22] Such an abridged stance has been historically estab-lished in a close tie with the modern Western assumption of the separation of religion and politics. This separation model has been influential in the West because many people simply adopted the dichotomous view that "the nature of

---

recovery of sight to the blind, to let the oppressed go free, to proclaim the year of the Lord's favor" (Luke 4:18–19).

21. John Howard Yoder, *The Politics of Jesus* (Grand Rapids, MI: Eerdmans, 1972), 61.

22. Richard A. Horsley, "Religion and Other Products of Empire," *Journal of American Academy of Religion* 71, no. 1 (March 2003): 13–44, here 17.

God's work is spiritual, not worldly." Bradley P. Hayton illustrates some of the catchphrases of this dualistic view as follows: "The redemption of the world doesn't hang on politics," "Politics is a dirty business," and "We ought not to identify our own specific political programs with the will of God."[23]

How do we overcome this abridged and myopic theological dualism? How could we reconstruct a more holistic and balanced political theology that addresses and transforms the structural injustice and systemic violence of this world? Where do we start our theological reconstruction? In answering these questions, Horsley is a helpful guide. In his book *Jesus and Empire*, he begins by arguing that the major problem with the standard interpretation of the historical Jesus is the depoliticization practiced in Western Christian theology and New Testament studies. He enumerates at least three types of depoliticization: that of Jesus, Judea and Galilee, and the Roman Empire. Why is depoliticization in the standard interpretation of the historical Jesus problematic? First, it prevents us from having a holistic understanding of who Jesus was and what his mission was for. Horsley analogically describes the methodological shortcomings of depoliticization, saying, "Trying to understand Jesus's speech and action without knowing how Roman imperialism determined the conditions of life in Galilee and Jerusalem would be like trying to understand Martin Luther King without knowing how slavery, reconstruction, and segregation determined the lives of African Americans in the United States."[24]

The immediate effect of depoliticization is the privatization of the Christian faith. If Jesus's activities and teachings did not have any political or socioeconomic significance as a result of a depoliticized reading of his gospels, how could we discover the political and socioeconomic relevance of his life, words, and ministry in our given context? Christian faith cannot but have only a personal or moral relevance, and the church's sole mission is, then, to save individual souls from sin and eternal death. This epitomizes the church's territorial thinking, which not only perpetuates but also consolidates the striated

---

23. Bradley P. Hayton, "Theopolitics: Theological Grounds of Political Action," *Journal of Christian Reconstruction* 12, no. 1 (1988): 140–66, here 142.

24. Richard A. Horsley, *Jesus and Empire: The Kingdom of God and the New World Disorder* (Minneapolis: Fortress, 2003), 13.

space of secular politics. It is right, then, for Horsley to write, "Alienated from the relations of production and no longer directly affecting the quality of political-economic-social life, religion became more of a privatized refuge and consolation." He argues that this Christian theological reductionism has to do with the lack of a sense of religious meaning felt by many Western Christians: "Given the reduction of religion to individual faith or spirituality, then, is it any wonder that many Westerns felt that something was seriously lacking in their lives and in their society?"[25]

Indeed, the reductionist view of the Christian faith is intrinsically tied to the religious separationist view that the church and the state have nothing to do with each other. The separationists argue that unlike the time of the Old Testament, in which Israel was living under a "theocracy," Christians in the New Testament period and today live under secular governments.[26] Under the separationist banner, the church cannot but develop an apolitical attitude toward worldly, or secular, matters in politics and economics. It no longer engages in various issues of structural injustice of this world from a prophetic perspective. I would call this situation the church's self-imposed exile because this type of morbidity is inculcated by its own misconceived theology. It seems evident that the first step toward the reconstruction of its deterritorial nomadic politics is to dismantle its depoliticized habitual reading of the New Testament.

What does it mean for us to read Jesus's gospels politically through the lens of theological deconstruction? It means that we bring the depoliticized Jesus back to his historical and sociopolitical context. To do so, we must first understand Roman imperialism and its significant political and economic impact on Jewish communities in which Jesus's life and mission were situated. The Romans controlled the life conditions of Galilee, where Jesus lived and carried out his mission. Roman armies invaded the area in the decades before Jesus was born, and they burned villages while enslaving many able-bodied people. Roman warlords appointed Herod as "king" and provided him with troops to conquer his subjects. The Roman emperor also installed Herod's

---

25. Horsley, "Religion and Other Products," 17.
26. Hayton, "Theopolitics," 144.

son Antipas, raised and educated at the imperial court, to rule over Galilee.[27] According to Horsley, Antipas launched a project to build two Roman-style cities in Galilee, which previously had neither cities nor a ruler resident in the territory. The needed money was funded with tax revenues extracted from Galilee. Roman governors, such as Pontius Pilate, had the power to appoint and depose the high priests, who ruled Judea from their base in the Jerusalem temple.[28] If we take this historical and sociopolitical context into consideration, we begin to see more clearly how Jesus's mission would have been deeply interconnected with the political-economic-religious context of his time. Horsley summarizes the contextualized Jesus's mission as follows: "Jesus worked among people subject to the Roman Empire. His renewal of Israel, moreover, was a response to the longings of those people, who had lived under the domination of one empire after another for centuries, to be free of imperial rule. Israelite tradition from which Jesus worked in his mission bore the marks of a prolonged struggle of the people both to adjust to and to resist the effects of the powers of empire."[29] From the vantage point of the contextualized Jesus's mission, the prophetic condemnation of structural injustice and economic exploitation looms large. For instance, the sharpest conflicts between Jesus and the Pharisees/scribes who "come from Jerusalem" in Mark 7:1–13 (Matt 15:1–20) illustrate that these contentions are not about Jesus's opposition to Judaism but about his continuation of the prophetic condemnation of structural (economic) injustice implied by their religious injunctions ("the tradition of the elders"). As Horsley points out, as representatives of the temple-state, the Pharisees and scribes were demanding poor villagers to enhance the wealth of the ruling class in the name of "devotion" to God and the temple.[30] Against this structural injustice, Jesus upholds the covenantal commandment to do justice to God's people.

---

27. Horsley, *Jesus and Empire*, 15.

28. Horsley, 15.

29. Richard A. Horsley, *Jesus and the Powers: Conflict, Covenant, and the Hope of the Poor* (Minneapolis: Fortress, 2011), 17.

30. Richard A. Horsley, "You Shall Not Bow Down and Serve Them: Economic Justice in the Bible," *Journal of Bible and Theology* 69, no. 4 (2015): 415–31, here 425.

Perhaps the most dramatic of Jesus's confrontations with structural (economic) injustice can be found in the case of his driving away the money changers and those who were buying and selling on the temple premises (Matt 21:12–17; Mark 11:15–17; Luke 19:45–48; John 2:13–16). It is plausible to imagine that there were connections between the high priests, who headed the temple-state, being appointed by the Roman governors, and the money changers. Undoubtedly, these money changers were given a financial monopoly through which they exploited the poor people, who were charged exorbitant rates when they exchanged standard Greek or Roman money for Jewish and Tyrian money to practice their religious beliefs. That is the reason Jesus calls the place "a den of robbers." Horsley argues that "Jesus's action in Herod's temple [is] not merely a 'cleansing.' It [is] rather a prophetic demonstration that symbolize[s] God's judgment."[31] God's ruling of structural injustice later composes one of two key aspects of the Pauline notion of *dikaiosyne* (righteousness), to which we will shortly turn.

Jesus's crucifixion becomes a crucial event in uncovering the nomos for the church's deterritorial nomadic politics against structural injustice and systemic violence. Caiaphas, a high priest, advises the Jews that it is "better to have one person die for the people" (John 18:14). His statement encapsulates how those who systemically set up the crucifixion of Jesus attempt to justify their social-religious sin of victimizing an innocent person for their own sake. Against the systemic force of structural injustice, what Jesus demonstrates at the courtyard of the high priests and Pilate's headquarters is not so much a defense of his innocence as his *resistance* to the structural injustice that attempts to subdue him to social-religious sin. It is Pilate, not Jesus, who finally succumbs to the systemic thrust of structural injustice. By resisting the systemic threat of structural injustice, Jesus not only fulfills but also reveals his righteousness. By resurrecting from death, however, he becomes a true hope to those who resist and stand up against the menacing power of structural injustice and social-religious sin.

From a theological perspective, Jesus's resistance to and confrontation with the structural injustice of Judean religious politics is in fact his acceptance and

---

31. Horsley, 425.

preservation of the prophetic tradition. It also reflects that he not only inherits Mosaic covenantal themes, such as God's deliverance, exclusive loyalty to God, and the social principles of righteousness and solidarity, but also renews them among his followers and hearers. Horsley argues that Luke 5:20–49 and the series of dialogues in Mark 10 are explicit statements of covenant renewal, and especially the former indicates the clear structure of the Mosaic covenant.[32] Jesus's covenant renewal ultimately aims at the reconstruction of the covenantal community, which was radically disrupted by the imperial rule of the Roman Empire and the corrupt religious governance of the temple-state. Facing against pervasive political-economic-religious structural injustices that radically disintegrate poor families and village communities, Jesus does and proclaims the renewal of the covenantal community, in which imperial rule is replaced by the leaders' just care rather than oppression while exploitative economic relations are superseded by the egalitarian economic relations empowering the community. It is indeed right for Horsley to say that it is "precisely in those circumstances of poverty and powerlessness that Jesus and his followers [find] it essential to struggle to practice those values and principles of justice, cooperation, and solidarity."[33]

We have explored key biblical sources to unearth the nomos for the church's deterritorial nomadic politics by focusing on the proclamations of Hebrew prophets and Jesus's life and words. In doing so, we have contextualized them against the backdrop of the Abrahamic-Mosaic covenant. The idea of righteousness or true justice looms large, which encompasses both saving (deliverance) and judging aspects vis-à-vis structural injustice and violence. What about the other voices in the New Testament, such as that of Paul, whose theology has decisively impacted the establishment of the Christian church in the West and beyond? Thanks to recent scholarship in New Testament studies, we are in a better position to discuss the importance of

---

32. Richard A. Horsley, *Jesus and the Politics of Roman Palestine* (Columbia: University of South Carolina Press, 2014), 122. The structure of the Mosaic covenant is as follows: "1. A statement of God's deliverance that evokes the peoples' gratitude and obligation; 2. Principles of exclusive loyalty to God and the principles of societal relations; 3. Sanctions as motivation for observance." Horsley, 122.

33. Horsley, 126.

Paul's political theology in constructing the idea of the church's deterritorial nomadic politics. In 1977, E. P. Sanders published *Paul and Palestinian
Judaism*, in which he argues that the traditional Lutheran understanding of
Paul's theology is fundamentally problematic, a thesis that kicked off the academic and public discourse on the "new perspective on Paul." Other New
Testament scholars, such as James D. G. Dunn and N. T. Wright, later joined
him in advancing the "new perspective" movement. The crux of this new
hermeneutic breakthrough lies in distinguishing between two interpretations
of what Paul might mean by "works of the law" (Rom 3:20 NIV; Gal 2:16).
While the traditional Lutheran and Reformed perspectives regard it as referring to human efforts toward performing good works to earn righteousness,
what Paul really alludes to is following traditional customs (such as circumcision, dietary laws, or observance of special days). Sanders summarizes his
point by differentiating two-word groups ("getting in" and "staying in"). He
writes, "In Paul's usage, 'be made righteous' ('be justified') is a term indicating getting in, not staying in the body of the saved. Thus when Paul says that
one cannot be made righteous by works of law, he means that one cannot, by
works of law, 'transfer to the body of the saved.' When Judaism said that one
is righteous who obeys the law, the meaning is that one thereby stays in the
covenant. The debate about righteousness by faith or by works of law thus
turns out to result from the different usage of the 'righteous' word-group."[34]

The theological significance of the new perspective movement is that it
can fundamentally change Christian engagement in various structural injustices of this world because this engagement is recognized as the works of
the new covenantal community established by Jesus. Whereas the works
of customs (circumcision, dietary laws, etc.) are rejected in having people
transferred to the new covenantal community, the works of the covenant
(justice, mercy, forgiveness, etc.) are as emphatically required to stay in the
new covenant of Jesus as in the old Jewish covenant. As N. T. Wright points
out, then, the works of the individual would matter in God's final judgment:
"Paul, in company with mainstream second-Temple Judaism, affirms that

---

34. E. P. Sanders, *Paul and Palestinian Judaism: A Comparison of Patterns of Religion* (Minneapolis:
Fortress, 1977), 544.

God's final judgment will be in accordance with the entirety of a life led—in accordance, in other words, with works."[35] James D. G. Dunn also writes similarly that the new perspective "reconciles Paul's teaching on justification by faith and *not works* with his teaching that judgment will be *according to works*."[36] According to Dunn, one of the most important continuing functions of the law for Paul is that it "will serve as the measure of God's judgment." In the end, then, "it is not enough to narrow the gospel down to 'imputation' (Protestant) while ignoring the important aspect of 'transformation' (Catholic), as in Rom 12:12. It is not enough [either] to dismiss any talk of human responsibility in the process of salvation as 'synergistic.'"[37]

Neil Elliott's 1994 *Liberating Paul: The Justice of God and the Politics of the Apostle* is another milestone in reinterpreting Paul's theology, especially his political theology. Although some of his arguments may be controversial, he presents a refreshing new perspective that Paul in fact proclaims and lives a gospel that is fully consonant with what liberation theologians call "the preferential option for the poor" by opposing the ideology of "empire" and the state-supported structural violence.[38] He writes, "After all, according to Paul's own account in the letter to the Galatians, when he met with the apostles in Jerusalem, he declared that being continually mindful of 'the poor' was 'the very thing I have made it my business to do' (Galatians 2:10, New English Bible)."[39] Elliott claims that Paul's theological understanding of the crucifixion and resurrection of Jesus is important for the liberation of the poor because the cross event reflects the revelation of God's ending of imperial powers: "Far from 'denationalizing' the cross, Paul has, so to speak,

---

35. N. T. Wright, "New Perspectives on Paul" (conference paper presented at Rutherford House, Edinburgh, August 2003), 1–17, here 8.
36. James D. G. Dunn, "A New Perspective on the New Perspective on Paul," *Early Christianity* 4, no. 2 (2013): 157–82, here 179.
37. Dunn, 179, 180.
38. For instance, while Elliott argues that Pauline passages such as 1 Cor 14:34–35 are pseudo-Pauline and even anti-Pauline, feminist scholars such as Antoinette Clark Wire and Elisabeth Schüssler Fiorenza claim otherwise. See Elliott, *Liberating Paul*, 52–53; Antoinette Clark Wire, *Corinthian Women Prophets* (Eugene, OR: Wipf & Stock, 2003); and Elisabeth Schüssler Fiorenza, "Rhetorical Situation and Historical Reconstruction in 1 Corinthians," *New Testament Studies* 33, no. 3 (1987): 386–403.
39. Elliott, *Liberating Paul*, 87.

internationalized it. He insists that the Roman colonists of Corinth, thousands of miles from the troubles in Judea, must mold their lives into a constant remembrance of one particular crucifixion in Judea because through that crucifixion God has revealed the imminent end of the Powers and has begun to bring 'the scheme of this world' to an end (1 Cor. 7:31)."[40]

With regard to the uncovering of the nomos for the church's deterritorial nomadic politics, what we learn from Elliott's provocative reinterpretation of Paul's "subversive theology and praxis" is that Paul's message is fundamentally political rather than a- or nonpolitical.[41] It is thus mistaken to read Paul's books, especially Romans, as dogmatic treatises on Christian salvation. He is not socially conservative at all because his "ideological intifada" not only promotes solidarity with the victims of the structural injustice of the Roman Empire but also encourages communal resistance to spurious Roman justice and its violence. In Paul's subversive political theology, God's justice is contrasted with that of the Roman Empire (*"The justice of God is not what the empire calls justice"*[42]). According to Elliott, Paul's message to the Roman congregation is summarized as follows: "While others suppress the truth in the service of injustice and violate one another's bodies in unspeakable acts, Christians are to yield their bodies to God 'as instruments of justice' (6:13–14). They must practice an ideological intifada, refusing to be coerced into conformity with the world and allowing their minds to be transformed (12:1–2)."[43]

As a result of our in-depth biblical investigation, we have discovered that the idea of righteousness (*dikaiosyne*) is a consistent biblical theme from Genesis to Paul's letters, which indeed should substantiate the nomos for the church's deterritorial nomadic politics. How could we, then, summarize the relational significance between the biblical notion of righteousness and the content of the nomos? I contend that a confessional resistance to structural injustice and systemic violence and an ecclesial engagement in healing and transforming

---

40. Elliott, 114.
41. Neil Elliott, "The Apostle Paul's Self-Presentation as Anti-imperial Performance," in *Paul and the Roman Imperial Order*, ed. Richard A. Horsley (New York: Trinity, 2004), 67–88, here 85.
42. Elliott, *Liberating Paul*, 195.
43. Elliott, 195.

the world should become the practical measures for the church's deterritorial nomadic politics. As for the former, we discover its original and ideal type from Jesus's life and words, especially his last moments of crucifixion and resurrection. By resisting the structural injustice of Jewish religious politics, which aims at subduing him to social sin, Jesus not only reveals his righteousness but also becomes the original model for the church's deterritorial nomadic politics of righteousness.

Paul's theological notion of righteousness, viewing it from the vantage point of the "new perspective on Paul," helps us uncover the other aspect of the nomos for the church's deterritorial nomadic politics—that is, its political engagement in healing and transforming the world. What does Paul's idea of righteousness have to do with the church's alternative politics? According to Sam K. Williams, it is not too much to say that "*dikaiosyne theou* [the righteousness of God in Rom 1:17] is the fundamental concept or the dominating theme of Romans."[44] He then goes on to say that there are three main views on what the apostle means by *dikaiosyne theou*, which he summarizes as follows: "'Righteousness of God' means (1) that human righteousness which 'counts' in God's eyes (*theou* being understood as an objective genitive), (2) God's own saving power or activity (*theou* taken as a subjective genitive), and (3) God's gift of righteousness (*theou* understood as a genitive-of origin)." Among these, the second view is particularly important because the "new perspective on Paul" makes it possible for us to conceptualize the church's deterritorial nomadic politics in such a way that, for the sake of staying in the new covenant of Jesus, the church continues to practice the "works of the covenant" through its politics. What are, then, these works? Shortly put, they include not only the works of justice, mercy, and forgiveness but also those of restoration, healing, and transformation in the world, affected by structural injustice and systemic violence. Since the righteousness of God signifies "God's own saving power or activity," these works are to reflect such salvific visions on all levels, including the social and political ones.

---

44. Sam K. Williams, "The 'Righteousness of God' in Romans," *Journal of Biblical Literature* 99, no. 2 (June 1980): 241–90, here 241.

Above, we have uncovered two key components of the nomos for the church's deterritorial nomadic politics: (1) resistance to structural injustice and (2) healing and transforming engagement in the world, affected by structural injustice. In the following chapter (chapter 4), I develop a more concrete model for the church's political practices by laying out the idea of its rhizomatic politics. Before moving forward, I reengage in a critical dialogue with recent voices of neo-Augustinian political theologies in the West to check out the possibility of consociating (in Luke Bretherton's terms) between these voices and the ideas of the church's deterritorial nomadic politics.[45]

NEO-AUGUSTINIAN POLITICAL THEOLOGIES AND JUSTICE OF THE CHURCH (*IUSTITIA ECCLESIAE*)

In this section, regarding the dialogical consociation between neo-Augustinian political theologies and the church's deterritorial political theology, I particularly engage with two political theologians—William T. Cavanaugh and Luke Bretherton. In recent years, they have further advanced neo-Augustinian political theologies by publishing a series of works (*Theopolitical Imagination*, *Field Hospital*, and *Migrations of the Holy* by Cavanaugh and *Resurrecting Democracy: Faith, Citizenship, and the Politics of a Common Life* and *Christ and the Common Life* by Bretherton). Indeed, they both significantly enhanced the church's theopolitical imagination regarding its political role in addressing social justice, democratic inclusion, and common life through their works and public discourses.

In his 2002 *Theopolitical Imagination*, Cavanaugh lays out the neo-Augustinian paradigm of theopolitics by attacking the liberal theopolitical position. The liberal paradigm is problematic because "'political theology' and 'public theology' have assumed the legitimacy of the separation of the

---

45. Luke Bretherton borrows the term *consociation* from the seventeenth-century Protestant political thinker Johannes Althusius, and it means "the art of living together." According to Bretherton, "A consociational vision rejects a unitary, hierarchically determined understanding of the state and a top-down, transcendent, monistic conception of sovereignty." The idea of consociation plays a central role as he develops the theologically ordained notion of democracy. See his *Christ and the Common Life: Political Theology and the Case for Democracy* (Grand Rapids, MI: Eerdmans, 2019), 167–68.

state from civil society, and tried to situate the Church as one more interest group within civil society."[46] There is a reason he attacks such a position. First of all, the liberal theopolitical assumption is questionable because it excludes Christian theological discourse from the putative public forum in the name of a "secular" neutrality, marginalizing the body of Christ in favor of a false public body centered in the state.[47] Against the false notion of a public body and the catholicity of the state, he develops an Augustinian counterargument that the church's role is not to "influence the public" but simply to *be* public. He reminds us that "for Augustine not the *imperium* but the Church is the true *res publica*, the 'public thing;' the *imperium* has forfeited any such claim to be truly public by its refusal to do justice, by refusing to give God his due." Cavanaugh points out that the Augustinian idea of *res publica* has to do with the political-theological notion of true justice. According to Augustine, the Roman Empire is not public at all because "its practices are not oriented toward the worship of God. A true *res publica* is based on justice, which must include giving God his due in sacrifice, for only when God is loved can there be love of others and a mutual acknowledgment of right."[48]

For Cavanaugh, then, the theopolitics of the church is established as the theopolitics of the true res publica, which pursues neither "Constantinian nor privatized" political space. It, rather, is shaped by its own "theopolitical imagination," which enables the church to create its "spatial story." By "spatial story," Cavanaugh means the transformation of the way space is configured. He writes, "To speak of the Church as a public space means, then, that Christians perform stories which transform the way space is configured."[49] Drawing on the Jesuit social theorist Michel de Certeau, Cavanaugh differentiates between the notion of place (*lieu*) and that of space (*espace*). Unlike place, which is arranged on a "static order" in a proper territory, a "space takes into account the vector of time, such that different spaces are created by

46. William T. Cavanaugh, *Theopolitical Imagination: Discovering the Liturgy as a Political Act in an Age of Global Consumerism* (New York: T&T Clark, 2002), 3.

47. Cavanaugh, 6.

48. Cavanaugh, 84, 90.

49. Cavanaugh, 70, 93. He borrows the term *spatial story* from the French religious historian and cultural critic Michel de Certeau, especially from his book *The Practice of Everyday Life*, trans. Steven Rendall (Berkeley: University of California Press, 1984).

the ensemble of movements and actions on them." De Certeau's notion of a spatial story can help us interpret Augustine's conception of the two cities not as a territorial conflict but as a movement of two different story lines that can coexist, occupying the same place (two spatial stories in one place or two cities on the earth). Cavanaugh thus writes, "In theological terms, we can think of de Certeau's work here as a gloss on Augustine's conception of the two cities. They do not exist beside each other on a territorial grid, but are formed by telling different stories about ends, and by thus using matter and motion in different ways."[50]

For Cavanaugh, liturgy, especially the Eucharist, becomes the core theological notion, symbol, and imagery that substantiates the spatial story of the res publica. He even states that without the Eucharist, there is no church: "The liturgy generates a body, the Body of Christ—the Eucharist makes the Church, in Henri de Lubac's words—which is itself a *sui generis* social body, a public presence irreducible to a voluntary association of civil society."[51] Why is, then, the Eucharist so important? How come it enables the church's theopolitical imagination? In what sense does the church's theopolitical imagination have to do with us and the world? In *Migrations of the Holy*, Cavanaugh answers these questions by saying, "Rituals enact our debt to the past, which we cannot pay via ritual, but only via fresh sacrifice. In contrast, the Christian liturgy is not merely cyclical but points forward to the eschatological consummation of history in which violence and division are overcome."[52] According to Cavanaugh, although the core of the Eucharist is the representation of Christ's foundational sacrifice, "it does not resacrifice Christ, nor is new blood sacrifice demanded of us"; instead, it directs us to the overcoming of violence and division. For this purpose, he claims, "we must not quarantine the liturgy into a 'sacred' space, but must allow it to shape the way we form our mundane communities, our goals, allegiances, purchases, and relationships."[53]

---

50. Cavanaugh, *Theopolitical Imagination*, 92.
51. Cavanaugh, 83.
52. William T. Cavanaugh, *Migrations of the Holy: God, State, and the Political Meaning of the Church* (Grand Rapids, MI: Eerdmans, 2011), 121.
53. Cavanaugh, 121, 122.

What is the specific and concrete imagery of the church's theopolitics, then? Cavanaugh answers this question by picturing the idea of a field hospital. He writes, "The kind of church I dream of goes out into the world and helps to bind wounds by taking on the suffering of others into the suffering body of Christ. All people, Christian or not, are members or potential members of the body of Christ." The imagery of the church as a field hospital offers us a hint that the church's spatial story cannot but have to do with the wounds of the world. Indeed, Cavanaugh says that *Field Hospital* deals with three kinds of wounds: "economic wounds, political wounds, and the wounds of violence." Given that wounds presuppose the existence of violence, whatever form it may be, how does Cavanaugh define it? According to him, "Violence comes from the refusal to see that all creation depends on the Creator for its true being. Violence is the attempt to seize and grasp at creation, turning away from recognition of our status as created and dependent."[54]

Cavanaugh's differentiation between "place" and "space" and the further development of the notion of "spatial story" give us an impression that his "theopolitical" imagination and operation are not caught up by what I call "territorial thinking." Yet I am not sure if his theopolitical imagination would be able to appropriate the idea of "deterritorial" intervention; instead, he seems to quickly adopt the "reterritorialization" of the church vis-à-vis the state's secular territory. Why is not there a critical "space" or "time variable" that would allow for the operation of deterritorial intervention in Cavanaugh's theopolitics? In my view, this lack of critical space for the church's deterritorial intervention is not accidental; it is, rather, expectable if we consider that he appropriates de Certeau's philosophical framework rather than Deleuze and Guattari's. Of course, Cavanaugh does not have to adopt the latter's methodical model as he develops the church's theopolitics. One should note that the idea of territory is neither place nor space. In *The Practice of Everyday Life*, de Certeau clarifies that "the opposition between 'place' and 'space' will rather refer to two sorts of determinations in stories." What are these determinations? He writes, "The first, a determination through objects that are ultimately reducible to the *being-there* of something dead, the law of

_____

54. Cavanaugh, *Field Hospital*, 5, 6, 229.

a 'place' (from the pebble to the cadaver, an inert body always seems, in the West, to found a place and give it the appearance of a tomb); the second, a determination through *operations* which, when they are attributed to a stone, tree, or human being, specify 'spaces' by the actions of historical *subjects* (a movement always seems to condition the production of a space and to associate it with a history)."[55]

The idea of territory cannot be replaced by de Certeau's place or space because unlike place and space, a territory is often determined not by "objects" or "historical subjects" but by seemingly inanimate "systems" or "structures." In this respect, territorial thinking cannot be replaced or substituted by spatial thinking or spatial stories. It is interesting to see that when he engages in dialogue with Deleuze and Guattari in his *Theopolitical Imagination* regarding the phenomenon of globalization, Cavanaugh does not go far enough to address deterritorialization while commenting on territorialization and reterritorialization.[56] By bypassing the critical step of looking into deterritorial phenomena, Cavanaugh does not fully capture the radical aspect of Deleuze and Guattari's transformative nomadic politics. Although his theopolitics exemplifies how the church becomes the true res publica against the state's secular politics, his theopolitics stops short of addressing the church's political engagement in structural injustice and systemic violence. According to Cavanaugh, the primary political task of the church is to become a field hospital in a wounded world rather than to dismantle the structural injustice that causes wounds to this world and its inhabitants.

While Cavanaugh's political theology is largely shaped by the theopolitical imagination, Bretherton's is characterized by his democratic political vision. Unlike Cavanaugh, whose Augustinianism is more of a classic kind, Bretherton ventures to establish a sort of cosmopolitan type. This characteristic difference is not unrelated to Bretherton's methodical distinction between "secularity" and "secularism." How does Bretherton differentiate the former from the latter? He begins by claiming that "as a theological term, the secular is that which is not eternity." He argues that it is a "Christian innovation"

---

55. De Certeau, *Practice of Everyday Life*, 118.
56. Cavanaugh, *Theopolitical Imagination*, 107.

that the current age is demarcated to be secular. He writes, "If something is secular, it can be both sacred and profane, rather than sacred or profane."[57] In this respect, secular time as a temporal moment is "ambiguous and contingent." Since "the secular is a synonym of the noneternal age before Christ's return," human history, then, becomes "secular" rather than neutral. In the realm of the secular, the church and the state coexist in a dyadic, not binary, manner. Bretherton's Augustinian influence becomes clear when he writes, "For Augustine, the city of God is an alternative yet co-terminus society to the earthly city. These two cities are two political entities coexistent in time and space and thus part of this noneternal age or *saeculum*."[58]

How, then, does secularity differ from secularism? According to Bretherton, "Secularity is a fruit of the entangled histories that shape processes of modernization around the world," which entails the commitment to and institutional configuration of a religiously plural and morally diverse common life.[59] In contrast, secularism refers to "a governmental and hegemonic project," and it "generates specific configurations of divisions between public and private, depends on a monistic and centralized conception of political sovereignty, and looks to the nation-state as both the normative form of polity and the primary focus of identity."[60] In this respect, as he emphasizes, secularism "seeks the active removal and exclusion of religious considerations from shared moral and political judgments."[61] While religion and religious practices can go with secularity, finding their space there, secularism does away with anything related to the religious. By distinguishing secularity from secularism, Bretherton reterritorializes the realm for the religious.

Bretherton's distinctive neo-Augustinian political theology is, then, established in light of its alignment with the notion of secularity. He thus writes, "Constructively and prescriptively I take secularity to be a political good that serves the formation and sustaining of a common life amid difference, disagreement, and asymmetries of power." Secularity as a political good enables

---

57. Bretherton, *Christ and the Common Life*, 231.
58. Bretherton, 237.
59. Bretherton, 251.
60. Bretherton, 251–52.
61. Bretherton, 252.

Bretherton to discover a new ground on which *mutual* rather than *neutral* democratic politics can be established. Of course, this requires a democratic commitment from all parties that exist within the realm. The church is certainly part of this ground, and according to Bretherton, this ground is what he means by the "secular," and in this sense, he claims that the secular "may be a form of 'the world' rather than inherently worldly."[62]

How does he, then, define politics and democratic politics? According to him, politics "refers to forming, norming, and sustaining some kind of common life between friends, strangers, enemies, and the friendless amid their ongoing differences and disagreements and as they negotiate asymmetries of various kinds of power." As a distinctive type of politics, Bretherton holds, democratic politics is characterized by "the radical extension of who is considered capable and worthy of being political agents." He thus writes, "Democratic politics thereby extends politics from being the preserve of the few to something undertaken by the many for the good of the whole."[63] Bretherton also distinguishes democratic politics from democracy. While democracy refers to a mode of statecraft or structuring government—such as "voting systems, parliamentary forms of government, etc."—democratic politics emphasizes a set of practices for generating nonviolent forms of relational power and cooperation by way of such acts as "community organizing, unions, cooperatives, demonstrations, etc."[64]

As M. T. Davila correctly points out, Bretherton's masterful, robust yet flexible understanding of a democratic political vision provides us with the promise of engaging diverse others in constructing the common good for all, especially those socially marginalized and disenfranchised others. Bretherton's thoughtful idea has essentially to do with his critique of "white, Eurocentric streams of political theology in relation to nonwhite, non-Eurocentric approaches."[65] His democratic political vision, thus, is formulated in such a

---

62. Bretherton, 254, 256.
63. Bretherton, 445.
64. Bretherton, 445–46.
65. M. T. Davila, "Dreaming of a Democracy Driven by the Preferential Option for the Poor," Political Theology Network, September 19, 2019, https://politicaltheology.com/dreaming-of-a-democracy-driven-by-the-preferential-option-for-the-poor/.

way to resist nearly all types of binaries, including those "between traditional and radical, conservative and progressive, mainstream and subversive, premodern and modern, Western and non-Western, or colonial and decolonial frames of references."[66]

Hopeful as it may seem, Bretherton's almost Hegelian attempt to integrate historical, social, and political binaries through democratic politics entails some serious questions that are not answered by his book. First, I cannot but agree with Davila's following statement: "While he periodically mentions the ways in which Christians have failed to make neighbors of enemies and strangers and to protect the humanity of all, I fail to see the robust critical self-reflection. . . . In my estimation, Bretherton fails to apply his radically biblical political theology, grounded in the transforming power and political possibility present in the life, death, and resurrection of Christ, to the earthly structures entrusted to teach and uphold such radical hope."[67] In my view, this critical failure involves his more fundamental failure to reckon with the church's historical sin of colonial complicity. Remembering is not reckoning. Although he is well aware of the negative legacy of colonialism, by interlinking it with and blaming "secularism," he stops short of engaging in the church's historical reckoning with it.[68] If Bretherton thinks that the world of "secularity" is exempt from this settlement (since secularism is blamed for colonialism), he is mistaken. Let me illustrate how he omits the white American church's reckoning with its own historical sin as he calls for a historical settling with white supremacy in his chapter on Black Power.

According to Bretherton, African Americans' Black Power movement is a representative "case" for his democratic politics, in that "the Black Power movement represents but one iteration of attempts to form a people/nation, through the pursuit of power via democratic politics, and how what it means

---

66. Bretherton, *Christ and the Common Life*, 27.

67. Davila, "Dreaming of a Democracy."

68. Bretherton, for instance, writes, "Moreover, the formation of liberal democratic nation-states in Europe was made possible by colonial political economies spread across the globe" (*Christ and the Common Life*, 5). He also states, "European political theology and, in particular, discussions of the relationship between Christianity and democracy have largely ignored or concealed the creolized nature of modern political terms and their colonial and racialized formation" (84).

to be a people/nation comes to be understood in nonessentialist terms." He then criticizes other secularist attempts to reckon with the historical sin of white supremacy. These attempts include "liberalism," "scientific Marxism," "social democracy," and "multicultural accounts." He says, "Each of these [secularist] approaches tends to ignore the specific history and experience of African Americans and thus fails to reckon with how integration into the political economy as currently structured reinscribes white normativity into the identity, performance, and rationality of democratic citizenship."[69] What is missing in his call for a historical reckoning with white supremacy is the white American church's ecclesial reckoning with its own historical sin of colonial complicity.

The most regrettable corollary of Bretherton's democratic politics is that the problem of structural injustice is not considered a key political-theological issue. Instead, he blames the ambiguous and contingent moral status of the people (the demos/*populus*) regarding the existence of social sin. For instance, when he describes the event of Jesus's crucifixion, he points out that "those who gathered before Pilate were not, as is mostly assumed, a mob. Rather, they constituted an assembly of the people whose cry of acclamation carried authorizing force in both the Jewish and the Greco-Roman world." He continues, saying, "Alongside Pilate (the one), the Sanhedrin (the few)—and the forms of human authority each represents—is ruled by the people (the many). Rule by the people is depicted as a key part of the proceedings by which Jesus is condemned."[70] It is the demos/*populus*, not structural injustice, that is blamable for Jesus's crucifixion. Bretherton claims that "while there is a clear preferential option for the poor and oppressed throughout Scripture, Scripture is skeptical of any beatification of the oppressed as somehow morally infallible or without sin. . . . The common people can be stiff-necked and act in either oppressive or self-destructive ways."[71]

I cannot but raise this question to Bretherton's account: If the church's primary responsibility in supporting democratic politics is not addressing the structural injustice of society and if the people (the demos/*populus*) are

---

69. Bretherton, 115, 114.
70. Bretherton, 406.
71. Bretherton, 407.

morally ambiguous and contingent, what are the specific tasks of the church in doing democratic politics in the world of secularity? In some sense, this question resonates with those Stanley Hauerwas raises at the end of his review of Bretherton's *Christ and the Common Life*: "(1) who did you write this book for? and/or (2) as people convinced by your argument, what do we now do?"[72]

CONCLUSION

In this chapter, we have not only explored key biblical sources to uncover the nomos for the church's deterritorial nomadic politics but also examined the possible consociation between neo-Augustinian political theologies and the church's deterritorial political theology. As a result of this biblical-theological investigation, we have arrived at the following conclusions. First, the biblical notion of righteousness (*dikaiosyne*), especially God's righteousness that condemns and dismantles structural injustice, constitutes the nomos for the church's deterritorial nomadic politics. We find its archetypal revelation in God's demand for the Jubilee Year. Second, an in-depth theological examination of Cavanaugh's and Bretherton's political theologies helps us see more clearly why we need to develop further the church's deterritorial nomadic politics. Both Cavanaugh and Bretherton begin to construct their political theologies by attempting to reckon with Western secularization in different ways. While Cavanaugh points out how the secular promises end up involving us in the even more serious problem of state violence, Bretherton emphasizes that the church should continue to create its spatial story in the place of secularity. They, however, stop short of digging deeper to reckon with the church's historical sin of colonial complicity. We should note that although Cavanaugh's *Torture and Eucharist* is a powerful political-theological statement concerning how the church should address the problem of structural injustice in a time of crisis, its context is South America (Chile before and during the military dictatorship of General Augusto Pinochet Ugarte, 1973–90), not North America.[73] I am not arguing that the

---

72. Stanley Hauerwas, "On God and Democracy: Engaging Bretherton's *Christ and the Common Life*," *Studies in Christian Ethics* 33, no. 2 (January 2020): 235–42, here 242.

73. William T. Cavanaugh, *Torture and Eucharist: Theology, Politics, and the Body of Christ* (Hoboken, NJ: Wiley-Blackwell, 2007).

Western church cannot imitate what non-Western churches are doing. I am only saying that imitation is not that simple. To do so, the Western church must do its homework first.

From the vantage point of the church's deterritorial nomadic politics, the Western church may not yet be well ready for facing and addressing the structural injustice and systemic violence in this world with Cavanaugh's eucharistic politics or Bretherton's democratic politics only. The first task of the Western church is to engage in its thorough and full historical reckoning. Until all the stories of the colonized people are told, it should keep reckoning with its historical sin no matter how long it takes. Along with this, it should also develop a more radical, practical, and interventive political-theological nomos for the church's political practice. Both Cavanaugh and Bretherton agree with the idea that the church (*ekklesia*) is neither polis nor *oikos* but an alternative imagination or public assembly that not only fixes the dichotomy between public and private but also promotes a common life. They, however, stop short of calling for the church's deterritorial intervention in regard to the structural injustice and systemic violence of this world. If the church's alternative politics is negatively conceived in such a way that it pursues neither "Christendom" nor "sectarian withdrawal," what is it, then? Cavanaugh and Bretherton both seek after the establishment of an alternative Christian politics, but they do not offer what the Western church should do specifically. This does not seem to be accidental; it looks, rather, inevitable because, in Deleuze and Guattari's terms, what they are doing is trying to reterritorialize the church's political space but without attempting to deterritorialize the existing striated space. In the following chapter, I lay out how the church's alternative politics is possible by introducing the idea of its rhizomatic politics.

4

THE CHURCH AND
RHIZOMATIC POLITICS

INTRODUCTION

On April 20, 2010, the largest marine oil spill in the history of the petroleum industry occurred in the Gulf of Mexico on the BP-operated Deepwater Horizon oil rig. As a result of this environmental disaster, eleven workers were killed, and seventeen others were injured. Before BP officially declared the oil well completely and permanently sealed on September 19, 2010, about 1,300 miles of the US Gulf Coast were covered in oil, and massive harm was done to wildlife in and around the region, including the deaths of an estimated eight hundred thousand birds and sixty-five thousand turtles. The courts later found that 3.19 million barrels of oil leaked during the spill, which is equal to over 130 million gallons.[1]

Although this case was widely publicized, many remain unaware of its backstory. In February 2009, BP filed a fifty-two-page exploration and environmental impact plan for the Macondo well (where the Deepwater Horizon rig was put) with the federal Minerals Management Service (MMS) and stated

---

1. Richard Pallardy, "Deepwater Horizon Oil Spill: Environmental Disaster, Gulf of Mexico [2010]," *Britannica*, July 9, 2010, https://www.britannica.com/event/Deepwater-Horizon -oil-spill/Cleanup-efforts.

repeatedly that it was "unlikely that an accidental surface or subsurface oil spill would occur from the proposed activities."[2] On April 6, 2009, the MMS granted BP's project "categorical exclusion" from the full environmental analysis normally required under the National Environmental Policy Act. *Reuters* reports that this exemption "ultimately resulted in the deadly Gulf of Mexico explosion and subsequent oil spill."[3] In their 2015 paper, the social scientists Russell W. Mills and Christopher J. Koliba confirm this report by saying that the explosion of the Deepwater Horizon rig has to do with "the failure of the regulatory network charged with overseeing deep-water oil exploration in the Gulf of Mexico."[4] Mills and Koliba also point out that unlike the United States, which adopts "market-based accountability mechanisms," in countries such as the United Kingdom, Norway, and Canada, high-risk industries (e.g., deepwater oil drilling) are regulated by a process-oriented approach that mandates firms to develop a "safety case" with items such as risk assessments and hazard mitigation plans. They conclude their study by saying, "A reliance on market-based accountability mechanisms, along with the lack of a fully implemented process-oriented regulatory regime, led to the largest oil spill in US history."[5]

One may wonder, then, how BP was categorically excluded from the full environmental analysis. Antonia Juhasz of the *Guardian* writes, "The oil major BP spends aggressively to influence US regulatory insight, and many would argue this has bought it leniency." She documents just how much money went toward their lobbying: "In 2009, the company spent nearly $16m on lobbying the federal government, ranking it among the 20 highest spenders that year, and shattering its own previous record of $10.4m set in 2008."[6] What is so

---

2. "BP Didn't Plan for Major Oil Spill," *CBS News*, April 30, 2010, https://www.cbsnews.com/news/bp-didnt-plan-for-major-oil-spill/.

3. Jeffrey Jones and Jeff Mason, "BP's US Gulf Project Exempted from Enviro Analysis," Reuters, May 6, 2019, https://www.reuters.com/article/us-oil-rig-leak-exemption-standalone/bps-u-s-gulf-project-exempted-from-enviro-analysis-idUKTRE64517H20100506?edition-redirect=uk.

4. Russell W. Mills and Christopher J. Koliba, "The Challenge of Accountability in Complex Regulatory Networks: The Case of the Deepwater Horizon Oil Spill," *Regulation & Governance* 9 (2015): 77–91, here 82.

5. Mills and Koliba, 78, 77.

6. Juhasz, "BP Spends Millions Lobbying."

outrageous about BP's lobbying is that the company spent at least $2 million on federal lobbying in the first quarter of 2011 (a year after the disaster) on a wide range of issues, "from advocating for an end to the offshore drilling moratorium imposed by President Barack Obama in the wake of the spill to caps on its contributions to the restoration of the Gulf Coast."[7]

In October 2018, American citizens and residents were taken aback as they saw on the news that thousands of Central American migrants (known as the migrant caravan) were walking, taking buses, and wading through rivers in a cross-continent effort to arrive at the southern US border.[8] According to BBC, the caravan grew to more than seven thousand people, and they finally arrived at the US-Mexico border in November after traveling more than 4,000 km (2,500 miles) from Central America. The phenomenon of the Central American migrant caravan quickly ignited a political debate ahead of the US midterm elections, and even before the first members of the caravan reached the US border, the then president Donald Trump began to label the movement an "invasion."[9] Conservative media, such as Fox News, followed Trump's lead by calling the caravan members "invaders," although many of them were women and children.

Before the political debate began to surface, the Trump administration had already made the so-called zero tolerance policy official in May 2018 and quietly started testing family separation as a sort of "shock and awe" against unauthorized migrant families. The purpose of this "test" was to use the policy as a "deterrent to families thinking about coming north and crossing the border."[10] As predicted, the impact of the policy was devastating to many migrant families. For instance, on June 9, 2018, a man from Honduras, after

7. Marcus Baram, "BP Spent $2 Million Lobbying on Offshore Drilling, Spill Liability, Other Regulations in First Quarter of 2011," HuffPost, April 21, 2011, https://www.huffpost.com/entry/bp-lobbying-2011-q1-2-million_n_851842.

8. Larisa Epatko and Joshua Barajas, "What We Know about the Latest Migrant Caravan Traveling through Mexico," *PBS NewsHour*, October 24, 2018, https://www.pbs.org/newshour/world/what-we-know-about-the-latest-migrant-caravan-traveling-through-mexico.

9. "Migrant Caravan: What Is It and Why Does It Matter?," *BBC News*, November 26, 2018, https://www.bbc.com/news/world-latin-america-45951782.

10. John Burnett, "How the Trump Administration's 'Zero Tolerance' Policy Changed the Immigration Debate," NPR: All Things Considered, June 20, 2019, https://www.npr

being separated from his wife and child, suffered a nervous breakdown and killed himself in a Texas jail.[11] According to the Southern Poverty Law Center, nearly two thousand children were separated from their parents or legal guardians between April 19 and May 31, 2018.[12]

These two cases illustrate how structural injustice is engendered and played out in socioeconomic and political systems (such as public policies and executive orders) in perfectly legal and legitimate manners. They also show that although the church responds to the devastating outcomes caused by the structural injustices of our socioeconomic or political system, it rarely addresses and problematizes the real and fundamental *source* of unjust social realities. Without a doubt, it is rightful for the church to engage in healing and advocating ministries for those who are affected or victimized by structural injustice. But why would not the church go further to challenge and speak up against the source of the problem? Why is its social and ecclesial activism typically characterized or idealized in the form of social caring and support but not in that of organized resistance or unified opposition to an unjust system and structural process? What renders it sheepish and sedentary rather than radical and transformative in facing and addressing the structural injustice of this world? What needs to be done to transform its long-cherished idealization of the *depoliticized* approach to structural injustice and systemic violence?

In this chapter, I develop a new practical-constructive paradigm for the church's political-theological engagement in the structural injustice of this world by critically appropriating Deleuze and Guattari's seminal notion of a rhizome. In so doing, I also introduce a new conceptual approach to the field of political theology, which has been largely characterized by the traditional binary model of the "church and state." The newly established

---

.org/2019/06/20/734496862/how-the-trump-administrations-zero-tolerance-policy -changed-the-immigration-deba.

11. Nick Miroff, "A Family Was Separated at the Border, and This Distraught Father Took His Own Life," *Washington Post*, June 9, 2018, https://www.washingtonpost.com/world/ national-security/a-family-was-separated-at-the-border-and-this-distraught-father-took -his-own-life/2018/06/08/24e40b70-6b5d-11e8-9e38-24e693b38637_story.html.

12. "Family Separation under the Trump Administration—a Timeline," Southern Poverty Law Center, June 17, 2020, https://www.splcenter.org/news/2020/06/17/family -separation-under-trump-administration-timeline.

political-theological paradigm (the "church vs. structural injustice") emphasizes the church's resistance to and confrontation with the structural injustice
in this world. In an age of rising neoliberalism—which has taken over virtually every aspect of our social, organizational, and ecological worlds, from
economics to politics, from culture to technology—the church can no longer
effectively address and cope with mounting structural injustice with the traditional church and state paradigm. The church's primary political-theological
task is to resist and confront structural injustice rather than to strike a balance
between itself and the state. Of course, the state may still be one of the formidable and primary agencies that can cause, inflict, and even perpetuate
structural injustice, but it is not the sole one anymore. Multinational corpo-
rations, interest groups, and even nongovernmental organizations can cause,
inflict, and perpetuate structural injustice by directly harming and indirectly
disrupting our world and the environment.

Since the "church and state" political-theological paradigm is originally
fashioned out of the so-called cataphatic (positive) theological tradition, which
is interwoven with various types of ontotheology, I develop the church's rhizomatic politics from a different theological perspective by appropriating the
apophatic (negative) theological tradition. Although there has been a rising
ecclesial and scholarly interest in apophatic theology in the Western world,
its political-theological appropriation has not been fully established yet, not
to mention its political-theological integration with the biological notion of
a rhizome.[13] Thus the rhizomatic politics that I am about to lay out will be
explorative and experimental rather than definitive and complete. In this
chapter, I will also attempt to illustrate what the church's rhizomatic politics
would be like by introducing some of the historical cases that can be found in
the relatively recent history of the Western world.

---

13. For instance, in his article "The Critical Value of Negative Theology," *Harvard Theological
Review* 86, no. 4 (October 1993): 439–53, John Peter Kenney writes, "Having established
a significant if sometimes recessive presence in Western theism, negative theology is again
an important element in contemporary philosophical theology" (439).

THE CHURCH, RHIZOME, AND ECCLESIAL POLITICS

What is a rhizome? How could we appropriate the notion of it in developing a new political-theological model? Since it is a biological/botanical concept, we first check on its original lexical meaning within its discipline. According to *The Gale Encyclopedia of Science*, the biological idea of the rhizome is defined as follows: "A rhizome is a root-like, underground stem, growing horizontally on or just under the surface of the ground, and capable of producing shoots and roots from its nodes. Rhizomes are most commonly produced by perennial, herbaceous species of plants, that die back to the ground at the end of the growing season and must grow a new shoot at the beginning of the next season. Rhizomes are capable of storing energy, usually as starch, which is used to fuel the regeneration of new shoots. Rhizomes are also sometimes called rootstocks."[14]

Deleuze and Guattari initially adopt the biological notion of a rhizome as "an underground root system that attaches itself to other root systems and scatters in all directions."[15] They, however, expand this biological idea into "an image of thought to describe an alternative way of conceptualizing the world."[16] They incorporate the idea of a "map" by contrasting it with the image of "tracing." While the image of a map is associated with the idea of the rhizome, the image of tracing is linked with the idea of a tree structure. It is critical to distinguish between these two ideas: rhizomes and trees. Deleuze and Guattari contrast between the rhizomatic system and what they call the "arborescent system" (referring to a tree structure). According to Peter Nikolaus Funke, "Unlike a tree structure, with only one path from one particular point to any other point, rhizomes represent non-hierarchical structures where any point can connect to any other point, generating links that can stretch, unevenly and asymmetrically, across spaces and times, scales, issues or strategies. As such, rhizomatic structures have 'multiple entranceways and

---

14. Lerner and Lerner, *Gale Encyclopedia of Science*, 3765–66.
15. Alice van der Klei, "Repeating the Rhizome," *SubStance* 31, no. 1 (2002): 48–55, here 48.
16. Peter Nikolaus Funke, "Building Rhizomatic Social Movements? Movement-Building Relays during the Current Epoch of Contention," *Studies in Social Justice* 8, no. 1 (2014): 27–44, here 29.

exits.'"[17] By "arborescent systems," then, Deleuze and Guattari mean any hierarchical or centralized systems in which "an element only receives information from a higher unit, and only receives a subjective affection along pre-established paths." Unlike these arborescent systems, rhizomatic structures refer to "acentered systems, finite networks of automata in which communication runs from any neighbor to any other, the stems or channels do not preexist, and all individuals are interchangeable, defined only by their state at a given moment—such that the local operations are coordinated and the final, global result synchronized without a central agency."[18]

The metaphor of a rhizome, especially its philosophically appropriated logic, is particularly important if we would begin to consider its ability to engender multiconnectivity as well as to mobilize heterogeneous formations. According to Deleuze and Guattari, these two ideas—connection and heterogeneity—compose the first two principles of the rhizome, and these principles become the philosophical foundation to give birth to new events or movements across borders and territories. Indeed, the seminal notion of a rhizome lies in its organic logic that can "accommodate the considerable diversity and the multiplicity of struggles and possible futures, bringing about amorphous sets of associated and loosely linked organizations, groups and movements including anti-war, labor, environmental, feminist, peasant, indigenous and student groups from the political Left that oppose corporate globalization and neoliberal capitalism, imperialism and war."[19] The rhizome is indispensably entangled with the idea of deterritorialization, which we have explored in chapter 2. Since a "rhizome ceaselessly establishes connections between semiotic chains, organizations of power, and circumstances relative to the arts, sciences, and social struggles," various forms of rhizomes cannot but be interlinked with the process of deterritorialization. For instance, Deleuze and Guattari write, "The book is not an image of the world. It forms a rhizome with the world, there is an aparallel evolution of the book and the world; the book assures the deterritorialization of the world."[20]

---

17. Funke, 29.

18. Deleuze and Guattari, *Thousand Plateaus*, 16, 17.

19. Funke, "Building Rhizomatic Social Movements," 29–30.

20. Deleuze and Guattari, *Thousand Plateaus*, 7, 11.

The inevitable correlation between a rhizome's transversal movement and the process of deterritorialization offers us an important clue as to why the church should appropriate the metaphor of a rhizome, especially regarding its engagement in structural injustice and systemic violence. One of the key features of structural injustice is that it commonly parasitizes the existing arborescent systems, such as governing, regulating, or justifying mechanisms, for its sustenance and further expansion. It does not come into being out of nowhere; it, rather, evolves itself by parasitically exploiting the existing arborescent systems, entailing systemic abuse and social sufferings. Unfortunately, since the onset of neoliberalism in the early 1980s, US society and its citizens have been gradually subject to the rising structural injustice virtually in all areas of their lives, including social, cultural, and political ones, not to mention their economic and financial ones. What is even more troubling in this downward trend is that most of the negative impact of the rising structural injustice has been concentrated on already socioeconomically and politically marginalized people.

Michelle Alexander's 2010 book, *The New Jim Crow*, provides painstakingly detailed realities of one of America's formidable structural injustices: mass incarceration. In his 2019 article, "From Mass Incarceration to Mass Coercion," Mark Jay offers an updated report on mass incarceration. He writes, "From the mid-1960s to the late 2000s, the number of people locked in U.S. prisons and jails, and forced onto parole or probation, increased from less than eight hundred thousand to more than seven million." Why is mass incarceration a matter of structural injustice? Because "the criminal justice system continues to target the most impoverished among us."[21] Socioeconomic inequality is closely interlinked with racial disparity, and this is starkly reflected in statistics. According to the American Civil Liberties Union, "One out of every three Black boys born today can expect to go to prison in his lifetime, as can one of every six Latino boys—compared to one of every 17 white boys."[22] Although these numbers unmistakably demonstrate the

---

21. Mark Jay, "From Mass Incarceration to Mass Coercion," *Monthly Review* 71, no. 7 (December 2019): 24–36, here 24.

22. "Mass Incarceration," ACLU, accessed January 17, 2022, https://www.aclu.org/issues/smart-justice/mass-incarceration.

existence of structural injustice in our criminal justice system, other factors, such as the private prison industry, help us see more clearly how structural injustice exploits the existing arborescent systems.

As Alexander points out, "Prisons are big business and have become deeply entrenched in America's economic and political system." Since these companies' revenues are directly related to the number of inmates held by their private prisons, "they are deeply interested in expanding the market—increasing the supply of prisoners—not eliminating the pool of people who can be held captive for profit."[23] It is no secret at all that as the public good suffers more with the rise of mass incarceration, private prison companies garner more government dollars, while private prison executives rake in greater compensation packages. Private prison companies are no longer shy about admitting that "their business model depends on locking up more and more people."[24] Although it is morally repulsive to make a profit by locking people in cages, it is perfectly legal that these private prison companies do what they are doing while spending millions of dollars in lobbying to increase the number of their prison beds. According to the *Washington Post* (April 28, 2015), the two largest for-profit prison companies—GEO and Corrections Corporation of America (which changed its name to CoreCivic in 2017)—and their associates have donated more than $10 million to political candidates since 1989 and have spent nearly $25 million on lobbying efforts. Unsurprisingly, "they now rake in a combined $3.3 billion in annual revenue and the private federal prison population more than doubled between 2000 and 2010, according to a report by the Justice Policy Institute."[25] It seems evident that structural injustice expands itself by taking advantage of the existing arborescent systems, such as governing, regulating, or justifying mechanisms.

We need to see clearly that while structural injustice can evolve and expand itself by taking advantage of the existing arborescent systems of the

---

23. Michelle Alexander, *The New Jim Crow: Mass Incarceration in the Age of Colorblindness* (New York: New Press, 2012), 230.
24. "Private Prisons," ACLU, accessed January 17, 2022, https://www.aclu.org/issues/smart-justice/mass-incarceration/private-prisons.
25. Cohen, "How For-Profit Prisons."

state, the church is categorically prohibited from doing so because its political theology is operated by the traditional binary model of the "church and state." This binary model takes it for granted that the church approves the so-called separation phrase commonly known as the "separation of church and state" or "wall of separation between church and state." From a critical perspective, separation means that the church is formally prohibited from becoming involved and interfering with the arborescent systems of the state. What is the implication of this prohibition?

The significance of this prohibition lies in the fact that even though the state's arborescent systems are exploited or even taken over by the rising structural injustice, there is virtually nothing that the church can do about it as long as its ecclesial politics is organized in an arborescent manner. This is the reason it stops short of addressing real and fundamental causes when it engages in responding to such structural injustice cases as the Deepwater Horizon oil spill and the Central American migration crisis. According to the church and state binary model, the church is not only prohibited from becoming involved and interfering with the arborescent systems of the state but also tempted to model itself after these systems. For the church to address the rising problem of structural injustice, it should first deterritorialize binary arborescent systems by incorporating the metaphor of a rhizome. If we consider that "rhizomes can engender both roots and shoots simultaneously without ever dissipating," the church may discover a new way of addressing the structural injustice and systemic violence in this world.[26] This, however, requires it to restructure its ecclesial politics from the arborescent to the rhizomatic model.

How does the church's appropriation of the biological notion of a rhizome influence its political theology, especially the development of a new ecclesial-political framework to address structural injustice and systemic violence? I answer this question by delineating two key elements: method and goal. Regarding the method, Deleuze and Guattari offer us some critical clues. They write, "Unlike the tree [arborescent system], the rhizome is not

26. Carl Raschke, *GloboChrist: The Great Commission Takes a Postmodern Turn* (Grand Rapids, MI: Baker Academic, 2008), 41.

the object of reproduction: neither external reproduction as image-tree nor internal reproduction as tree-structure. The rhizome is an antigenealogy. It is a short-term memory or antimemory. The rhizome operates by *variation, expansion, conquest, capture, and offshoots*." They go further, saying, "The rhizome is an *acentered, nonhierarchical, nonsignifying* system without a General and without an organizing memory or central automaton, defined solely by a circulation of states. What is at question in the rhizome is a relation to sexuality—but also to the animal, the vegetal, the world, politics, the book, things natural and artificial—that is totally different from the arborescent relation: all manner of 'becomings.'"[27]

How does the church, then, practice and fulfill the political acts of "variation, expansion, conquest, capture, and offshoots" in an acentered, nonhierarchical, and nonsignifying manner? The idea of an "assemblage" becomes crucial in answering this question. The concept takes a key position in Deleuze and Guattari's political philosophy, especially concerning the ideas of deterritorialization and reterritorialization. Rhizomatic assemblages emerge from the arranging of heterogeneous elements into a productive or machinic entity, unlike arborescent assemblages, which are structurally unified by hierarchical force and representational logics (capital, state, corporation, etc.). Since rhizomatic assemblages arise in multiplicities and operate through desire, which is the organizing energy that produces connections, the emergence of assemblages is possible only when the arrangement of multiple desires is unaffected by arborescent social production or representation. This is how rhizomatic assemblages are distinguished from repressive, alienated, and mediated types. In this respect, Athina Karatzogianni and Andrew Robinson write, "The political goal of Deleuzian theory is to actualize the active social logics entirely, hence to take them to the point where they construct the entire social/ecological field, hence to release these forces from their entrapment within or submersion beneath other social logics."[28] The church's rhizomatic politics is conceived in such a way to practice the call to deterritorialize a territory controlled and colonized by parasitized arborescent systems and

27. Deleuze and Guattari, *Thousand Plateaus*, 21 (emphasis added).
28. Athina Karatzogianni and Andrew Robinson, *Power, Resistance and Conflict in the Contemporary World: Social Movements, Networks and Hierarchies* (London: Routledge, 2010), 13.

structures. In other words, the church's ecclesial politics strives after the deterritorialization of the structural injustice of an arborescent system through its rhizomatic networking and emerging assemblages.

Since the church's deterritorial ecclesial politics targets structural injustice and systemic violence, it is intrinsically related to the theological notion of liberation. For instance, Philip Goodchild illustrates that Deleuze and Guattari's political thought effects a triple liberation from the idea of humanism: first, liberation from the "mastery of nature"; second, liberation from the "model of representation or reflective knowledge"; last, liberation from "capital." Among these, Goodchild calls the last the "most significant," in that capital "exerts a determining role over political ecology."[29] We need to go a little deeper to understand what this means. In *Anti-Oedipus*, Deleuze and Guattari analyze how capital has deterritorialized the socius by unleashing its own (capitalist) flow of desire, resulting in the creation of a new mode of (arborescent) representation and a posthumanist subjectivity. It is worth citing their critical comments: "Hence, unlike previous social machines, the capitalist machine is incapable of providing a code that will apply to the whole of the social field. By substituting money for the very notion of a code, it has created an axiomatic of abstract quantities that keeps moving further and further in the direction of the deterritorialization of the socius. Capitalism tends toward a threshold of decoding that will destroy the socius in order to make it a body without organs and unleash the flows of desire on this body as a deterritorialized field."[30]

There is a reason Goodchild calls the liberation from capital the most significant. Capital substitutes the entire arborescent system of the state's power politics with its own quasi-rhizomatic politics of desire. The capitalist desire, however, should be differentiated from the Nietzschean "the will to power." Marc Roberts, for instance, writes, "As an unconscious and dynamic 'play

---

29. Philip Goodchild, "Philosophy as a Way of Life: Deleuze on Thinking and Money," *SubStance* 39, no. 1 (2010): 24–37, here 29.

30. Gilles Deleuze and Félix Guattari, *Anti-Oedipus: Capitalism and Schizophrenia* (New York: Penguin Classics, 2009), 33. By "body without organs," they mean a body or an entity that has an unregulated potentiality due to the absence of an organizational structure of organs. One, however, should be aware that this potentiality can be cancerous as well.

of forces,' a 'becoming' that constitutes life itself, 'the will to power' is to be understood as the 'instinct' of all living things for 'growth and expansion,' the unconscious drive 'to become more.'" He goes further, saying, "In so far as it is explicitly identified with 'the will to power,' 'desire' is to be understood as the principle that 'underlies' the world, existence, life, and hence the 'real' itself." Unlike this real desire identified with "the will to power," capitalist desire is marked by its own impotence, lacking the ability "to become more, to become other or to become different."[31] It thus tends to degenerate into mere interests.[32] Although it differs from Deleuzian real desire, since capital plays an essential role in taking over the entire arborescent system of the state by deploying the quasi-rhizomatic politics of desire, Goodchild emphasizes that liberation from capital is the most significant one.

The church's rhizomatic politics neither pursues the Nietzschean desire of "the will to power" nor assumes a Marxian liberation. As we will see shortly, the church's deterritorial ecclesial politics is practiced in a multiplicity of rhizomatic assemblages energized by apophatic faith ("abstract machines," in Deleuze and Guattari's terms). On the other hand, Deleuze and Guattari's rhizomatic politics is distinguished from Marxist revolutionary politics. From Deleuze and Guattari's perspective, Marxist politics is quintessentially arborescent rather than rhizomatic.[33] Athina Karatzogianni and Andrew Robinson capture the arborescent nature of Marxist politics by calling it "projects of counter-hegemony."[34] Deleuze and Guattari's rhizomatic politics or deterritorial assemblages do not pursue any hegemonic control as their political goals. This is the reason their rhizomatic politics diverges from other contemporary

---

31. Marc Roberts, "Capitalism, Psychiatry, and Schizophrenia: A Critical Introduction to Deleuze and Guattari's Anti-Oedipus," *Nursing Philosophy* 8 (2007): 114–27, here 116.

32. According to Karatzogianni and Robinson, "The mistake made by those who view capitalism as schizoid and desire-affirmative is that they fail to distinguish desires from interests. This distinction is, however, clearly articulated in capitalist subjectivity" (*Power, Resistance and Conflict*, 45).

33. By poignantly pointing out their disagreement with all types of arborescent social movements, including Marxist politics, Deleuze and Guattari write, "We're tired of trees" (*Thousand Plateaus*, 15).

34. Karatzogianni and Robinson, *Power, Resistance and Conflict*, 11.

Marxist political projects, such as Michael Hardt and Antonio Negri's.[35] For Deleuze and Guattari, Hardt and Negri's "concept of the multitude is a seed that wants to grow into an oak tree." Nicholas Tampio thus characterizes Deleuze and Guattari's rhizomatic politics as follows: "Deleuze and Guattari create the concept of assemblage to help the left envision political bodies that may 'gently tip' society in the direction of freedom and equality. Left assemblages can still effect profound changes—e.g., to address global warming or to distribute global wealth—but they recognize that 'a too-sudden destratification may be suicidal.' For Deleuze, leftists must comport themselves with both militancy and self-restraint, a desire for transformation and care."[36]

Deleuze and Guattari's innovative concept of the rhizome and its ecclesial appropriation can become a new paradigm for the church's deterritorial political-theological engagement in structural injustice as a non-Marxist social transformative movement. The idea of this new political-theological paradigm, however, is in much need of an in-depth theological verification and elaboration. How could we *theologically* ground Deleuze and Guattari's idea of rhizomatic politics? This is a crucial issue we need to discuss in the following section.

APOPHATIC THEOLOGIES AND RHIZOMATIC POLITICS

How could we theologically justify and substantiate the church's rhizomatic politics? What does it mean for us to establish this idea theologically? I argue in this section that it is not only theologically verified but also ecclesiastically required for the church to become itself. I will critically appropriate some of the key theological insights of the church's apophatic theological traditions, including both classic and contemporary thought. I will address three

---

35. Michael Hardt and Antonio Negri have copublished their neo-Marxist project in a series of books: *Empire* (Cambridge, MA: Harvard University Press, 2000); *Multitude: War and Democracy in the Age of Empire* (New York: Penguin, 2004); *Commonwealth* (Cambridge, MA: Harvard University Press, 2009); and *Assembly* (New York: Oxford University Press, 2017). They explicitly outline their allegiance to Marx's method in *Multitude*, 140–53, whose section is titled "In Marx's Footsteps."

36. Nicholas Tampio, "Assemblages and the Multitude: Deleuze, Hardt, Negri, and the Postmodern Left," *European Journal of Political Theory* 8, no. 3 (2009): 383–400, here 395.

questions. First, what is apophatic, or negative, theology? Second, why is the church's rhizomatic politics established and operated apophatically? Last, how does apophatic theology specifically support and substantiate it? If we successfully answer these questions, we will then be able to ground the idea of the church's rhizomatic politics as a theologically justifiable paradigm for the church's political practices.

Apophatic, or negative, theology is "a name given to a tradition within Christianity that confesses God to be so utterly transcendent, so beyond our concepts and names for God, that we must in fact 'negate' them to free God from such cramped categories."[37] In early Christian history, the Greek Cappadocian Fathers—Basil the Great (330–79), Gregory of Nyssa (ca. 335–95; Basil's younger brother), and Gregory of Nazianzus (329–89)—are commonly recognized as classic figures. Pseudo-Dionysius the Areopagite (late fifth to early sixth century), Maximus the Confessor (ca. 580–662), and Nicholas of Cusa (1401–64) are also widely regarded as major apophatic theologians.

We should note that although these classic figures are frequently categorized under the banner of apophatic theology, their apophatic recognition of God's transcendence is variable among themselves. For instance, "for Maximus, the apophatic recognition of God's transcendence does not lead to *endless progress* as it does for Gregory, or directly to *union with* the unknown God as it does for Dionysius, but rather to Christ as the *incarnate revelation* of God."[38] We also should note that even though apophatic theology lies in an opposite position to cataphatic, or affirmative, theology from a methodological perspective, they are not separable from each other for two reasons. Charles M. Stang notes, "First, they are inseparable because the practitioner must have something to negate—namely, God's self-disclosure or revelation, be that revelation in the natural world, in the scriptures or, as in the case of Christian negative theology, in the incarnation of Christ. . . . Second, negative and

---

37. Charles M. Stang, "Negative Theology from Gregory of Nyssa to Dionysius the Areopagite," in *The Wiley-Blackwell Companion to Christian Mysticism*, ed. Julia A. Lamm (Hoboken, NJ: John Wiley & Sons, 2013), 161–76, here 161.

38. Paul Rorem, "Negative Theologies and the Cross," *Harvard Theological Review* 101, nos. 3–4 (2008): 451–64, here 460 (emphasis added). Rorem goes on, saying, "Where the first [Gregory of Nyssa] outcome invoked endless time and the second [Dionysius] featured ecstatic eternity, this third [Maximus the Confessor] emphasizes salvation history" (460).

affirmative theologies are inseparable because negation is not an operation performed once, but rather is a commitment to the perpetual affirmation *and* negation of God's revelation."[39] John Peter Kenney summarizes the disparate yet interrelated relation between the apophatic and the cataphatic theologies as follows: "It may even be said that apophasis without kataphasis is empty, and kataphasis without apophasis lacks mystery and depth."[40]

What, then, does apophatic theology have to do with the idea of the church's rhizomatic politics? What theological significance does apophatic theology provide to us as we develop it? Although there are many different voices and types of apophatic theology in the Christian theological tradition, one of the most important contributions that it has brought to the church is that it helps the church critically distinguish its deterritorial political theology from the types of ontotheology.[41] What is ontotheology? Martin Heidegger uses the term to criticize the problematic approach of Western metaphysical thinking in general. In his *Identity and Difference*, he outlines the problem of metaphysical thinking by saying, "What characterizes metaphysical thinking which grounds the ground for beings is the fact that metaphysical thinking departs from what is present in its presence, and thus represents it in terms of its ground as something grounded."[42] Heidegger holds that in the Western philosophical tradition, the goal of metaphysics has always been searching for unifying "ground" that makes beings possible. This ground becomes "the place from which the beings of our experience derive and upon which they are grounded." Such a grounding reality or ultimate substance has always been differently explored, conceived, and named in Western philosophical traditions. As Anthony J. Godzieba succinctly summarizes, Heidegger brings a philosophical indictment against such a metaphysical way of thinking because "it ignores the phenomenality of beings, their sheer giveness as modes of presencing, and persists in formatting

---

39. Stang, "Negative Theology," 161.

40. John Peter Kenney, "The Critical Value of Negative Theology," *Harvard Theological Review* 86, no. 4 (1993): 439–53, here 448.

41. For instance, Bruce Milem introduces four different theories of negative theology. See his "Four Theories of Theology," *Heythrop Journal* 48, no. 2 (March 2007): 187–204.

42. Martin Heidegger, *Identity and Difference*, trans. Joan Stambaugh (New York: Harper & Row, 1969), 70–71.

reality along the lines of dualistic oppositions (ground/grounded, sources of presence / what is present)."[43]

Metaphysical thinking is particularly problematic when "it considers beings as grounded in Being, Being as somehow graspable by the intellect on analogy to beings, as made transparently clear by being represented as *something*—as *archē*, foundation, whatever." Now it becomes more evident how Western metaphysical thinking is then linked with ontotheology. Godzieba writes, metaphysics "exhibits the propensity to think this ground, this ulti-mate stable unifying principle as the 'highest being,' as the divine ground. Here is where metaphysics becomes 'ontotheologic.'" Ontotheology becomes possible as "God enters philosophy having been identified with Being, by functioning as the generative Ground of the perduring of beings, as that which is different from and which unifies what is grounded."[44] Carl Schmitt's *Political Theology* exemplifies how ontotheology can be problematic and even dangerous to democracy. By secularizing the notion of sovereignty, which is the image of the sovereignty of the ontotheologically conceived God, Schmitt justifies the secular state's sovereign right to sacred violence.[45]

Deleuze and Guattari's political philosophy has already deterritorialized the metaphysical terra of ontotheology with such concepts as "imminence," "difference," "multiplicity," and so on. They not only oppose Platonism but also valorize the Nietzschean death of God as the dismantling of ontotheo-logical thinking. Consequently, the metaphysical concept of "being/Being" is replaced by "becoming," and the "plane of imminence" is introduced in opposition to "transcendence." Without a doubt, with their "pure meta-physics" (a metaphysics of imminence) and "entirely positive, affirmative

---

43. Anthony J. Godzieba, "Ontotheology to Excess: Imagining God without Being," *Theologi-cal Studies* 56, no. 1 (1995): 3–20, here 6, 7.

44. Godzieba, 7.

45. Schmitt, for instance, writes, "All law is 'situational law.' The sovereign produces and guar-antees the situation in its totality. He has the monopoly over this last decision. Therein resides the essence of the state's sovereignty, which must be juristically defined correctly, not as the monopoly to coerce or to rule, but as the monopoly to decide. The exception reveals most clearly the essence of the state's authority. The decision parts here from the legal norm, and (to formulate it paradoxically) authority process that to produce law it need not be based on law." Carl Schmitt, *Political Theology: Four Chapters on the Concept of Sovereignty* (Chicago: University of Chicago Press, 2005), 13.

ontology" (there is no need to negate on the plane of imminence), Deleuze and Guattari effectively disassociate the idea of rhizomatic politics from the disrupting influence of ontotheology.[46] If this is the case, then, why should we specifically appropriate the method of *via negativa* in laying the ground for the church's rhizomatic politics theologically? Why apophatic theology? If Deleuze and Guattari have already dismantled any conceptual interfusions between the church's rhizomatic politics and ontotheology, what specific role could apophatic theology play in justifying and ratifying the church's rhizomatic politics?

Indeed, Deleuze and Guattari's Nietzschean atheism or death of God has conceptually prevented any types of ontotheology from seeping into the unfolding of rhizomatic politics.[47] All the positive names and ideas of God have been already cleared from the plane of imminence. Their philosophical atheism, however, also results in the clearance of all idols and subsequently all forms of idolatry from the plane of imminence. Deleuze and Guattari write, "Only friends can set out a plane of immanence as a ground from which idols have been cleared."[48] What we need to see is that although this clearance of idols and idolatry is effective regarding the philosophical plane of imminence, idols and idolatry are very much real in the world of power, capital, law, and attention. This is the reason apophatic theology becomes indispensable in laying a theological ground for the church's rhizomatic politics. The territorial world percolated by structural injustice and systemic violence is yet to be folded into the plane of imminence, and apophatic theology is constantly called to guide the church's rhizomatic politics to remain on it while the church ventures to deterritorialize the world of power, capital, law, and attention.

Giorgos Vlantis helps us see more clearly how apophatic theology could intervene and prevent idolatry by asserting that "apophaticism is the most

46. Christopher Ben Simpson, *Deleuze and Theology* (London: Bloomsbury, 2012), 12.
47. Deleuze and Guattari write, "Atheism is not a problem for philosophers or the death of God. . . . Atheism is not a drama but the philosopher's serenity and philosophy's achievement" (Gilles Deleuze and Félix Guattari, *What Is Philosophy?* [New York: Columbia University Press, 1994], 92).
48. Deleuze and Guattari, 43.

persistent human resistance against the temptation of self-divination." "By reminding us of human limitations," Vlantis writes, "it dictates an attitude of humility and respect towards the other and their opinion."[49] In a similar fashion, Yountae An points out that "the method of negation [*via negativa*] testifies to the fact that truth can be glimpsed only through a humble epistemological surrender to one's limits."[50] We should note that idolatry is always fueled by our tendency to absolutize or centralize our views, voices, or places, and the church is not exempted from such a temptation. In this respect, Vlantis is right to say, "If idolatry is the absolutization of the relative, . . . apophatic consciousness could help guard the church against this temptation, as well as from confessional arrogance and aggressiveness."[51] John Peter Kenney argues that apophatic theology "subverts our deep human tendency to settle for idols, reminding us that all theology can function properly only as an icon of the divine, leading the spiritual self into the immediacy of God." We should not miss the critical point that although "dogmatism" often turns out to be a religious form of idolatry, we may not see it clearly without the eyes of apophasis. This is the reason Kenney writes, "Apophasis saves us from idolatry by serving as an antidote to dogmatism."[52]

Besides this critical value of negative theology (saving us from idolatry), there is another important reason the church's rhizomatic politics should be grounded on an apophatic plane of imminence. According to Vlantis, apophasis helps us resist not only the temptation of self-divination but also structural injustice and systemic violence. He writes, "The fight of Christians against poverty and social injustice, the totalitarianism of dictatorships and of wars, racism, and xenophobia expresses a deeply eschatological and therefore apophatical ethos." He goes further, saying, "Apophaticism postulates the refusal of compromises with the powers of evil in this world; it gives a creative feeling of dissatisfaction, always having in mind the perspective

---

49. Giorgos Vlantis, "The Apophatic Understanding of the Church and Ecumenical Dialogue," *Ecumenical Review* 62, no. 3 (October 2010): 296–301, here 300.
50. Yountae An, *The Decolonial Abyss: Mysticism and Cosmopolitics from the Ruins* (New York: Fordham University Press, 2016), 32.
51. Vlantis, "Apophatic Understanding," 300.
52. Kenney, "Critical Value of Negative Theology," 441.

of the future that God has promised to the world."[53] Given that "little has been written on the political significance of negative theology," Vlantis's bold interpretation of *via negativa* is a welcome advancement of political theology, especially regarding the church's rhizomatic politics.[54]

We have seen two reasons the church's rhizomatic politics needs the critical voice of apophatic theology. First, the practice of *via negativa* saves the church from the temptation of idolatry; second, it also helps the church proceed to resist structural injustice and systemic violence. How does, then, apophatic theology specifically lay a theological ground for the church's rhizomatic politics? What does it mean for the church to unfold its rhizomatic politics on the apophatic plane of imminence? What is this apophatic plane of imminence on which the church rolls out its distinctive rhizomatic politics? I answer these questions by integrating the apophatic theology of the "incarnation" and the Deleuzian concept of "becoming." As for the former, I will particularly focus on Maximus the Confessor and his modern-day Orthodox disciple Nikolaos Loudovikos. From the perspective of this integration, the church's rhizomatic politics is understood as a continuum of Christ's *incarnation*, which has no end. This integration also helps us see that the church's rhizomatic politics is indeed a way (a "line of flight," in the Deleuzian sense) through which the church *becomes* itself. How, then, is this theological-philosophical integration possible?

Many commentators believe that the apophatic tradition is centrally concerned with mystical experience and thus implicitly apolitical. David Newheiser, however, argues that "although negative theology does not offer direct prescriptions for modern politics, it exemplifies an ethical discipline with political implications."[55] Although Newheiser does not provide us with a specific prescription regarding how negative theology exemplifies it, we may conjecture that this exemplification is not merely possible but also inevitable because where there is idolatry, there is always a shadow of violence. Thematizing idolatry cannot thus be separated from addressing this shadow.

---

53. Vlantis, "Apophatic Understanding," 300.
54. David Newheiser, "Why the World Needs Negative Political Theology," *Modern Theology* 36, no. 1 (January 2020): 5–12, here 10.
55. Newheiser, 11.

Grounding in the apophatic plane of imminence, the church's rhizomatic politics is, then, expected to tackle both idolatry and the shadow of violence. One should be warned not to miss that the "politics" in the phraseology (the church's rhizomatic politics) is determined by a rhizome, and thus it differs from its traditional meaning. To put it negatively, the politics of the church's rhizomatic politics is neither organized nor characterized by arborescent systems.

The feminist apophatic theologian Catherine Keller exemplifies how apophatic political theology is possible. She claims that "theology is not politics," then immediately adds, "But it is *always already political.*"[56] According to her, while politics refers to the "structures of the state, and so with institutions that religious practice may shape, sanctify, question, or protest," the political that cannot be reduced to politics is defined as "the struggle for a more common good."[57] Although Keller does not use the term *rhizomatic politics*, she clearly illustrates that the church's apophatic political theology is established as its rhizomatic endeavor (through "social movements") to uphold the common good. She states, "There will be no political transformation for a more common good unless we build upon the social movements *growing as cells anywhere, networking virtually everywhere, and spilling as crowds into the streets.*"[58] In developing an apophatic political theology, Keller particularly appropriates the Greek Cappadocian Father Gregory of Nyssa and his seminal work *The Life Moses*. The metaphor of the "cloud" becomes crucial as she develops her apophatic political theology. The all-inclusive yet explosively enfolding image of the cloud becomes an apophatic plane of imminence that encompasses "every register of our relations, every economy, every politics, every social or ecclesial movement, every ecology."[59] In the third part ("Implications") of her *Cloud of the Impossible*, then, Keller explores the possibility of apophatic

---

56. Catherine Keller, *Political Theology of the Earth: Our Planetary Emergency and the Struggle for a New Public* (New York: Columbia University Press, 2018), 8.
57. Keller, 30.
58. Keller, 63 (emphasis added).
59. Catherine Keller, *Cloud of the Impossible: Negative Theology and Planetary Entanglement* (New York: Colombia University Press, 2015), 30.

political engagement in such topics as politically/religiously sponsored violence, global economics, and the ecological crisis.[60]

Insightful and illuminating as Keller's apophatic theology is, the church's apophatic calls and tasks are not fully addressed in her works. This is the reason we are to engage with other theological voices to develop a more comprehensive and inventive apophatic ecclesiology for the church's rhizomatic politics. In this respect, Nikolaos Loudovikos becomes an important guide for us, especially his *Church in the Making*, in which he develops the church's profound and convincing apophatic vision by appropriating Maximus the Confessor's apophatic ecclesiology. He writes, "Already at the beginning of his *Mystagogy*, his most important ecclesiological work, Maximus boldly attempts, first, a complete connection between apophaticism and ecclesiology."[61] How does Maximus, then, lay out his apophatic ecclesiology? What makes the church's apophatic ecclesiology possible as well as sensible?

In *Mystagogy*, Maximus first defines the apophatic nature of God by writing, "For nothing whatsoever, whether being or nonbeing, is linked to him as a cause. . . . He has in fact a simple existence, unknowable and inaccessible to all and altogether beyond understanding which transcends all affirmation and negation." According to Maximus, "Holy Church bears the imprint and image of God since it has the same activity as he does by imitation and in figure." He subsequently describes the activities of God as follows: "[God] leads all beings to a common and unconfused identity of movement and existence, no one being originally in revolt against any other or separated from him by a difference of nature or of movement, but all things combine with all others in an unconfused way by the singular indissoluble relation to and protection of the one principle and cause."[62] For Maximus, the incarnation of the Word of God becomes pivotal in establishing an apophatic ecclesiology because Christ not only "knows the Father by essence" as the "messenger of the great counsel" but also becomes the head of the church that imitates the

60. Ilsup Ahn, *Theology and Migration* (Leiden, Netherlands: Brill, 2019), 54.
61. Nikolaos Loudovikos, *Church in the Making: An Apophatic Ecclesiology of Consubstantiality* (New York: St. Vladimir's Seminary, 2016), 43.
62. George C. Berthold, ed., *Maximus Confessor: Selected Writings* (Mahwah, NJ: Paulist, 1985), 186.

"activity" of God, "as the image reflects its archetype." Maximus continues, "The great plan of God the Father is the secret and unknown mystery of the dispensation which the only-begotten Son revealed by fulfilling in the incarnation, thus becoming a messenger of the great plan of God the eternal Father."[63]

Loudovikos develops further Maximus's apophatic ecclesiology by emphasizing the Trinitarian imprint of the apophatic church as well as its "becoming" nature. According to Loudovikos, Maximus's concept of ecclesiological consubstantiality "presents the *Trinitarian* ecclesial event as fundamentally Christological and consequently pneumatological . . . that is to say, as consubstantial manifestations of the whole Christ, in the Spirit according to the goodwill of the Father." The church, then, exists in the form of apophatic mimesis of or participation in a great mystery of God's free love, charisms, or "divine energy." The idea of "apophatic" thus signifies "participable, possible, gradual, indeterminate, and free manifestation, relative to the degree of free 'imitation' of the divine energy."[64] From the perspective of "consubstantiality," Loudovikos continues, "the eucharistic incarnation of Christ within his Church that follows is correlated very closely with the unfolding of these charisms in the Spirit in their absolute and consubstantial christological plenitude and communion."[65]

Two important themes—"becoming" and "plenitude"—emerge in Loudovikos's apophatic ecclesiology of consubstantiality, and they are indispensable to lay an apophatic theological ground for the church's rhizomatic politics. According to Loudovikos, it is critical to differentiate between "coordination" and "consubstantial perichoresis" because the latter "signifies a specific ontological status that can verify the ability of a charism to function in relation to its apophatic participation in the consubstantial mode of the divine energy."[66] Since the ecclesial structure or ecclesial body is not simply given but rather apophatically linked with the divine consubstantiality in a mode of "participation in the divine energy," the ecclesial structure turns out to be

---

63. Berthold, 187, 152.
64. Loudovikos, *Church in the Making*, 58.
65. Loudovikos, 59.
66. Loudovikos, 50.

in the mode of dynamic "becoming," not of static "being." Loudovikos further defines the notion of becoming by evoking the image of "church in the making." He writes, "This is what an apophatic ecclesiology of consubstantiality means, describing Church in the making, that is, Church as an icon/image of the kingdom being realized in the course of an imitation/mimesis/participation in Christ's members/energies/charisms in the Spirit."[67] While the concept of becoming refers to the imitating and participatory mode of the church in relation to the divine consubstantiality, the notion of plenitude denotes the excess of charism, which originates in the divine consubstantiality. The excess of charism is liturgically demonstrated by the practice of the divine Eucharist. Loudovikos writes, "It is thus in the divine Eucharist that we learn the modes of the *plenitude* of our charisms, and it is the divine Eucharist that supports and also judges this *plenitude* as a consubstantial manifestation of Christ in each one and in the communion of each with each other."[68]

We have developed an apophatic political theology for the church's rhizomatic politics. In doing so, we have engaged in an in-depth critical dialogue with the classic apophatic theologian Maximus the Confessor and modern-day apophatic theologians Catherine Keller and Nikolaos Loudovikos. While Keller helps us see how the unfolding epiphany of the mystery of God becomes the apophatic call for the church's rhizomatic movements that enfold all the social, economic, political, and ecological planes, Loudovikos offers us a methodological perspective regarding how an apophatic ecclesiology is possible as an imitation and manifestation of divine consubstantiality. The construction of an apophatic ecclesial-political theology, however, requires more than a simple integration between Keller's *apophatic political theology* and Loudovikos's *apophatic ecclesiology*. To construct a more holistic apophatic ecclesial-political theology that addresses structural injustice and systemic violence, Keller's apophatic political theology should make more room for harboring the church's apophatic "becoming," whereas Loudovikos needs to extend the church's apophatic intervention into the wider territories of

---

67. Loudovikos, 51. He later sums up his apophatic ecclesiology by asserting, "The Church is always in the making" (58).

68. Loudovikos, 59 (emphasis added).

116

economy, politics, culture, and ecology. In the following section, I attempt to bridge these two apophatic planes to lay a more holistic theological groundwork for the church's rhizomatic politics.

APOPHATIC INCARNATION, BECOMING THE CHURCH, AND RHIZOMATIC POLITICS

How can we bridge Keller's apophatic political theology and Loudovikos's apophatic ecclesiology? I argue that the answer lies in Maximus's insightful theological idea that was not fully uncovered by Loudovikos. There is a key statement on the "incarnation" made by Maximus, and it is as follows:

> The Word of God is called flesh not only as having become incarnate but as God the Word understood simply in the beginning with God the Father, who possesses the clear and naked forms of the truth of all things and does not include riddles or enigmas or need allegorical stories. When he is present to men who cannot with their naked mind reach naked spiritual realities, and converses in a way familiar to them in a variety of stories, enigmas, parables, and dark sayings, then he becomes flesh. Our mind does not in this first encounter hold converse with the naked Word, but with the Word made flesh, certainly in a variety of languages; though he is the Word by nature he is flesh to the sight, so that many think they see flesh and not the Word even if he is truly the Word. For the understanding of Scripture is not what appears to the many but is otherwise than it appears. For the Word becomes flesh through each recorded word.[69]

In this passage, Maximus helps us see that there are two ways of understanding the incarnation of Christ: cataphatic and apophatic. The cataphatic view of the incarnation is for those "who cannot with their naked mind reach naked spiritual realities," and because of this given limitation, God the Father uses their familiar ways, such as "stories, enigmas, parables, and dark

---

69. Berthold, *Maximus Confessor*, 159–60.

sayings," to converse with them, and this is how the Word becomes flesh. Maximus calls it the "first encounter," in which our minds hold converse with the Word made flesh in a variety of languages but not with the naked Word itself ("Many think they see flesh and not the Word"[70]). Unlike the cataphatic view, the apophatic view helps us understand the "naked Word" as such, not the Word made flesh. Maximus then summarizes the idea of this apophatic understanding of the incarnation by emphasizing the invisible Word itself rather than the visible flesh. Here is what he says: "For the understanding of Scripture is not what appears to the many but is otherwise than it appears."[71]

After distinguishing the two ways of understanding the incarnation, Maximus proceeds to connect them by proposing an idea of apophatic progression from the cataphatic to the apophatic type. He acknowledges first that "the beginning of religious discipleship for men is directed at the flesh." Why is it so? According to him, it is because "in our first acquaintance with religious devotion," we tend to approach it in the letter, not the spirit. Indeed, without the eyes of faith, one cannot easily see the Word even if Christ is truly the Word. Maximus thus writes, "Gradually going on in the spirit we strip off the grossness of the words to find finer meanings and so arrive purely at the pure Christ." How is it possible for us to look on Christ not according to the flesh but according to the spirit? Maximus emphasizes the importance of clearing away one's own perceptions, prejudices, or worldviews. He writes, "By means of the simple encounter with the Word without the veils of the mind covering him, we progress from knowing the Word as flesh to 'his glory as the only-begotten of the Father.'"[72]

What, then, is the difference between one who knows the "Word" or the "pure Christ" and one who knows the "Word as flesh"? How would their lives differ from each other? How would they act differently in this world? Maximus answers the question by declaring that "the One who is living a life in Christ has gone beyond the righteousness of both the Law and of nature, as the divine Apostle has pointed out in these words, 'For in Christ there is neither circumcision nor uncircumcision.'" He then immediately adds,

---

70. Berthold, 160.
71. Berthold, 160.
72. Berthold, 160.

"By circumcision, he [Christ] meant the righteousness of the Law, and by uncircumcision, he signified in an obscure way the equality that comes from nature."[73] This short yet profound response offers us a glimpse of how an apophatic ecclesial-political theology can be possible. If we interpret "the One who is living a life in Christ" as the church, "the righteousness of . . . the Law" as religiously sanctioned righteousness, and "the righteousness of . . . nature" as politically appropriated justice, then Maximus's response insinuates that the church should go beyond any politically appropriated legal justice as well as religiously sanctioned moral righteousness. This means that the genuine church of apophatic incarnation stands against injustice, especially structural injustice, which religious institutions and politics fail to address by their moral and legal standards.

We discover an archetype of this apophatic ecclesial-political practice in Jesus's cleansing of the Jerusalem temple (Mark 11:15–19; Matt 21:12–17; Luke 19:45–48; John 2:13–22) and the subsequent event of Jesus's standing before the assembly of the elders and Pilate. We should recall that structural injustice commonly parasitizes the existing arborescent systems, such as governing, regulating, or justifying mechanisms, for its sustenance and further expansion. When Jesus overturns the tables of the money changers and the seats of those who sell doves, those who plot to kill him are not money changers and dove sellers. Interestingly, they are "the chief priests and the scribes" (Mark 11:18). Later, when Jesus is bound and handed over to Pilate by the council, although Jesus does not defend himself, Pilate comes to know that the whole process has been set up by the chief priests out of their jealousy (Mark 15:10). The series of events that lead to Jesus's crucifixion demonstrates how Jesus stands up against structural injustice that has parasitically taken over arborescent systems of religion and politics and also why the church as the body of the "only-begotten Son" should go beyond fragile justice of the worldly politics. The idea of the church's rhizomatic politics emerges out of this theological reflection. From this perspective, the church's practice of rhizomatic politics becomes an event in which the invisible Word is apophatically

---

73. Berthold, 160.

incarnated. In the following chapter (chap. 5), we will investigate further the hidden political-theological meaning of this event by reading René Girard.

What about Keller's apophatic cloud that unfolds the impossible? The image of this cloud signifies not only our "nonknowing" but also our boundless, alternative, and all-inclusive impossible knowing. This alternative knowing, however, emerges with an apophatic call to entangle with the ecological world as well as the political and economic worlds. Keller also claims that the cloud of our nonknowing encompasses every ecclesial movement. What really transpires in the apophatic cloud is, then, the unfolding of alternative knowing and new possibilities. She writes, "Such a theology performs its negations for the sake of the most positive relations possible. This nonknowing is to its alternative knowing as im/possibility—the most impossible possible—is to its possibility."[74] The critical questions we cannot but raise are, then, Where could we find this cloud? Is it still available out there? If yes, where is the site of it so that we may enter to experience the unfolding of alternative knowing and new possibilities?

Keller's answer to these questions is short and clear—potentially everywhere. The nature of this cloud is neither accidental nor intentional; it is more likely evental or eventful and cannot be contained or measured. Her answer has to do with the idea of "apophatic panentheism," which develops by critically appropriating Paul's panentheism. She writes, "Panentheism [not pantheism] signifies one thread looping together vastly disparate schemes under a name the originative authors do not use. That would also be true of a more distant ancestor, Paul." According to Keller, Paul lays out his panentheism in his first letter to the Corinthians, especially 1 Corinthians 15:28: "so that God may be all in all." As she points out, "God being *in all* isn't quite the same as God being *all in*." She goes on, saying that Paul's panentheism is presaged by his idea of human interconnectivity: "in its 'all in Adam,' by which a failure went contagious; and then, enliveningly, in its all 'in Messiah,' as in, 'so all will be made alive in Christ.'"[75]

---

74. Keller, *Cloud of the Impossible*, 3.
75. Keller, *Political Theology of the Earth*, 145.

After outlining Paul's panentheism, by drawing on her apophatic process theological perspective, Keller moves on to reinterpret 1 Corinthians 15:28, particularly the theological meanings of the words "may be." She writes, "The 'may be' may signify that God can become something God is not always already. But this becoming would happen precisely not as an exception that proves the rule of substance metaphysics. It seems instead to presume a divine becomingness that must somehow always be in play."[76] Keller's apophatic panentheism and her apophatic political theology are focused on the relation between God and the world rather than the church and structural injustice. This is the reason it is hard to see the church in her apophatic political theology even though she actively engages in "worldly" matters, including politics, economics, culture, and ecology. At a glance, it appears that her apophatic theology is a type of political theology without the church. This, however, is not entirely true because the church is not absent in her political theology; it is, rather, subsumed by the apophatic space between God and the world. The church is there, but it is largely buried beneath the apophatic plane of imminence. Keller's subsumed ecclesiology renders the metaphor of "a rhizome" even more relevant and apposite in conceptualizing the church's alternative ecclesial politics vis-à-vis structural injustice and systemic violence. While the metaphor of the cloud seems most seizing to describe God's apophatic imminence in the world, the metaphor of a rhizome appears to be most capturing to denote the church's apophatic engagement in structural injustice. In this respect, we may call Keller's buried and thus invisible church a rhizome.

Although Keller does not say much about the subsumed ecclesiology, she offers us some critical insights about the unfolded role of the church buried beneath the apophatic plane of imminence. In doing so, she draws on Paul again. She, however, has a major concern regarding Paul's Christ in 1 Corinthians 15:24–25, which reads, "When he hands over the kingdom to God the Father, after he has destroyed every ruler and every authority and power. For he must reign until he has put all his enemies under his feet." Without a doubt, she is worried about the church's captivity to Christian triumphalism by upholding "Christ-exceptionalism." But she argues that Paul himself

---

76. Keller, 146.

dismantled an "exceptionalist christos." She writes, "It is all the more surprising that Paul immediately pulls the rug out from under its sovereign feet: 'When all things are subject to him, then the Son himself will also be subjected to the one who put all things in subjection under him.'"[77] We need to see here that Paul's counterexceptionalist christos does not do away with his "counter-imperial" Jesus. Keller cites N. T. Wright, "The christological titles Paul uses here for Jesus (saviour, lord, Messiah) are blatantly counter-imperial, with the word 'saviour' in particular . . . echoing around the Mediterranean world with the claims of Caesar," who called himself "savior, indeed 'divine son of God, redeemer, lord . . .'"[78] Keller's subsumed ecclesiology is now more evident. According to her, as the body of Christ, the church must desist "Christ-exceptionalism," but it should continue to be "blatantly counter-imperial." Keller helps us see more clearly why we should lay the ground for the church's rhizomatic politics apophatically. From a Deleuzian perspective, the church becomes itself by practicing rhizomatic politics.

CONCLUSION

I have outlined the concept of the church's rhizomatic politics as an ecclesial response to the rising structural injustice of this world. In doing so, I critically engaged in Deleuze and Guattari's seminal philosophical works on the politics of immanence. As Paul Patton points out, their political philosophy "does not conform to the disciplinary norms of anglophone normative political philosophy or German Critical Theology." Patton emphasizes that the political ideas formulated in *Anti-Oedipus* and *A Thousand Plateaus* "do not directly address the macropolitical public domain."[79] Their seminal concept of "micropolitics" certainly provides us with a new perspectival paradigm concerning how the church should respond to the rising structural injustice of our world. Trapped by the traditional binary logic of the church

---

77. Keller, 152.
78. N. T. Wright, *The Resurrection of the Son of God* (Minneapolis: Fortress, 2003), 232.
79. Paul Patton, "Deleuze's Political Philosophy," in *The Cambridge Companion to Deleuze*, ed. Daniel W. Smith and Henry Sommers-Hall (Cambridge: Cambridge University Press, 2012), 198–219, here 198.

and state separation, the Western church has long been confined by this ideological straitjacket. In this respect, the concept of a rhizome and its ecclesial appropriation (the church's rhizomatic politics) become a liberating yet challenging breakthrough for those churches that care about justice.

We also laid a theological ground for the church's rhizomatic politics by drawing on both classic and contemporary apophatic theologies (Maximus the Confessor, Catherine Keller, Nikolaos Loudovikos, et al.). The method of apophasis saves the church from what Keller calls "the deeper idolatry" and dogmatism. Meanwhile, it empowers the church to be what N. T. Wright calls "blatantly anti-imperial."[80] Apophatic theology is indispensable to develop the idea of rhizomatic politics because without it, the church may tend to turn a blind eye to or even take sides with the arborescent systems of religion and politics parasitically taken over by structural injustice. Since the church's rhizomatic politics fulfills the apophatic unfolding of justice, the metaphor of a rhizome is deeply entangled with the idea of "becoming the church" in apophatic political theology. Although we have laid a theological ground for the church's rhizomatic politics, there are still many questions to be answered and explored—such as, Who will carry it out? How do they fulfill such an apophatic call? I attempt to answer these questions in the following chapter.

---

80. Wright, *Resurrection*, 232.

5

THE CHURCH AND
RHIZOMATIC ORGANIZING

INTRODUCTION

In the previous chapter, we examined not only the conceptual identity of the church's rhizomatic politics but also its theological backdrop, justification, and necessity by constructively integrating Deleuze and Guattari's notion of a rhizome and the church's apophatic theological tradition. In this chapter, we examine the agential aspect of the church's rhizomatic politics. Without those who organize it, there cannot be such a thing called rhizomatic politics. We can refer to these distinctive organizers using different terms, such as *rhizomatic organizers*, *rhizomatic leaders*, *community organizers*, and so on. They can be interchangeably used, but by adopting Saul D. Alinsky's distinction between the leader and the organizer, I will coin the term *rhizome organizers* to refer to those who organize rhizomatic politics.[1] Who are these rhizome organizers?

---

1. Alinsky differentiates the leader and the organizer as follows: "The leader goes on to build power to fulfill his desires, to hold and wield the power for purposes both social and personal. He wants power himself. The organizer finds his goal in creation of power for others or use." Rhizome organizers, thus, can be defined as those who utilize rhizomatic networks to promote social-ecological justice and communal-environmental solidarity in society. See Saul D. Alinsky, *Rules for Radicals: A Pragmatic Primer for Realistic Radicals* (New York: Vintage, 1989), 80. Although rhizome organizers and community organizers are

What does it mean for one to become a rhizome organizer? What are the key qualifications to become a rhizome organizer for the church? How could we theologically ground this idea?

In answering these questions, I first define the notion of rhizome organizers and lay out a compelling reason church leaders should identify themselves as such by looking at two historical cases that illustrate what happens if they fail to become so in critical times. To be more specific, I critically examine the cases of housing apartheid and Japanese American internment. This examination is followed up by a critical summary and analysis of my early 2021 in-depth interviews with four church leaders: Rev. Dr. Liz Theoharis, the cochair of the Poor People's Campaign and the director of the Kairos Center for Religions, Rights, and Social Justice at Union Theological Seminary in New York City; Rev. Dr. Michael Nabors, the senior pastor of Second Baptist Church in Evanston, Illinois, and the president of the Evanston/Northshore NAACP (National Association for the Advancement of Colored People); Rev. John Fife, the former senior pastor of Southside Presbyterian Church in Tucson, Arizona, and a founding organizer of the Sanctuary Movement; and Rev. Kaji Douša, the senior pastor of Park Avenue Christian Church in New York City and the chair of the New Sanctuary Coalition New York City. I conducted these interviews to explore what it means to become a rhizome organizer in the real world. Through them, I develop a more specific and realistic idea of the church's rhizome organizers.

By what biblical and theological foundation could we formulate church leaders as rhizome organizers? I answer this question by conversing with René Girard, especially focusing on his innovative ideas on mimetic desire and scapegoating violence. I also investigate the forgotten virtue of parrhesia as part of constructing the idea of a rhizome organizer. Speaking the truth in the face of risk becomes a key rhizomatic virtue for the church's rhizome organizers.

---

almost identical, the word *rhizome* provides us with a distinctive nuance that it is not confined to a certain locality or shared identity.

PASTORS AS RHIZOME ORGANIZERS

One of the key structural injustices in the United States is the racially engineered wealth gap between Black and white households. According to a 2020 Brookings Institution report, "The net worth of a typical White family ($171,000) is nearly ten times greater than that of a black family ($17,150) in 2016." This gap is not accidental, since such a disparity is the outcome of "accumulated inequality and discrimination, as well as differences in power and opportunity that can be traced back to this nation's inception."[2] In other words, the wealth gap between Black and white households is a form of structural injustice. Although we can trace the origin of it back to the earliest history of this nation, a more explicit and concrete historical origin goes back to the 1930s—to the federal housing policies started under the New Deal. In 1933, the federal government launched a new housing program to increase America's housing stock, but the efforts were primarily designed to provide housing to "middle- and working-class White families."[3] According to Richard Rothstein, as a result of these discriminatory housing policies, African Americans and other people of color were not allowed to move to the new suburban communities; they were instead forced into overpopulated urban housing projects, effectively creating segregated communities.[4]

The federal Home Owners' Loan Corporation adopted a discriminatory housing policy known as "redlining," and it resulted in a practice of color-coding maps to designate certain neighborhoods as the best or worst for mortgage lending. For instance, "borrowers buying in White Communities—colored green for being safest for lending—could get loans backed by the federal government. Black neighborhoods—colored red—were deemed too risky for mortgage lending."[5] Since banks would not lend to Blacks because they were

---

2. Kriston McIntosh et al., "Examining the Black-White Wealth Gap," *Brookings Institution*, February 27, 2020, https://www.brookings.edu/blog/up-front/2020/02/27/examining-the-black-white-wealth-gap/.

3. Richard Rothstein, *The Color of Law: A Forgotten History of How Our Government Segregated America* (New York: Liveright, 2017), 20.

4. Rothstein, 18.

5. Michelle Singletary, "Being Black Lowers the Value of My Home: The Legacy of Redlining," *Washington Post*, October 23, 2020, https://www.washingtonpost.com/business/2020/10/23/redlining-black-wealth/.

discriminated against from the federal guarantee, they were often forced to purchase homes under predatory contracts that eventually led many to be evicted.[6] How specifically does the legacy of redlining effectuate the establishment of an enormous wealth gap between Black and white households? Rothstein illustrates the decisive impact of redlining on the discriminatory construction of this gap. According to him, although the 1968 Fair Housing Act prohibited future discrimination, the patterns of segregation had been firmly established, and the act did not enable African Americans to relocate themselves to the suburbs from which they had been excluded.[7] He then summarizes what happened to the US housing market:

> Those homes sold for about $8,000 a piece or $100,000 more or less in today's currency. African Americans, working-class families could have bought those homes. Today though, those homes sell for $300,000, $400,000. They're no longer affordable to working-class families. In the ensuing two generations, the White families who moved into those homes gained that $200,000, $300,000 in equity appreciation.
>
> African Americans living in rented apartments, prohibited from moving to the suburbs, gained none of that appreciation. The result is that today nationwide, African American incomes on average are about 60 percent of white incomes, but African American wealth is about 5 to 7 percent of white wealth. That enormous difference is almost entirely attributable to unconstitutional federal housing policy practiced in the mid-20th century.[8]

Other social scientists, such as Lauren Joy Krivo and Robert L. Kaufman, affirm Rothstein's historical discovery. For instance, Krivo and Kaufman write, "We found that past exclusion from the housing market (as evidenced

6. Singletary.
7. "'The Color of Law' Details How U.S. Housing Policies Created Segregation," NPR: All Things Considered, May 17, 2017, https://www.npr.org/2017/05/17/528822128/the-color-of-law-details-how-u-s-housing-policies-created-segregation.
8. "'Color of Law.'"

in lower rates of previous homeownership, particularly among Blacks) is an important source of the lower home equity that is subsequently attained."[9]

What, then, did white Christian churches do during this historical period of systemic housing discrimination? The Christian ethicist Joe Pettit calls the government's discriminatory housing policy "housing apartheid," which he defines as "the multi-dimensional creation of zones of opportunity growth limited almost exclusively to white people and the creation of zones of opportunity destruction and extraction limited almost exclusively to non-White, especially Black people." According to Pettit, during the decades of housing apartheid, "the White churches of the United States, along with their denominational expressions, were active participants in it, as well as explicit and implicit proponents and beneficiaries of it."[10] How did white churches participate in, promote, and benefit from the government's discriminatory housing policies? It is worth looking at Pettit's explorative research more closely. He points out that there was an "explosive" growth of the white churches during the period of housing apartheid. For example, according to James Hudnut-Beumler, "a National Council of Churches report noted that over the years 1926–1949 the percentage of the population who were church members had increased 51.6 percent, while the population itself grew less than 30 percent."[11]

The growth of the white suburban churches, however, entailed the gradual abandonment and systemic negligence of the nonwhite churches in the cities. Gibson Winter remarks, "Protestant gains in membership through movement to the best residential areas were counterbalanced by heavy losses

9. Lauren Joy Krivo and Robert L. Kaufman, "Housing and Wealth Inequality: Racial-Ethnic Differences in Home Equity in the United States," *Demography* 41, no. 3 (August 2004): 585–605, here 601. Krivo and Kaufman go further by saying that "consistent barriers to homeownership for Blacks over the course of history continue to impede their potential to generate wealth" (601).

10. Joe Pettit, "Blessing Oppression: The Role of White Churches in Housing Apartheid," *Journal of the Society of Christian Ethics* 40, no. 2 (2020): 291–309, here 294–95, 299.

11. James Hudnut-Beumler, *Looking for God in the Suburbs: The Religion of the American Dream and Its Critics, 1945–65* (New Brunswick, NJ: Rutgers University Press, 1994), 33, quoted in Pettit, "Blessing Oppression," 299–300.

in churches and memberships in the central areas of the cities."[12] What is disturbing about this counterbalance between the churches of the white suburban areas and those of the colored inner cities is that individual churches and church leaders adopted an opportunist position during housing apartheid. Pettit critically points out this by writing, "It was not uncommon to find individual churches and church leaders taking active roles in advancing Whites-only communities and in denying housing opportunities to Blacks." Why did not the church and church leaders stand up and oppose such a discriminatory social policy and structural injustice? One of the key reasons was the "increased wealth" for the churches. Intoxicated by increased wealth as well as by increased church membership, the white suburban churches and church leaders not only kept their silence about the social-structural injustice but also went further to render their members complicit in such a social sin. Pettit states, "What every one of these churches has done on behalf of the cause of housing apartheid is to allow the consciences of their members to rest easy. . . . These churches served the purpose of comforting their members, allowing them to be active participants in housing apartheid without ever suggesting that anything was amiss."[13] These churches' and church leaders' complicity during the period of housing apartheid reminds us of the historical legacy of the Western churches' and church leaders' complicity during the colonial period, which we have investigated in chapter 1. Unfortunately, the white churches missed another chance to reckon with historical sin during this period. One may ask the following question, though: Would the white churches' reckoning have brought any meaningful change to the structural injustice of housing apartheid? Pettit offers us a definite answer to this question: "White churches were essential to the very organization of suburban life. . . . Had the churches refused to locate in any community that excluded non-Whites, housing apartheid in the United States could not have happened."[14]

---

12. Gibson Winter, *The Suburban Captivity of the Churches* (New York: Macmillan, 1962), 49, quoted in Pettit, "Blessing Oppression," 300.
13. Winter, *Suburban Captivity of the Churches*, 301.
14. Winter, 299.

The internment of Japanese Americans during World War II is another historical case that illustrates how America's churches engaged in federally engineered structural injustice. In 1942, in the wake of Japan's attack on Pearl Harbor, the then president Franklin D. Roosevelt issued Executive Order 9066, which rounded up 120,000 Japanese Americans on the West Coast and relocated them to "concentration camps" or "war relocation camps." Although the government justified the order by calling it a "military necessity," it was motivated by anti-Japanese xenophobia. We should note that from the early Asian immigration history, many Asian immigrants and their US-born children had to suffer from various racial discriminations motivated by anti-Asian xenophobia. For instance, the Chinese Exclusion Act of 1882 was perhaps the most explicit anti-immigration policy that targeted nonwhites, and many Asian immigrants underwent racially motivated systemic discrimination until 1965, when the Immigration and Nationality Act finally eliminated racial/ nationality-based discrimination in immigration quotas. The internment of Japanese Americans should be understood against this historical backdrop. Erika Lee summarizes the Japanese American internment as follows:

Long before Pearl Harbor, Japanese immigrants had been treated as undesirable and dangerous foreigners in the United States and throughout the Americas. Considered racially inassimilable like other Asians, Japanese were confronted with immigration restrictions and laws that curbed their rights in the United States. They were feared for their supposed loyalty to Japan during the war, and the US government treated them as both a racial problem and a national security one. The US response was harsh: the forced relocation and mass incarceration of 120,000 Japanese Americans, two-thirds of whom were American-born citizens, from their homes and into prison camps as "prisoners without trial" for the duration of the war. Like Mexican Americans, an entire generation of Japanese Americans was de-Americanized.[15]

---

15. Erika Lee, *America for Americans: A History of Xenophobia in the United States* (New York: Basic Books, 2019), 184.

Even the Supreme Court upheld the legality of the 1942 exclusion order. Fred Korematsu was twenty-three years old when it was issued, but he did not comply with it, refusing to leave his home and job. He not only changed his name to Clyde Sarah but also had plastic surgery on his eyes to alter his appearance. On May 30, 1942, despite his resistance, he was arrested by the FBI, and while waiting in jail, he decided to allow the American Civil Liberties Union to make his opposition "a test case to challenge the constitutionality of the government's order." He ultimately appealed to the Supreme Court to hear his case, and on December 18, 1944, it upheld, in a 6–3 decision, the constitutionality of the exclusion order by ruling that the detention was a "military necessity," not based on race.[16] Although the ruling was made against Korematsu, Justice Robert Jackson, in a strongly worded dissent, calls the exclusion order "the legalization of racism," which indeed sums up the whole process of the Supreme Court's ruling. What, then, did the church do in response to Roosevelt's Executive Order 9066?

The historian Anne M. Blankenship documents the white churches' responses to the Japanese American internment by categorizing them into three groups: Quakers, mainline Protestants, and Catholics. According to Blankenship, even before the bombing of Pearl Harbor, Quaker leaders, such as those of the West Coast section of the American Friends Service Committee (AFSC), warned of the potential "caustic backwash of war hysteria" in case the United States were to enter into a Pacific war. They thus "organized conferences in Seattle, Los Angeles, San Francisco, and Honolulu to bring attention to the challenges facing Nikkei in the spring of 1941." Quakers' wartime advocacy for Japanese Americans was proactive, decisive, and ardent. They even tried to prevent Executive Order 9066 from being issued. Blankenship writes, "As rumors of Executive Order 9066 spread, the Seattle AFSC office protested the policy in telegrams to the secretary of war, the attorney general, Eleanor Roosevelt, and three congressmen. . . . Two weeks after FDR signed Executive Order 9066, the AFSC sent delegates to Washington D.C. as a 'last-minute effort to revoke the evacuation scheme.'"

---

16. "Facts and Case Summary—Korematsu v. U.S.," United States Courts, accessed January 18, 2022, https://www.uscourts.gov/educational-resources/educational-activities/facts-and-case-summary-korematsu-v-us.

By Blankenship's assessment, "Quakers in the United States took decisive actions to defend Nikkei's civil rights and minimize the damage caused by the incarceration. In public and internal statements, the AFSC apologized for the injustice and pledged solidarity and material supports."[17]

How, then, did mainline Protestant churches and church leaders respond to the internment of Japanese Americans? According to Blankenship, "Many mainline Protestant churches skirted condemnation of the incarceration during its first months," although they immediately tried to defend Japanese Americans after the attack on Pearl Harbor. For instance, Congregational churches judged the executive order to be "favoritism among God's children," but they conceded that the eviction of Japanese nationals could be "justified" for the sake of national security.[18] The Seattle Council of Churches issued a statement in which even though the members write that they "feel very definitely opposed to mass evacuation," they qualify it by adding "unless it is a military necessity." Other church groups, such as the Portland Council of Churches and a panel of white Protestant leaders in San Francisco, responded in a similar manner, either offering no judgment of the eviction or citing religious justifications for it. At that time, *Christian Century*, a representative voice of mainline American Christianity, "did not condemn the government's decision or fight to end the incarceration in the late spring of 1942," echoing the mainline churches' general stance.[19]

What about Catholic churches and their leaders? Most Catholics working with Japanese Americans in the United States during the time were affiliated

---

17. Anne M. Blankenship, *Christianity, Social Justice, and the Japanese American Incarceration during World War II* (Chapel Hill: University of North Carolina Press, 2016), 19, 22, 27.
18. Blankenship, 31.
19. Blankenship, 29, 32. We should note that there were some dissenting voices among mainline Christian churches. For example, Blankenship writes, "A group of ministers in Santa Maria, California, argued that the 'highest patriotism' requires Christian citizens to reject the incarceration for its 'totalitarian methods.'" Under the leadership of Clarence Gillett, the group cited "both practical and ethical reasons why an incarceration should not occur" (31). In an apparently opposite position, however, Frank Herron Smith, superintendent of the Japanese Methodist churches in California, scolded Nikkei pastors who resisted the government's racist policy, writing, "Some [of you] are running around like chickens with their heads cut off. Keep calm. . . . War is terrible and you should be thankful it will not be worse for you. Let us as Christians keep our heads, cooperate with the authorities" (35).

with the Maryknoll mission society, and unlike Protestant churches, due to the hierarchy within Roman Catholicism, "decisions to speak against the incarceration relied on authorization from bishops and higher authorities."[20] For instance, Bishop James E. Walsh, the father general of Maryknoll, was originally open to the possibility of protesting discriminatory actions to the federal government, but "for unclear reasons," he insisted later that "religious workers on the West Coast 'ignore local proposals until they become fact.'" His instruction was the voice of the council, which "did not want to interfere with what it believed were necessary security precautions." Why did Catholic churches and their leaders stop short of providing more rigorous support for their Japanese parishioners victimized by the unjust governing authority? Blankenship writes, "Bishop Walsh and the Maryknoll Council feared making statements that might be interpreted as 'unpatriotic.' Since nativist groups still questioned Catholics' loyalty to the United States, Catholic religious leaders felt particular pressure to support government policy."[21]

What is the significance of these two cases? What do they have to do with the conceptual constitution of the ideal type of church leader as a rhizome organizer or a rhizomatic politician? These cases demonstrate that without committed rhizome organizers, the church's rhizomatic politics is not possible, and arborescent systems of social and systemic injustice are likely to continue to victimize people and their communities. Although the church attempts to neutralize, objectify, or even justify structural injustice by intentionally or unintentionally turning away from it, it ultimately ends up becoming an accomplice to "social sin." By so doing, it becomes non-church because victimized people find no hope there. If people, especially the victimized, cannot find hope there, where are they supposed to go? In this respect, the work of a rhizome organizer is critical not only for the church but also for those whom Jesus calls "the least of these" (Matt 25:45). They cannot be separated from each other.

The investigation of the two cases also helps us see more clearly what it means for church leaders to become rhizome organizers as well as why they

---

20. Blankenship, 39.
21. Blankenship, 40.

should identify themselves as such in facing historical or structural injustice in our world. Unlike arborescent politicians (public officers, political leaders, etc.), who run the social, political, and economic systems, rhizome organizers of the church focus on advocating for victims' voices and rights while attempting to transform structural and systemic injustices. In this respect, church leaders must accept and acknowledge that they are more than priests, more than storytellers, and more than caregivers; they are ordained as well to become story makers, community organizers, and activist theologians. Since what we discover from the above two cases is the wholesale absence of rhizome organizers on the part of Christian churches, we should perhaps look for different stories in which we may discover a more positive and definitive image or ideal type of the church's rhizome organizers. For this reason, I have interviewed four individuals whom I regard as rhizome organizers of our time to have a better understanding of what it means to be a rhizome organizer of the church today.

REAL-WORLD RHIZOME ORGANIZERS OF THE CHURCH

Above we have investigated two cases that demonstrate negatively how critical the ecclesial leadership and organizational work of rhizome organizers can be in the church's social ministry to resist structural injustice as well as to advocate for victims. In this section, I explore real examples of rhizome organizers, what they are up to, and how they practice distinctive rhizomatic politics. These rhizome organizers and their engagement in different rhizomatic politics are unique and distinctive, but I believe that there are certain commonalities among their works and theologies. The purpose of these interviews is thus intentionally pedagogical, in that by narrating their stories, I aim to help pastors, ministers, and lay leaders be awakened from the traditional model of ecclesial leadership and become new and transformative rhizome organizers of the church.

Rev. Dr. Liz Theoharis is the founder and codirector of the Kairos Center for Religions, Rights, and Social Justice and coordinator of the Poverty Initiative at Union Theological Seminary in New York City. She is also an ordained minister in the Presbyterian Church (USA) and cochair of the Poor People's Campaign: A National Call for Moral Revival with Rev. Dr. William Barber II. As she emphasized in my interview, "The work of the Poverty Initiative and the Kairos Center is focused on raising generations of religious and community leaders—especially more leaders and clergy and leaders of poor people's organization—who are dedicated to building a social movement led by those most impacted by injustice to address and overcome racism and poverty, ecological devastation, militarism, and this distorted, this kind of false narrative of religious nationalism."

In her 2017 book, *Always with Us? What Jesus Really Said about the Poor*, Theoharis explains how she began her earlier work of community organization. She was working with a group of homeless families with the Kensington Welfare Rights Union in the winter of 1995; they broke the locks and moved into St. Edward's Catholic Church in North Philadelphia. She recalls that the church takeover was an embodiment of what Rev. Dr. Martin Luther King Jr. called a Freedom Church of the Poor, and the collective action was "a proactive response to the failure of organized religion to take poverty seriously either theologically or practically." As expected, the takeover sparked a debate in the city of Philadelphia, but it also elicited corroborators. Later, she writes, "the Catholic archdiocese moved its offices from downtown to a poor area in North Philadelphia, and new evangelical Christian, mainline Christian, and interfaith groups began to partner with poor people to end poverty."[22]

Three key elements characterize the ideal type of the church's rhizome organizers, and we could confirm that Theoharis's ecclesial grassroots movement and leadership have demonstrated these three aspects. First, she and her organizations are very clear about the specific form of structural injustice that they aim to address and dismantle through their rhizomatic activism. Although they target a range of structural injustices, from systemic racism to ecological devastation and voter suppression, she mentioned that the poverty issue takes a central position in her ecclesial and community activism. She

22. Liz Theoharis, *Always with Us? What Jesus Really Said about the Poor* (Grand Rapids, MI: Eerdmans, 2017), 2.

said, "I myself have been engaged in grassroots antipoverty organizing for twenty-five or thirty years. I got my start with the National Union of the Homeless and the National Welfare Rights Union efforts for homeless people, low-wage workers, and welfare recipients. And it was from those organizations and those movements that I actually learned about the last campaign, or last crusade. They said Dr. King was a part of the launch of the Poor People's Campaign back in 1967 and 1968."

Second, as Theoharis kept emphasizing in my interview, while addressing various structural injustices, she and her organizations have constantly reached out to and built grassroots alliances with other organizations and communities across the country, even beyond the national boundaries. Indeed, reaching out to and building up people's grassroots movements against structural injustice and systemic violence are essential aspects of the church's rhizomatic politics, and the work and responsibility of rhizome organizers are therefore critical. In my interview, Theoharis exemplified the rhizomatic nature of her work and organizations as follows:

The reason we have titled our campaign the Poor People's Campaign: A National Call for Moral Revival is that we really believe we need a moral revolution of values that are rooted in our constitutional and sacred texts and values. You know, the campaign has about twenty national faith bodies that are behind it and have endorsed it—you know, the Union for Reform Judaism, the largest national group, representing millions of Jewish people; the Islamic Society of North America; networks of Muslims, of Sikhs, of Hindus, of Buddhists; and then more than a dozen, probably more like sixteen or so, of the different Christian denominations as an ecumenical group, everything from the Presbyterian Church (USA), which is my denomination, to the Church of Christ, the Disciples of Christ, the Episcopal Church, the AME Church—many, many different denominations not just on a local level, not just on a congregational level, but on a national kind of faith body level. So that's important. And we have poor and low-income people helping run our coordinating committees in forty-five states, we have activists and advocates, and we also, in the leadership of those committees, have moral leaders and clergy from different religious traditions.

Lastly, she unveiled the third element of the church's rhizome organizers by highlighting the importance of theological reflection and engagement in biblical and sacred texts. She said, "But we also believe that we have to engage in theological and biblical and sacred texts, work, as well as organizing faith communities toward the practice of justice." One of the key purposes of this theological and biblical engagement is to dismantle what she called "the false narrative of religion." She remarked, "And we see one of the injustices that interlocks and that needs to be transformed is this false narrative of religious and especially kind of White evangelical Christian nationalism." She gave me a specific example of how she and her organizations are actively engaging in the work of deconstructing false religious narratives. She mentioned, "In the pandemic, for instance, alongside all the work we're doing, building in support of the campaign, we have launched a cohort of community leaders and pastors and scholars called Reading the Bible with the Poor. It's kind of a form of doing biblical and theological interpretation and praxis—you know, connecting in community—but then also challenging some of the misuses of texts and traditions." Among many false narratives, she is particularly devoted to dismantling the popular misperception related to Matthew 26:11 ("For you always have the poor with you"). She pointed out the toxic misinterpretation of this passage by saying, "Poverty is an unfortunate reality, but it's inevitable." In her book *Always with Us?*, she successfully dismantles this false narrative by launching an intertextual investigation between Deuteronomy 15 and Matthew 26. She summarizes her work as follows: "Deuteronomy 15 continues and says that because people will not follow those commandments, there will always be poor among you. So, when Jesus quotes this phrase, he isn't condoning poverty, he is reminding us that God hates poverty and has commanded us to end poverty by forgiving debts, by outlawing slavery, and by restructuring society around the needs of the poor."[23]

---

23. Theoharis, 73.

Rev. Dr. Michael Nabors is the senior pastor of Second Baptist Church in Evanston, Illinois, and the president of the Evanston/Northshore branch of the NAACP. According to its website, Second Baptist Church is the first Black Baptist church, established on November 17, 1882, and since then, "more than 100 ministers have been trained, ordained and sent to serve in venues across the United States and globally." It also notes that the church is "known for its powerful preaching, excellent music ministry and wide-ranging missions work"; it is "a revitalized congregation" that "became even more progressive and community-minded in the 1970s."[24] In my interview with Nabors, I sensed that there was a good fit between a socially open-minded church and a theologically progressive pastor. Nabors made it clear that one of his ministerial goals is to address and dismantle one of America's most formidable structural injustices: systemic racism. In my interview, he said, "On the first Sunday of January 2018, I stood before the congregation after having written something to them and stated, 'I am declaring an all-out war on racism. And I will not stop in my battles against racism until racism has ended or until my voice has ended.'" Nabors emphasized several times that he is passionate about social justice, especially racial justice.

His passion for social justice led him to engage in community activism in Evanston after several years of focusing on his congregational care and program reconstructions. The word *community* takes a central position in his congregational-social ministry as well as his practical theology. He told me a story about how he grew up in a traditional African American Baptist church and how he recognized that there was an intersection between Black churches and communities in Kalamazoo, Michigan, and the issues of social justice. He then said, "That intersection came through an organization that I'm still involved with, the National Association for the Advancement of Colored People, the NAACP, so [did] my first recognition that the church was more than just people coming to worship on Sunday."

After reorganizing the church programs as well as focusing on congregational care for five years, which enabled the church members to have extra

---

24. "A Summary History of Second Baptist Church," SBC, accessed January 17, 2022, https://www.secondbaptistevanston.org/history.

time and money, they began to reach out into the community. Nabors told me this story:

> What resulted was a sort of shift in our consciousness so that we understood the gospel of Jesus Christ now is not just about saving souls. It is. But it is just as much about transforming the community. And I think maybe they knew that before, but just to be able to make that shift through our ministries and our outreach that allowed them to give me the freedom to really be much more involved and focused in community outreach. That's when I became the president of the NAACP. That is when . . . I was asked to join different boards and communities around the city and all of that. And each time, I would go back to the leaders of the church and say, "Now this has been asked of me. What do you all think?" And they would say, "By all means, yes, we think that's important." And what they did is they created an infrastructure to give the pastoral ministry help at Second Baptist. So now I have a full-time executive minister, who helps run the day-to-day functions of the church. He oversees the staff of the church. We have twenty-seven people who are on the payroll, and that's not my gift anyway. It's not my gift. You know, my gift is being a community activist. And so that created an opportunity for me to really begin to do more in the town of Evanston on behalf of the church.

One of the remarkable outcomes of the community work in the city of Evanston, where Nabors has been involved, is the city council's resolution to make reparations available to eligible Black residents for what it describes as harm caused by "discriminatory housing policies and practices and inaction on the city's part." As a result of this historic resolution, voted to pass in November 2019, the first phase was established in March 2021, which involved giving sixteen residents $25,000 each for home repairs or property costs. This housing program is the first initiative in a historical plan to distribute $10 million in reparations to Black residents of Evanston. In my interview, Nabors emphasized that the more significant aspect of this community work is that it has established a model for other communities. He told me this:

"I think it's going to end up being a snowball effect. There are now communities and societies around the nation saying, 'We ought to do the same thing.' So the secretary of state in California, Dr. Shirley Weber, has introduced legislation to California for reparations throughout the entire state. Milwaukee is introducing legislation for the city. Chicago is introducing legislation for the city. A church in Baltimore and the Episcopal Church have already set aside $500,000 to do repair work in the Black community of the church's zip code that they know they have discriminated against in the past."

At the beginning of my interview, Nabors named three theologians who have influenced the establishment of his theological perspective: James Cone, Cornel West, and Michael Eric Dyson. He explained how the Second Baptist Church engages in Bible study in conjunction with themes of social justice. He went further, saying,

> This Lenten season, we are studying one of Dr. Cone's books for our Bible study, and it's his latest book before he died, *The Cross and the Lynching Tree*, and it is absolutely riveting. We have eighty people who have been on our Zoom Bible study for the past five weeks representing both churches [the other church is a white congregational church called Lake Street Church, which was once called First Baptist Church], and it's just been a very, very powerful social justice journey, especially as it relates to race relations and racism and building an antiracism environment here in Evanston.

One of the striking theological views Nabors shared with me was his critical stance on the relationship between the church and the state or religion and politics. Let me quote what he said:

> In my estimation, coming out of the experience and tradition of the Black church, there has never been a division between church and state. It's a misperception. I'm looking at the earliest churches that began but particularly Black churches in this country, particularly Bethel AME Church in Baltimore. Richard Allen and Absalom Jones—they walked out of a worship service at St. George's

[Methodist] Episcopal Church in 1786 because they were denied the right to pray until white parishioners had finished praying. So that is how much of the Black church began as a result of entrenched racism. That was not so much St. George's Episcopal Church but the racism that was entrenched into the very structure of the earliest US government, its policies, its procedures. Indeed, from the very beginning, Black people were described as three-fifths of a person in the Constitution of the United States. . . . The very existence of the Black church is a response to the discrimination and the racism that the state has meted out against [Black people]. So we refuse to be separate from the state because if we do, then that will give [it] the freedom and the isolation to legislate, to form policy, to create judicial acts that will continue to deny us our freedom, and so the earliest Black leaders of churches were also greatly involved in politics. The first Black senators of the United States of America during the Reconstruction were preachers: [Hiram Rhodes] Revels out of Mississippi, James Lynch out of Mississippi. P. B. S. Pinchback was the lieutenant governor of Louisiana—all in the 1870s. They came out of the church. And even now this tradition continues. Raphael Warnock, the pastor of Ebenezer Baptist Church in Atlanta, becomes the latest junior senator in the United States.

Rev. John Fife is a retired Presbyterian minister living in Tucson, Arizona. He is well known as one of the key figures who launched the Sanctuary Movement in the 1980s. He also helped start the Samaritan Patrol along the US-Mexico border in Arizona in 2002, which later became a part of the larger border-monitoring organization No More Deaths, which aims to relieve the suffering of migrants by offering food and water while advocating a more humane border policy. As we have already seen above, Fife and his church have engaged in one of the key structural injustices of our society—migration justice.

In my interview with him, Fife told me about the history of Southside Presbyterian Church and how he became the pastor there, where he served for thirty-five years:

Well, Southside Church is a unique church in the Presbyterian family at any rate. It is located in the oldest and poorest barrio in Tucson. So it's a great place to be a church, and it has a fascinating history. It was founded as a Native American mission church, and Native Americans were not allowed to live in the city of Tucson. So where the church is located now was the Native American village outside the city. It was started as a Presbyterian mission congregation to Native American families, and it remained that with a series of mission pastors until after World War II, when the city of Tucson had grown around that area, and instead of a Native American village, it became a Native American and Mexican American barrio and remains the oldest and poorest barrio in Tucson, and they were trying to find a pastor after World War II, and the only guy they could find who wanted the job was a Mexican American pastor from Texas, and he said, "Well, if you call me, I'm gonna, of course, reach out to the whole community and Mexican Americans." They said, "Well, that'll never work; they don't even speak the same language," but he did. He spent, I don't know, seven or eight years here, and the church incorporated other Mexican Americans and Native Americans from the community, and you're not gonna believe this, but it's true: the bunch of Mexicans and Native Americans called in an African American pastor. This was 1956!

He, of course, became the president of the NAACP and led the congregation into desegregation campaigns in the early 1960s and added African Americans and some white folk gringos to the congregation. So I knew it back in the 1960s, when I did an internship in West Tucson for the Presbyterian Church—I thought at that point that it was just an ideal place to do ministry and had this unique history of inclusion and diversity that are not typical of Presbyterian churches, and so after seminary, I heard at a meeting that Southside Church was needing a pastor, and so I called and reached all the contacts I had in Arizona from the internship site and got the job, but unfortunately, the pastor who had succeeded the African American pastor had not done well at all. When I came, there were only about twenty-five people who were left, and we had a lot of work to do, but I still thought it was an ideal place to be a church, and I loved the history of the church, and so we went to work to reconstruct a diverse congregation—Native Americans and Latino Americans and African Americans and as diverse a group as we could put together and Koreans and Chinese and others. So when we declared ourselves a "sanctuary," we had reestablished a viable church. And I'd been there twelve years. So they had begun to trust me. It always takes a while to be trusted by a congregation if you're going to do serious ministry. So it was an opportune moment to begin to do something significant.

During my interview, I came to realize that it was not accidental for South-side Presbyterian Church to become the beacon of the Sanctuary Movement. It was indeed an extension of the community-building ministries Fife began to organize in his earliest ministerial years. Let me quote another testimonial narrative from Fife:

I think one of the things I have always tried to do as a pastor is get the people in the congregation into a relationship, whatever the community is or [whoever] the people are who need our help. One needs to help us understand what their plight is and what their issues are. Yeah. And we had done that. From the time I became the pastor, we organized and donated the land for the first Native American housing—urban housing—program in the country, and built houses for Native Americans in the area. And then we became deeply involved in the Chicano Movement. There was a golf course in the barrios that was designed so that businesspeople and bankers from downtown could get to the golf course easily from their offices and had no relationship at all to the needs of the barrio. So some Chicano organizers and priests and I occupied the golf course so they couldn't play off till they built a recreation center and an education center for the people of the barrio rather than the bankers downtown. And we had been involved in a number of issues like that—Native American treaty violations, those sorts of issues. So we'd had some practice as a congregation.

144

I was particularly inspired by his answer to my question about how he and his church got involved with the Sanctuary Movement. Instead of paraphrasing it, let me quote his own words:

When refugees from the Central American conflicts began to show up at the border, we had worked with barrio legal aid organizations to help undocumented, primarily Mexican, families who were living in the barrio and a couple who were members of our congregation get their status legalized. So it was kind of a natural move to meet with those legal aid entities in the barrio and say, "What do we need to do to help these new refugees [who] are showing up the border?" And then it just escalated from a legal aid program to my involvement with this damn Quaker by the name of Jim Corbett, who came to me and said, "John this legal aid strategy is not going to work because nobody is getting political asylum no matter what legal representation we provide them if they're from El Salvador [and] Guatemala. The US government is just refusing anyone asylum if they're from the allied countries in Latin America," and so he said to me, "I don't think we have any choice under the circumstances except to help people cross the border without being captured by border patrol because once they're captured, we can delay their deportation, but we can't stop it." So I basically said, "Really, how do you do that?" And he pointed to two times in history: the abolition movement, when some church people and pastors formed an underground railroad to help runaway slaves cross the border safely and to move them to safer and safer places. And he said, "As we read history, John, they got it right. They were faithful in their time," and I said, "Well, yeah, that's how I read history, Jim." Then he pointed to almost a total failure of the church to protect Jews in Europe in the 1930s and 1940s. He said, "That's one of the worst chapters in church history. It was a complete, complete failure of the European church to be faithful," and I said, "Well, yeah, that's how I read history, Jim," and he looked me right in the eye, and he said, "I don't think we can allow that to happen on our border in our time, can we?" And I did what I was taught in seminary. I said, "Well, I have to pray about that," and that's whenever pastors are stalling. But finally, after some sleepless nights, I went back to [him] and said, "Yeah, you're right. We really don't have any choice, do we, if we're going to be faithful?" So we started smuggling people across the border very, we thought, very secretively.

In my interview with him, I could sense that Fife and his ministry demonstrated all the key components of the rhizomatic organizing of the church, such as addressing structural injustice, organizing the community, and grounding justice ministry theologically. I asked him if he ever had any moments of sensing the presence of God during his time involved with the Sanctuary Movement. He replied, "Yes," then began to tell me a story of how he had a "conversion experience" in Central America:

That experience was a conversion experience for me. To do the work we were doing here on the border, I had to build relationships in El Salvador and Guatemala—with the church there and with human rights organizations there—because we couldn't make decisions about who we would cross and who we could not without a trusted relationship there because I had to know what the risk was to the person who was seeking our help. Here I'm a gringo. I'm just an old white guy, and I sure couldn't make those decisions. So I had to have those kinds of trusted relationships in Central America. So I spent six weeks there, learning and building those relationships, but the learning was of this liberation theology and how it had formed the mission of the church there. And I saw and experienced this amazing [and] strengthened spirituality of the church under persecution there. And that was a conversion experience for me. I came back, and the first Sunday in the pulpit at Southside, I said to them, "I'm grateful to be back among you. There is a great deal of work we have to do, but the most important thing is, I think, I've recently been converted to the Christian faith. I will try to explain that to you as we go along. I know—I've been your pastor for twelve years. Thank God I've recently discovered the Christian faith among campesinos in El Salvador, and I'll try to explain that as we go along here." So for me, it was a complete conversion experience of that kind of relationship with the persecuted church in Central America and their faith and their reading of Scripture and their theological reflections on that intense experience of life and death in the church there. So for this North American gringo, it was a complete conversion experience and changed my whole life.

The Sanctuary Movement of the 1980s was later revived in the name of the New Sanctuary Coalition in 2007 as a multifaith immigrant-led organization by bringing together citizens, volunteers, and immigrants. Rev. Kaji Douša is the senior pastor of Park Avenue Christian Church in New York City and now a chair of the New York City–based New Sanctuary Coalition. In December 2018, Douša had participated in a forty-day sanctuary caravan to offer aid to Central American asylum seekers in the migrant caravan. On January 2, 2019, when she attempted to return to the United States, a Customs and Border Protection officer detained and interrogated her. According to *Christian Century*, "Douša and several others are listed in a government database of activists, journalists, and lawyers. Douša's name and photo appear with a yellow X across her face, indicating that her pass allowing for expedited screening along the Southwest US-Mexico border has been revoked."[25]

In my interview with Douša, I sensed that her engagement in the church's rhizomatic politics, particularly for immigrant rights, was almost predestined. Her grandfather was the first Black man to graduate with a PhD from Boston University School of Theology and also a good friend of Dr. King. He helped Dr. King's civil rights movement in Greensboro, North Carolina, by becoming involved in the NAACP while Dr. King was the president. His daughter, her mother, was also a field organizer and national communications director for the Student Nonviolent Coordinating Committee, and her father was one of the people at Morehouse College who took over the administration at the end of the 1960s (with actor Samuel Jackson). It was fascinating to hear her family stories and how she was brought up with such a unique family background.

---

25. "Kaji Douša," *Christian Century* 136, no. 9 (April 24, 2019): 18.

In my interview with her, I realized how important community organization and involvement are in addressing the needs of those victimized by structural injustice. Douša told me her story about how she got involved in the New Sanctuary Coalition:

So the whole reason I got involved back in 2008, although at a different church, was something that was replicated in that time. You know, during 2009, during the Obama administration, when a bunch of us in New York City had people who were being targeted with deportation and we didn't know what to do—so I was part of a congregation that had somebody who was rejected from every New York City social service / immigrant service organization . . . and nobody would help him. And then finally, New Sanctuary would. And so that was how I got involved. And I think many congregations have a similar story, where there's somebody in their community who needs support. . . . So many congregations found that to be the experience—that we grew from a movement of, like, twenty of us at Judson Memorial Church, where it started, to a movement of thousands and many thousands of us, you know, New Sanctuary. I really credit not myself but Ravi and the work he did by making us the sanctuary city and then a sanctuary state, and then for that to spread across the country—it really started with this, in response to what John Fife did in Arizona, you know, and not just John Fife but, like, the whole movement out there in Tucson. And I spent some time walking in the desert. I didn't get to see John on that trip, but in my time with his successor, Alison Harrington, [she] was amazing and a good friend and [so were] people from the organizations that they work with, and they had me do water drops.

Douša also shared her theological views, especially her critical-theological reflection on the danger of the church's confusion between forgiveness and reckoning:

And I think that the problem, though, that church causes is that it confuses forgiveness with reckoning. . . . If tables are to be turned over [referring to Jesus's overturning the tables of the money changers], it sends a message, right? Like, this is not OK. Or if something is to be condemned, if a cross needs to be picked up and carried and it means following [Jesus], which might mean that your family will hate you, you know, that's part of the reckoning. And it's not about making friends. It's not about, like, currying favor. It's not about getting money or contracts. It's about picking up your cross, following him, and making sure nobody else gets hung on a cross like that. Reckoning may lead to some forms of restoration. And I'm still praying about what that looks like with God's help. But it certainly doesn't mean that we gloss over something. Forgiveness as a gloss—yeah, it's such a damaging practice in the church, which is used constantly and controls people. . . . When we rush to forgiveness, it only serves one perspective, and that's not where we go. Some forgiveness, being confused with reconciliation and also with reparations, is a real problem that the church needs to figure out.

These rhizome organizers share three commonalities. First, they all had a very clear goal of their rhizomatic politics; they were devoted to addressing and changing a specific type of structural injustice—poverty issues for Theoharis, racial justice for Nabors, and migrant rights for Fife and Douša. Second, they all were also deeply involved with community organizing and participation in protecting and advocating the rights of people who were victimized by structural injustice and systemic violence. During my interviews, I sensed that their coordinated works of community engagement are what substantiate the church's rhizomatic politics. Finally, these rhizome organizers were all equipped with clear and strong theological viewpoints on various topics, including the church's role and responsibility related to social justice and solidarity. For instance, Fife said, "The church has always been at its most sinful when it has been supportive for empire. Those periods of time when the church allied itself with the empire and blessed the empire were the most sinful aspects of church history." Their political-theological views were epitomized by their critical understanding of who Jesus was. For instance, Theoharis said in my interview, "[Jesus] was working to transform society from the bottom up and was seen as a threat by the ruling elite." As she said this to me, she emphasized that we should not forget the theological meaning of crucifixion. In her own words, "Crucifixion is punishment for revolutionaries. It's not for murderers, robbers, or common criminals. It's for those who have been deemed a threat." It was clear that for Theoharis, Jesus's crucifixion has a much greater and deeper meaning than a soteriological concern. In a similar vein, Douša also said, "[We] are followers of the movement Jesus started back in the day. . . . What we see with Jesus is that the tables always have to keep overturning. It wasn't a onetime deal. And if we're not willing to examine and keep turning those tables, . . . it feels to me that we are resisting God's Spirit."

BECOMING A RHIZOME ORGANIZER

Although these four rhizome organizers did not specifically verbalize it, they all seemed to agree that the *way* Jesus died and the *reason* he died cannot be separated from each other. The traditional atonement theories, however, are heavily focused on the latter, resulting in a narrow understanding of salvation: saving the soul. In the following, I examine why this seeming agreement (the inseparability between the *way* Jesus died and the *reason* he died) matters and how this critical understanding of Jesus's crucifixion becomes an indispensable theological backdrop against which the idea of a rhizome organizer is conceived as an ideal type in conjunction with the construction of the church's rhizomatic politics.

In so doing, I draw on René Girard and his seminal notions of memetic desire, the scapegoat mechanism, and the nonsacrificial death of Christ. Girard's distinctive biblical-theological reinterpretation of Jesus's crucifixion offers us a new perspective regarding the structural aspect of sin, which goes beyond the scope of the traditional notion of individual sin or original sin (e.g., perversion of the will, transgression of the eternal law, or guilt of disobedience to God). Uncovering the social and structural nature of sin is critical in conceptualizing the idea of the rhizome organizer as an ideal type because if Christ's death would have nothing to do with the social and structural nature of sin, then the church's raison d'être will eventually be reduced to a narrowly conceived soteriology with a neutral or disinterested position on engaging structural injustice and its transformation. Hence it seems necessary for us to construct the idea of the church's rhizome organizers on a new biblical and theological ground. In my view, we find a critical pathway for doing this in Girard's innovative biblical and theological hermeneutics as well as anthropological insights.

According to Girard, one of the key functions of human life is desire, and it is deeply social, in that humans do not simply desire a certain object, but instead, they learn to desire specific objects through a process of imitation, which Girard describes by employing the ancient Greek term *mimesis*. The imitation of another person's desire may entail contradictory outcomes. While it can be the source of mutual interest and friendship, it also can lead to conflict. Girard writes, "Plato is right to see it [mimesis] as both a force of cohesion and a force of dissolution."[26] The universal human phenomenon of desire is therefore transformed into mimetic desire by Girard, and its realization takes on a triangular relationship involving a subject, a model, and an object. How does this triangular relationship work? We first identify in someone else a model that we are inclined to imitate; this model can be their parents, elites, leaders, and so on. The triangular structure of mimetic desire then implicates two different aspects: desiring a particular object or desiring a general goal (status, acclaim, or a level of competence). Girard calls the former "acquisitive mimesis" and the latter "metaphysical mimesis."[27] We can conjecture that acquisitive mimesis may easily turn into a dangerous conflictual mimesis, which "quickly escalates into violence, blows, and murder, confronting people with not just physical death but a truly frightening destruction of all hierarchy, custom, and order in the community."[28]

---

26. René Girard, *Things Hidden since the Foundation of the World*, trans. Stephen Bann and Michael Metter (Stanford, CA: Stanford University Press, 1987), 17.

27. Raymond Bryce, "Christ as Second Adam: Girardian Mimesis Redeemed," *New Blackfriars* 93, no. 1045 (May 2012): 358–70, here 360. See also René Girard, *Deceit, Desire, and the Novel: Self and Other in Literary Structure*, trans. Yvonne Freccero (Baltimore: Johns Hopkins University Press, 1965), 17.

28. Frank C. Richardson and Nicolette D. Manglos, "Reciprocity and Rivalry: A Critical Introduction to Mimetic Scapegoat Theory," *Pastoral Psychology* 62, no. 4 (2013): 423–36, here 426.

The idea of scapegoating emerges as a mechanism to resolve the rising violence caused by what Girard calls "mimetic rivalry." According to P. J. Watson, the effects of mimetic desire cannot be confined to dyads, as mimesis will encourage entire communities to converge on the same objects.[29] In the absence of the sorting-out process, individuals' acquisitive mimesis inevitably grows into a more widespread collective form of mimetic rivalry, leading to communal acts of aggression: "Individuals increasingly will become identical models of conflict. A plague of violence will threaten the group with a crisis of undifferentiation. Social solidarity will move inexorably toward collapse in a war of all against all."[30] What, then, should be done in an escalating violent situation that may lead to the destruction of the entire social life? Girard argues that from ancient times, humanity has tried to resolve this natural yet mutually destructive problem by incorporating the scapegoat mechanism. How does the scapegoat mechanism work? Daniel Cojocaru succinctly summarizes a Girardian response: "At the height of the mimetic crisis, just as the mimetic doubles are about to turn against each other, the violence is unanimously redirected onto one single victim. The choice of victim is ultimately arbitrary but is based on the unanimous mob's perceived difference of the victim."[31]

Regarding Girard's historical-anthropological analysis of the scapegoat mechanism, we need to pay special attention to two critical aspects. First, although this scapegoat is an arbitrary victim as Girard perceives him,[32] he cannot be considered as innocent and impotent. Girard writes, "[The victim] must be perceived if not necessarily as a culprit in our sense, at least as a creature truly responsible for all the disorders and ailments of the community, in other words for the mimetic crisis that has triggered the mimetic mechanism

29. P. J. Watson, "Girard and Integration: Desire, Violence, and the Mimesis of Christ as Foundation for Postmodernity," *Journal of Psychology and Theology* 26, no. 4 (1998): 311–21, here 314.
30. Watson, 314.
31. Daniel Cojocaru, "Mimetic Theory and the Miners' Strike: Probing Implications of René Girard's Theory on Political Religion," *Religion Compass* 6, no. 1 (2012): 72–81, here 73.
32. Girard writes, for instance, "The creature that excited its fury is abruptly replaced by another, chosen only because it is vulnerable and close at hand" (René Girard, *Violence and the Sacred*, trans. Patrick Gregory [Baltimore: Johns Hopkins University Press, 1977], 2).

of scapegoating." Second, what is even more important is that for the scapegoat mechanism to work, the scapegoaters should not know that they are scapegoating. Girard writes, "Scapegoating has never been conceived by anyone as an activity in which he himself participates and may still be participating even as he denounces the scapegoating of others. Such denunciation can even become a precondition of successful scapegoating in a world like ours, where knowledge of the phenomenon is on the rise and makes its grossest and most violent forms obsolete."[33] The significance of these two critical aspects of the scapegoat mechanism lies in the point that they are not nonsensical or irrelevant to the case of structural injustice in our world. In fact, in many aspects, modern-day structural injustice and systemic violence largely replicate and represent similar traits of the scapegoat mechanism. For instance, concerning structural poverty in a neoliberal society, while the poor are commonly blamed for their economic struggles, the society takes it for granted that the growing economic gap and inequality are sort of a given nature of a capitalist society, especially in a neoliberal context. When it comes to the case of immigration justice, while migrants, especially those with no legal documents, are commonly blamed for social unrest, many citizens seem to normalize the criminalization of these people as a legal necessity. It does not seem too much to say that at the core of structural injustice and systemic violence lies a Girardian hidden scapegoat mechanism.

What, then, does the Girardian scapegoat mechanism have to do with his understanding of Jesus's passion? Was Jesus not crucified on the cross as a scapegoat? According to Girard, the recurring phenomenon of scapegoating did happen on the cross, but this event was not for the sake of ancient theories of religious or mythical sacrifice but for the sake of the termination and

---

33. René Girard, "Mimesis and Violence," in *The Girard Reader*, ed. James Williams (New York: Crossroad, 1996), 9–19, here 15. It is right for Jaeyeon Lucy Chung to write, "In fact, persecutors do not realize that they chose their victims for inadequate reasons, or perhaps for no reason at all: if they realize it, then the dispersal of the violence that has built up in the community would not occur. The operation of the scapegoat mechanism ultimately depends on concealing how it functions" (Jaeyeon Lucy Chung, "When Xenophobia Spreads like a Plague: A Critical Pastoral Theological Reflection on Anti-Asian Racism during the COVID-19 Pandemic," *Journal of Pastoral Theology* 31, nos. 2–3 [2021]: 159–74, here 166).

annihilation of its unjust practices. He writes, "First of all, it is important to insist that Christ's death was not a sacrificial one. To say that Jesus dies, not as a sacrifice, but in order that there may be no more sacrifices, is to recognize in him the Word of God: 'I wish for mercy and not sacrifice.'"[34] Girard emphasizes that reading Jesus's passion as a mythical sacrificial ritual is none other than the act of reading the Gospels in light of myths. The mythical reading of Jesus's passion is deeply problematic because it not only reduces the transformative work of Christ to another perpetual form of mythical sacrifice but also justifies the scapegoating violence. The mythical reading of the Gospels only represents the point of view of the persecuting community, not the perspectives of the victims. The Gospel testimonies are unique because they represent the victims' voices, not the persecutors' false and deceitful views. The scapegoat mechanism is epitomized by the so-called Caiaphas principle: "You know nothing at all! You do not understand that it is better for you to have one man die for the people than to have the whole nation destroyed" (John 11:49–50).

We should recall that there are two core components of the scapegoat mechanism: the victims cannot be considered innocent, and the scapegoaters should not know that they are scapegoating. Scapegoating should be hidden from scapegoaters. Jesus's passion once and for all shatters this ancient communal belief. Although the violence of the passion resembles the violence of mythical sacrifices, in which the victims are always guilty, the Gospels testify that Jesus was innocent and guiltless.[35] While Pilate's public act of washing his hands (Matt 27:24) demonstrates that Jesus's innocence was publicly recognized even by the Roman authority, the release of Barabbas (Matt 27:26) exemplifies how deeply flawed and unjust Jesus's scapegoating was. Yet for all this, the Gospel text testifies that Herod and Pilate were united to scapegoat Jesus in the name of bringing order and peace ("That same day Herod and Pilate became friends with each other; before this they had been enemies," Luke 23:12). Referring to this, Girard writes, "From a historical viewpoint

---

34. Girard, *Things Hidden*, 210.
35. René Girard, "Satan," in Williams, *Girard Reader*, 205.

the information is insignificant but, in regard to the effects of the unanimous mimetic violence upon the participants, it is enormously significant."[36]

What does this Girardian interpretation have to do with the idea of a rhizome organizer? Jesus's passion narrative becomes the biblical and theological foundation on which the ideal type of the church's rhizome organizers is established. How is it so? Two key elements stand out in regard to grounding the idea of a rhizome organizer biblically as well as theologically. First, the source of the scapegoating violence and its injustice inflicted upon Jesus was structural. Second, the overall process and way he died reveal that he paradigmatically demonstrated his archetypal resistance to structural injustice and his condemnation of scapegoating violence.[37] When Herod and Pilate "became friends" colluding to scapegoat Jesus, they both represented the unholy alliance between religious and political powers, and this alliance reflects the reality of structural injustice. We should note that when Girard uses the term *collective* in his analysis of Jesus's passion, he means what we call *structural* or *systemic*. For instance, he writes, "The Passion is presented as a blatant piece of injustice. Far from taking the *collective* violence upon itself, the text places it squarely on those who are responsible for it."[38] He says, "The two *collective* murders (Jesus and John the Baptist) portrayed in the Gospels are mimetic and so are the deaths of the biblical prophets that the Gospels explicitly associate with Jesus."[39]

How come we can interpret Jesus's passion as an act of resistance to the collective violence unjustly inflicted upon him? The first step toward this resistance was his revelation of the structural matrix of religious scapegoating, whose goal is to sacralize and mystify scapegoating sacrifice. Girard emphasizes that unveiling and rejecting the scapegoat mechanism is a continuous

36. Girard, 201.
37. According to Robyn Henderson-Espinoza, resistance does not merely have a negative notion. They write, "Resistance not only creates conditions of possibility for a new world to materialize but also helps us shift our politics and practices, so that our life is framed by the restorative work of reparations and the deeply transformative work of changing ourselves so that we change the world" (Robyn Henderson-Espinoza, *Activist Theology* [Minneapolis: Fortress, 2019], 25).
38. Girard, *Things Hidden*, 170 (emphasis added).
39. Girard, "Satan," 197 (emphasis added).

thread outlined in the Old Testament: "For instance, the averted sacrifice of Isaac; the Joseph story; the prophets' condemnation of scapegoating the widow, the weak, or the foreigner; the complaints of Job against false accusations; and the Psalms' focus on the innocent victim of collective violence—they all unmask the mechanism of victimization at the intersection of religion and society and refuse them."[40] In this respect, when the Gospels speak of sacrifices, their purpose is "to reject them and deny them any validity."[41] Revealing and unmasking the hidden structural injustice of scapegoating violence thus become key aspects of the church's rhizomatic politics. For Jesus, resistance is not merely a matter of moral integrity; it has a much greater theological significance than that. It was an archetypal demonstration of revealing and unmasking structural sin as such to reject and uproot it: "The rejected stone is the scapegoat, who is Christ. By submitting to violence, Christ reveals and uproots the structural matrix of all religion."[42]

The purpose of revealing and unmasking the structural injustice of scapegoating violence is to reject and stop it so that there would be no more victims of it. One of the key missions of the kingdom of God must be fulfilling this purpose. Unless the church would practice this mission, then it may exist only as a physical entity, but it cannot be the church established by the Christ of resistance and liberation. Girard sums up the theological significance of Jesus's revelation of the structural injustice of the scapegoat mechanism as follows: "By providing us with an accurate portrayal of the mimetic process behind the death of Jesus, and secondarily the death of John the Baptist, the Gospels reveal something which, in the long run, is bound to discredit not one particular lie about one particular victim of collective persecution only but all lies rooted in the victimage mechanism, in the grotesquely deceptive scapegoat misunderstanding."[43] Although, as Girard points out, we have fewer and fewer myths all the time thanks to the demythologizing effects of the Gospels,[44] we should not ignore that "injustice and arbitrariness are still with us,

---

40. Chung, "When Xenophobia Spreads," 167.
41. Girard, *Things Hidden*, 180.
42. Girard, 178–79.
43. Girard, "Satan," 207.
44. Girard, *Things Hidden*, 174.

no doubt, and the greatest massacres in history, the most scandalous persecutions are just as characteristic of our world as the vindication of victims." If we consider what is going on in our neoliberalized world now, it is right for him to say, "There is no denying that immense forces have tried and are still trying to nullify our concern for victims, and these forces are not only outside of us but in all of us."[45] The need for the church's rhizomatic politics and the urgency to raise our rhizome organizers cannot be emphasized enough.

Above, we saw how the idea of a rhizome organizer is established as an essential biblical and theological concept following after the archetypal model of Jesus and his demystifying resistance to scapegoating violence and its sacralization. It becomes more evident why we just cannot say that the church's justice ministry is only for so-called progressive churches, and the leaders of this ministry are assigned only to those who are interested in promoting social justice. No Christian churches are exempted from the call to become churches established by the Christ of resistance and liberation, and no church leaders are released from the mimetic responsibility to imitate Christ (1 Thess 1:6). Speaking up against any form of the scapegoat mechanism and structural injustice is an essential aspect of the church established by the Christ of resistance and liberation. Of course, there are differences in ecclesial characters and ministerial focuses among all the churches and church leaders, but all are part of the transformative and liberative ministry in some way or another.

What does it take to become a rhizome organizer of the church based on the Christ of resistance and liberation? What is the most foundational quality we need to nurture and embody to become an "imitator of God"? Answering this question in full perhaps deserves a book-length discussion and exploration. Before concluding this chapter, I want to zero in on an essential but largely forgotten virtue that seems most needed for any rhizome organizer of our church—the virtue of parrhesia (speaking the truth in the face of risk). The French philosopher and political activist Michel Foucault popularized the term in the 1980s. In 1983, both in Paris and in Berkeley, he delivered a series of public lectures on this topic and elevated people's awareness of its

---

45. Girard, "Satan," 208.

importance concerning the protection and development of a democratic culture and politics. In his Paris lecture on January 12, 1983, Foucault summarizes the Greek philosophical notion of parrhesia as follows:

> One of the original meanings of the Greek word *parrēsia* is to "say everything," but in fact, it is much more frequently translated as free-spokenness (franc-parler), free speech, etcetera. You recall that this notion of *parrēsia*, which was important in practices of spiritual direction, was a rich, ambiguous, and difficult notion, particularly insofar as it designated a virtue, a quality (some people have *parrēsia* and others do not); a duty (one must really be able to demonstrate *parrēsia*, especially in certain cases and situations); and a technique, a process (some people know how to use *parrēsia* and others do not). . . . In other words, *parrēsia* is a virtue, duty, and technique which should be found in the person who spiritually directs others and helps them to constitute their relationship to self.[46]

Alongside the Greek *parrhesia*, the prophetic tradition of the Old Testament is a key forerunner of contemporary critical discourses. According to Tom Boland and Paul Clogher, "Prophetic discourse claims to reveal injustice and idolatry and speaks from a position of transcendence within immanent historical moments." Indeed, the prophets demonstrated the spirit of parrhesia by opposing the delusions of others and false prophets.[47] In the New Testament, parrhesia is an essential virtue for those who are called to follow Jesus and his devictimizing transformative ministry. As Paul Scherz points out correctly, Jesus himself exemplifies parrhesia when he defends himself to Annas, saying, "I have spoken openly to the world; I have always taught in synagogues and in the temple, where all the Jews come together. I have

---

46. Michel Foucault, *The Government of Self and Others*, trans. Graham Burchell (New York: Palgrave Macmillan, 2011), 43.
47. Tom Boland and Paul Clogher, "A Genealogy of Critique: From Parrhesia to Prophecy," *Critical Research on Religion* 5, no. 2 (2017): 116–32, here 116.

said nothing in secret" (John 18:20).[48] Jesus's disciples also demonstrated the virtue of parrhesia as they continued to spread Jesus's gospel. An in-depth reading of Paul's letters offers us an undoubtable sense of his high integrity and continuous practice of parrhesia. Acts 4:29–31 also tells us that in the face of persecution in Jerusalem, the apostles displayed parrhesia: "When they had prayed, the place in which they were gathered together was shaken; and they were all filled with the Holy Spirit and spoke the word of God with boldness" (v. 31).

What distinguishes the biblical instances of parrhesia from those of Greek political society is that the Bible testifies that parrhesia is a gift of God rather than a demonstration of an individual's willpower. Timid and fearful as they were before having the Pentecostal experience (Acts 2), Jesus's disciples became spirit-filled apostles who no longer remained in the old religious paradigm and selfhood. Likewise, Saul became Paul after a life-changing encounter with Jesus on his way to Damascus (Acts 9). This means that the church's rhizomatic politics should be organized and practiced by those who are spiritually awakened as well as theologically renewed. The church's rhizomatic politics is also the work of the Spirit.

CONCLUSION

The rhizome organizer is the ideal type of church leader who organizes the church's justice ministries against structural injustice and systemic violence. To have a more tangible and realistic picture of this ideal type, I interviewed four church leaders whom I identified as rhizome organizers of our church. Through these interviews, I have discovered certain commonalities in their ecclesial leadership. They were all clear about a specific type of structural injustice they attempt to address and transform. They were also unequivocally devoted to the work of community organizing and participation. They all shared a certain liberative and transformative political theology that resists the Girardian scapegoat mechanism and mimetic violence. I have noted the

---

48. Paul Scherz, "The Legal Suppression of Scientific Data and the Christian Virtue of Parrhesia," *Journal of the Society of Christian Ethics* 35, no. 2 (2015): 175–92, here 184.

importance of theology while having these interviews. Theology matters. It is foundational to practicing the church's rhizomatic politics against structural injustice and systemic violence. Yet theological knowledge alone does not simply render it possible. Years of community engagement experiences as well as spiritual growth and maturation are required. I discover the ideal type of rhizome organizer in Jesus and his ministry, and I lay the biblical and theological ground for a rhizome organizer based on his model. Although briefly addressed, the importance of rhizomatic virtues, especially parrhesia, should never be ignored. Without nurturing rhizomatic virtues, the church's rhizomatic politics would be greatly curtailed. Indeed, it takes the whole church to raise a rhizome organizer.

6

A PUBLIC CHURCH FOR A POST-CHRISTENDOM ERA

INTRODUCTION

On August 20, 2004, a tragic accident occurred in Wise County, Virginia. In the early morning, a stray boulder from an A & G Coal surface mine rolled down directly into a home in the valley below, killing three-year-old Jeremy Davidson in his sleep. According to Joseph D. Witt, "Stray boulders had been a point of concern for many anti–surface mine activists since the earliest days of surface mining in Appalachia—they had been known to damage property."[1] This tragedy is part of a much bigger and more complex structural problem related to what is known as "mountaintop removal coal mining." According to Earthjustice, a nonprofit public interest organization, mountaintop removal coal mining is "strip mining on steroids" and is "an extremely destructive form of mining that is devastating Appalachia."[2] Referring to any method of surface coal mining that removes a mountaintop or ridgeline,

---

1. Joseph D. Witt, *Religion and Resistance in Appalachia: Faith and the Fight against Mountaintop Removal Coal Mining* (Lexington: University Press of Kentucky, 2016), 11. A & G paid a fine of $15,000 for the accident, which was the legal maximum for such an incident at that time.

2. "What Is Mountaintop Removal Mining?," Earthjustice, accessed January 17, 2022, https://earthjustice.org/features/campaigns/what-is-mountaintop-removal-mining.

it involves the use of heavy explosives to remove hundreds of vertical feet of a mountain to access thin seams of coal underneath. Huge machines called "draglines" are used to scoop up and push rocks and dirt into nearby streams and valleys, forever burying waterways. As a result of the decades-long practice of this method, over five hundred mountains have been leveled, and "over 2,000 miles of streams and headwaters that provide drinking water for millions of Americans have been permanently buried and destroyed."[3]

Shortly after the death of Jeremy Davidson, several Appalachian activists organized a public memorial calling for justice in the Davidson case while attempting to present the dangers and costs of mountaintop mining to others beyond the Appalachian region. Several environmental organizations—such as Kentuckians for the Commonwealth, Coal River Mountain Watch, the Ohio Valley Environmental Coalition, and Katuah Earth First! (a southern Appalachian branch of Earth First!)—got involved with the 2004 rally, and the Appalachian activists began to organize regular meetings and develop more strategic goals and strategies. In 2005, they successfully mobilized the first Mountain Justice Summer, and it became a turning point in the long-standing resistance movement to surface mining in Appalachia. Witt assesses their work as follows: "Within only a few years of the first Mountain Justice meeting, the issue of mountaintop removal moved from what was considered one of the most 'censored stories' of the century to an internationally known environmental and social justice concern. While rallies, legislative efforts, and legal cases were ongoing, this period marked a reemergence of civil disobedience in the movement, which in turn possibly contributed to increasing national and international media attention."[4]

As Witt addresses in his book, *Religion and Resistance in Appalachia*, the church engaged and participated in the works of seeking environmental justice and caring for creation. For instance, as mountaintop removal became a more public issue, several national denominations issued official statements opposing the corporate mining practice from the perspective of ecological justice. These denominations include the Evangelical Lutheran Church in

---

3. Witt, *Religion and Resistance*, 11.
4. Witt, 11, 12.

America, the Episcopal Church, the United Methodist Church, the Presbyterian Church (USA), the Religious Society of Friends (or Quakers), and the Unitarian Universalist Association. Although these denominational statements signal that North American Christian institutions were increasingly aware of the religious significance of environmental problems, they also have limitations, in that these denominations were not based in Appalachia. Witt points out that "denominational institutions in Appalachia remained overwhelmingly silent about mountaintop removal in the 1990s and 2000s, with two major exceptions: the Catholic Committee of Appalachia [CCA] and the West Virginia Council of Churches [WVCC]."[5] While the CCA had already taken strong stands advocating for reform of the coal industry and service to the poor and needy of Appalachia, the WVCC focused more on stricter enforcement of present laws, such as the Clean Water Act and the Surface Mining Control and Reclamation Act of 1977.[6]

The case of Appalachian mountaintop removal helps us see an important issue we have not explored yet in developing the church's rhizomatic politics. The issue is how the church should involve or work together with nonreligious organizations and institutions in practicing and advancing rhizomatic politics. The purpose of this chapter is threefold: First, I argue that to dismantle structural injustice, the church should proactively engage in multilateral community organizing with other groups, including nonreligious, or secular, organizations. Second, this requires the church to reinterpret the theological meaning of the Great Commission (Matt 28:16–20) and its related passages, such as Acts 1:8. I especially focus on two significant biblical terms: the "end of the age" and the "ends of the earth." Lastly, I develop further the idea of a "public church" in light of this new biblical reinterpretation and the concept of rhizomatic politics that has been constructed above. I contend that the future of the Christian church lies in knowing what it means for the church to be public and to live it out by becoming itself based on this knowledge.

---

5. Witt, 80.
6. Witt, 80, 82.

THE CHURCH AND COMMUNITY ORGANIZING

Community organizing is an essential part of the church's rhizomatic politics because it is "profoundly theological in its foundations and can be politically effective." Despite its importance, it has received less attention from public theologians. As Katie Day explains, "Community organizing has benefited over the last decades from the human resources and social capital of communities of faith, but less so from the attention of public theologians." In the same vein, she also points out the limitations of academic theological education in the real world. According to her, it is limited and thus inadequate because it "creates cultural, institutional and psychic distance from the on-the-ground, from-the-pews-into-the-streets organizing."[7] For the church's rhizomatic politics to be practical and real, the church's engagement in community organizing is indispensable. Community organizing is currently experiencing a resurgence as the destructive power of neoliberalism, such as structural poverty, tightens and the demand for democracy grows globally.[8]

Saul D. Alinsky is famous (and infamous) for his fieldwork on community organizing as a community activist as well as a political theorist. After studying archaeology and criminology, Alinsky began his work as a union organizer. By the late 1930s, he was able to see local communities and neighborhoods as social networks in which people share more common concerns than in the workplace, "yet there were no strong social processes in place whereby neighbors could band together to challenge and change the quality of their life together." This is how he started organizing communities in Chicago to address the social ills and problems of their areas, which eventually led to the creation of the Industrial Areas Foundation (IAF) in 1940. Day identifies Alinsky as "a humanist in the truest sense of the word."[9] How, then, does Alinsky describe community organizing? What is his political philosophy of it?

At the beginning of his book *Rules for Radicals: A Pragmatic Primer for Realistic Radicals*, Alinsky claims that it is for those "who want to change the world from what it is to what they believe it should be." The word *change* becomes the

---

7. Katie Day, introduction to *Yours the Power: Faith-Based Organizing in the USA*, ed. Katie Day, Esther McIntosh, and William Storrar (Leiden, Netherlands: Brill, 2013), 1–15, here 2.
8. Day, 2.
9. Day, 3.

central notion of his book, and he argues that the first step toward community organizing for social change is to recognize the world as it is. He writes, "The basic requirement for the understanding of the politics of change is to recognize the world as it is. We must work with it on its terms if we are to change it to the kind of world we would like it to be. We must first see the world as it is and not as we would like it to be. We must see the world as all political realists have, in terms of 'what men do and not what they ought to do,' as Machiavelli and others have put it."[10] As a fierce realist, Alinsky emphasizes that change comes from power, and power comes from organization. In order to act, people must get together.[11] He then clearly lays out a road map for community organizing: "The disruption of the present organization is the first step toward community organization. Present arrangements must be disorganized if they are to be displaced by new patterns that provide the opportunities and means for citizen participation. *All change means disorganization of the old and organization of the new.*"[12]

Two key elements characterize his community organizing. First, by "community," he does not mean a physical community, such as towns, counties, and so on. Instead, he says that we must understand that in a highly mobile, urbanized society, such as a cosmopolitan city, the word *community* means "community of interests." Of course, there are some exceptions, and he specifies such cases as ethnic ghettos, where segregation has resulted in physical communities that coincide with their communities of interests and political districts during political campaigns.[13] The significance of his definition of a community lies in the point that the idea of community organizing is quintessentially teleological, and the attainment of the community's strategic goal always lies at the forefront of its political mobilizations.

Second, community organizing is more than a goal-oriented strategic action; it should be also ethical from the beginning to the end. Alinsky calls the ethical principle of community organizing "the ethics of means and ends" by claiming that "the real and only question regarding the ethics of

---

10. Alinsky, *Rules for Radicals*, 3, 12.
11. Alinsky, 113.
12. Alinsky, 116.
13. Alinsky, 120.

means and ends is, and always has been, 'Does this *particular* end justify this *particular* means?'" One should not make a quick judgment that Alinsky's ethics is plainly utilitarian. Indeed, he affirms the utilitarian ethos of his ideas by saying that "to me, ethics is doing what is best for the most."[14] He, however, emphasizes that the interests of a community should be grounded on "high values" that can be universally approved, such as "freedom, equality, justice, peace, the right to dissent," and other "values in our own Bill of Rights."[15] He also includes religious values by specifically saying, "These values include the basic morals of all organized religions; their base is the preciousness of human life."[16] The inclusion of religious moral values has helped him and his organization (the IAF) enjoy strong support and participation from religious communities, especially the Roman Catholic Church, which had a large presence in urban areas.[17]

Public theologians generally approve of Alinsky's realist and pragmatic activism of community organizing. Luke Bretherton, for instance, argues against Walter Kloetzli, who saw Alinsky's approach as amoral, and the American New Left, which accused Alinsky of lacking an ideology and a transcendent vision, by saying, "Alinsky's pragmatism was neither amoral nor lacking in vision." Bretherton particularly appreciates Alinsky's insight that people can only act together within traditions and institutions. Evidently, they can learn to trust and cooperate within particular contexts. Bretherton concurs with Alinsky, saying, "Only by working with the grain of the institutions and traditions already in place can real change be effected. This necessitated both avoiding top-down, ideologically or theoretically driven political programs and inductively deriving specific policy proposals from the lived experience of the people those policies would effect."[18] Hak Joon Lee also approves Alinsky's social philosophy of community organizing by adopting it as a modern form of grassroots organizing in a democratic society. According

---

14. Alinsky, 24, 33.

15. Alinsky, 47.

16. Alinsky, 46.

17. Day, introduction, 4.

18. Luke Bretherton, "Alinsky and Augustine: Connecting Organizing and Theology," in Day, McIntosh, and Storrar, *Yours the Power*, 132–50, here 136.

to Lee, Alinsky's community organizing "has proven to be a practical and effective tool for social change, and a worthy partner for critical dialogue and comparison with covenantal organizing." Lee holds that "Alinsky is worthwhile for an academic study of community organizing as well as collaboration between community organizers (participants) and Christians."[19]

As a secular Jew raised in a secular environment, Alinsky did not develop his community organizing and social activism for the church or religious institutions. Despite this background, the church may discover key inspirational visions and mobilizing tactics from his books and legacy of social activism. His community organizing is particularly well suited to the church's rhizomatic politics, which is established in contrast to any form of arborescent politics, including both religious and nonreligious mobilization, and Alinsky's community organizing opposes any top-down political programs. Indeed, there is a tactical and formative affinity between the church's rhizomatic politics and community organizing. In this respect, it does not seem too much to say that the work of community organizing composes the key aspect of the church's rhizomatic politics. For this reason, I agree with Day, Bretherton, and Lee that the church should be more affirmative and willing to embrace and appropriate Alinsky's social philosophy of community organizing. As Lee observes, "Inspired by Alinsky's work, many Christians are working at a local grass-roots level to address the many social issues that affect the lives of ordinary citizens."[20] How does the church, then, embrace and appropriate Alinsky's community organizing? Would there be any difference between the church's community organizing and Alinsky's nonreligious, or secular, model of it?

It is my contention that the church should learn and adopt Alinsky's social activism and community organizing when it mobilizes rhizomatic politics, but it needs to do so with a grain of salt. The renowned Christian community organizer Rev. Dr. William Barber II offers us a clear illustration of what this means. In his 2016 book, *The Third Reconstruction*, he writes that although he and other members of his faith-based community organizing took important lessons from "the old organizer's playbook," they also learned that it does not

---

19. Hak Joon Lee, *God and Community Organizing: A Covenantal Approach* (Waco, TX: Baylor University Press, 2020), 11.

20. Lee, 11.

always have the answer they need for a new moment. Barber holds, "Saul Alinsky and his community organizing tradition had shown us the importance of building power and only tackling 'winnable issues.' His power analysis was crucial as we considered tactics and time. But the moral power of standing by that which is good and right could not always be easily calculated beforehand. We hadn't known how long it would take to win on public education. But we had known we were right. So we had pressed forward."[21]

Barber's many experiences of church-related community organizing and his theological reflection provide us with a critical perspective that the church's community organizing does not need to always coincide with Alinsky's model. This, of course, does not mean that the church should part ways with Alinsky when it comes to its own community organizing. On the contrary, Barber emphasizes that it should learn from and work with "folk outside the church." Without a doubt, this includes Alinsky's community organizing. What makes Barber's Christian community organizing distinct from Alinsky's nonreligious, or secular, community organizing? While Alinsky's is based on organizers' pragmatic-realist calculation in determining goals and means, Barber grounds his in what he calls "moral dissent" without necessarily negating or depreciating realist endeavors. We should note that Barber's moral dissent is deeply rooted in the African American Christian traditions of Black spirituality and faith, which have been transmitted to him through his family and the Black community. By calling himself a "son of a preacher man," he talks about his family as follows: "For my family, it was also always a matter of faith. I cannot remember a time when I did not know God both to be real and to be about bringing justice in this world."[22]

Barber explains that his moral dissent biblically originates in Psalm 94, which he read intently after his first loss of the fight for the union movement in Martinsville, Virginia, against corporate bosses. He confesses that the words of Psalm 94 kept resounding in his ears: "Who rises up for me against the wicked? Who stands up for me against evildoers?" In his critical self-reflection, he acknowledges that he was naïve and inexperienced, yet he

---

21. William Barber II and Jonathan Wilson-Hartgrove, *The Third Reconstruction: How a Moral Movement Is Overcoming the Politics of Division and Fear* (Boston: Beacon, 2016), 81–82.

22. Barber and Wilson-Hartgrove, 38, 6.

could not compromise his moral stance despite the loss: "Though I knew we had lost the fight, I couldn't shake the moral analysis that remained so clear."[23] As a political science major himself in college and also a volunteer on a lieutenant governor's campaign during graduate school, he admits first that the knowledge of realpolitik and Reinhold Niebuhr's Christian realism have equipped him with strategies and practical skills. Yet he also realizes that they have limitations. He writes, "But even as I was learning from the analysis of Christian realism, I also knew that I could not trust its basic assumption that faithful action is determined by political effectiveness. I could admit that we had lost, and I wanted to learn from my mistake. But I also knew that standing for the union had been the right thing to do."[24]

His discovery of "something more than Christian realism" eventually led him to anchor his community organizing in moral dissent rather than in an effective and calculable outcome. In this respect, he discovers his own language to describe what moral dissent is about. For instance, he clarifies it as follows: "When we raise a voice of moral dissent, we don't only stand with Moses against Pharaoh. We also stand with William Lloyd Garrison, the nineteenth-century abolitionist who denounced slavery when its abolition was a political impossibility." Barber goes further, saying, "In the American struggle for justice and freedom, moral dissent has always seemed impractical when it began."[25] Now we can see that there is a subtle yet meaningful difference between Alinsky's social philosophy of community organizing and Barber's political theology of community organizing. For Barber, the true origin of Christian community organizing is Jesus, whom he calls a "practitioner of moral dissent." Barber writes, "Teaching Jesus as a practitioner of moral dissent helped me to identify strategies and tactics to sustain people in their struggle, both in and beyond the church." How, then, does Barber's moral dissent accord with pragmatic-realist calculation and appropriation? Barber answers this thorny question in a simple yet critical manner. He asserts, "While realism cannot determine the goals of our faith, it must shape our strategy in movements of moral dissent." For him, moral dissent is faith based, and faith cannot be delimited by what seems

---

23. Barber and Wilson-Hartgrove, 20, 19.
24. Barber and Wilson-Hartgrove, 20.
25. Barber and Wilson-Hartgrove, 20–21, 22.

reasonable and practical. He writes, "Faith-rooted moral dissent requires that we always look forward toward the vision of what we know we were made to be. But defeat can and must invite us to question our means."[26] Barber inherits Alinsky's ethical framework of "means and ends" but injects into it a theological and spiritual moral power and urgency.

Along with the notion of moral dissent, what makes Barber's community organizing distinctive is his idea of fusion coalitions. Indeed, they are central components of his social ministry. A fusion coalition is the inclusion and solidification of all people across all the lines to uphold justice. Barber writes, "Yes, we needed dedicated church folk with faith that not only motivated them but also gave them a distinct, prophetic vision for their work in the community. But we also needed community partners." He emphasizes that "we needed to come together with banks and businesspeople, with other people of faith and with people of no particular faith." From the early abolition movement to the civil rights movement, from the suffrage movement to the recent Black Lives Matter movement, US society has witnessed various types of fusion coalitions across the country. A fusion coalition is established in various forms and manners, such as the "formation of an interfaith coalition," "the coalition of secular and ecclesial authorities," "interorganizational coalitions," and so on. His conviction in them is clearly illustrated by his own words: "Only a fusion coalition representing all the people in any place could push a moral agenda over and against the interest of the powerful. But such coalitions are never possible without radical patience and stubborn persistence." Again, Barber confesses that he learned the importance of fusion coalitions from his own social ministry of community organizing: "I was learning the awesome power of what happens when people come together. And I was learning it in the church."[27]

For Barber, fusion coalitions are not merely a matter of organizational skill or strategic action. They are theological as well as organizational. According to him, the development of the holistic community is rooted in the power of the Holy Spirit, and the Spirit stirs up people and the community, transcending the line between the church and the secular world. He sums up his

26. Barber and Wilson-Hartgrove, 24.
27. Barber and Wilson-Hartgrove, 38, 28, 35.

pneumatological understanding as follows: "The Spirit blows where it will, working in, through, and beyond the church." Perhaps the most significant aspect of his experience-based pneumatology is that the church neither has a "monopoly on God's dream" nor is confined by the walls of the church. He confesses, "When we went to share with others the vision we'd received from the Spirit, we found that the Spirit was often already moving them."[28]

We have compared Alinsky and Barber to formulate a suitable community organizing model for the church's rhizomatic politics. In my view, although the church's rhizomatic politics cannot be reduced to the work of community organizing, the church's prophetic and liberative ministry is not possible without its proactive participation in community organizing. This critical comparison helps us see more clearly why the church should take seriously Alinsky's broad-based community organizing with a grain of theological salt. As Barber points out, while Alinsky's pragmatic-realist framework may not determine the goals of our faith, it certainly helps the church shape its strategy "in movements of moral dissent." Barber's notion of fusion coalitions is especially important for the practice of the church's rhizomatic politics. Without the concerted effort of all related parties, it is unlikely for the church or any other organization to dismantle structural injustice by itself. Of course, those who are most directly affected or related are to engage in rhizomatic politics more proactively. Without having others' support and rhizomatic solidarity, however, no organization, including the church, can accomplish its goals. It is right for Barber to say that in a fusion coalition, "when workers spoke up for the right to organize and engage in collective bargaining, the civil community would be there with them. And when civil rights leaders petitioned for the expansion of voting rights for people of color, white workers would stand with them."[29] To put it bluntly, the church's rhizomatic politics is about building relationships and connections among all the related parties across all the dividing lines. In this regard, both Alinsky's and Barber's community organizing models offer us indispensable tools concerning how the church would practice its distinctive rhizomatic politics.

---

28. Barber and Wilson-Hartgrove, 35.
29. Barber and Wilson-Hartgrove, 53.

THE GREAT COMMISSION AND
THE ENDS OF THE EARTH

There are various factors that keep local churches from organizing or participating in rhizomatic politics. It is beyond the scope of this chapter to investigate all those factors, reasons, or backgrounds, but I will focus on the most
challenging yet important factor with the purpose of dismantling it. I contend
that the most daunting stumbling block resides inside the church rather than
on the outside and is quintessentially theological. It is a narrow and reductive
understanding of what is known as the Great Commission, which is the direct
instruction given by the resurrected Jesus Christ to his disciples to spread the
gospel to all the nations of the world. Matthew 28:16–20 (Mark 16:14–18;
Luke 24:36–49; John 20:19–23; Acts 1:6–8) describes a meeting in Galilee
to charge the disciples with a mission that will endure throughout the age. It
reads as follows: "Now the eleven disciples went to Galilee, to the mountain
to which Jesus had directed them. When they saw him, they worshiped him;
but some doubted. And Jesus came and said to them, 'All authority in heaven
and on earth has been given to me. Go therefore and make disciples of all
nations, baptizing them in the name of the Father and of the Son and of the
Holy Spirit, and teaching them to obey everything that I have commanded
you. And remember, I am with you always, to the end of the age'" (Matt
28:16–20). The significance of this particular passage cannot be overempha-
sized concerning the formations of Christian theology, biblical scholarship,
ecclesial mission, liturgical tradition, seminary education, and so on. There
is an enormous volume of literature that deals with the Great Commission
in many languages, including "thousands of books, monographs, essays, and
articles."[30] Cynthia M. Campbell even remarks, "This text, often called 'The
Great Commission,' has long served as a 'job description' for the church."[31]

---

30. Mookgo S. Kgatle, "Globalization of Missions: An Exegesis on the Great Commission
(Mt 28:18–20)," *In die Skriflig* 52, no. 1 (2018): 1–7, here 1, https://www.researchgate
.net/publication/326340973_Globalisation_of_missions_An_exegesis_on_the_Great
_Commission_Mt_2818-20.

31. Cynthia M. Campbell, "Matthew 28:16–20," *Interpretation: A Journal of Bible and Theology*
46, no. 4 (October 1992): 402–5, here 402.

As long as the church continues to regard the narrow meaning of evangelism and mission as its central task, the works of social transformation and different types of rhizomatic politics will be most likely relegated to the back seat, even if it favorably views such works. Thus when I am asserting that the Great Commission is the most formidable stumbling block for the church's rhizomatic politics, what I am pointing at is not the Great Commission as such but rather the way the church has theologically interpreted and ecclesiastically appropriated it into the ecclesial life and structure. Two issues are, then, at stake here: first, the problem of how the church interprets the Great Commission, and second, the problem of how it appropriates such an interpretation. While the former is more likely a theological issue, the latter is an ecclesial one. Unless the church resolves these conjoined problems, it will never fully activate its rhizomatic politics in a world that desperately needs its full deployment.

Yonghan Chung summarizes the church's traditional interpretation of the Great Commission as follows: "The best of Matt 28:18–20, the so-called Great Commission, plays a crucial role as a motif in almost every Christian gathering, causing people to recall the significance of mission and evangelism."[32] Concurring with Chung's summary, Mookgo S. Kgatle goes further, saying that the history of interpretation of this passage shows us clearly that "the Great Commission in Matthew 28:18–20 is a call to global mission."[33] It is not my intention, however, to introduce various scholarly exegetical works in this section. What I intend to do here is to argue that it is time now to reinterpret the passage because the traditional interpretation fails to capture a hidden yet more holistic aspect of Jesus's Great Commission due to its narrow and reductionist understanding. What is the content of this holistic yet hidden meaning, and how is it possible to uncover that? I answer these questions by attempting to reread the passage in light of Girard's novel interpretation of the Bible, especially his mimetic reading of the Gospel.

David L. Turner notes that as we begin to interpret Matthew 28:16–20, we are immediately struck with the repetition of the word "all":

---

32. Yonghan Chung, "A Postcolonial Reading of the Great Commission (Matt 28:16–20) with a Korean Myth," *Theology Today* 72, no. 3 (2015): 276–88, here 276.

33. Kgatle, "Globalization of Missions," 1.

1. Jesus has been given *all* authority (28:18).
2. Disciples are to be made of *all* nations (28:19).
3. Such disciples are to be taught to obey *all* that Jesus commanded (28:20).
4. Jesus will be with his disciples *all* the days until the end of the age (28:20).[34]

Turner's keen observation of the recurring word "all," however, ends as a mere observation without further investigating its deeper meaning. Inadvertently, though, he reveals how he interprets its meaning without intentionally verbalizing it. For Turner, the seemingly emphatic use of "all" involves the importance of mimesis in the lives of those who follow Jesus, especially disciples. In other words, disciples and, by extension, all the followers of Jesus are expected to imitate him in *all* aspects of their lives by modeling after his acts and teachings. In this respect, we can say that mimesis in fact takes the central position in the Great Commission. Turner writes, "The disciples' central responsibility is to *reproduce* themselves. The other tasks (going, baptizing, teaching) describe how disciples are made. A disciple is literally one who follows an itinerant master, as have Jesus's disciples."[35]

If there is an intrinsic relation between the emphatic use of "all" and the centrality of "mimesis" in Matthew 28:16–20, one cannot but realize that those verbs (*going, baptizing, teaching*) are not comprehensive enough to encompass every scene and section of Jesus's ministerial life on earth. In other words, those key verbs are not an exhaustive list of Jesus's thoughts and acts, which his followers are to imitate in their lives. What about Jesus's bold act of confronting his adversaries (Pharisees)? What about his conscientious act of resisting Roman rulers (Pilate) in Jerusalem? What about his advocating act of defending children who were coming to him? Those verbs (*confronting, resisting, advocating*) are not listed in the Great Commission, but this does not mean that the followers of Jesus are exempted from the commanded mimetic task of practicing them in this world, even "to the end of the age." One may

---

34. David L. Turner, *Matthew* (Grand Rapids, MI: Baker Academic, 2008), 687.
35. Turner, 689 (emphasis added).

respond that those unlisted tasking verbs are implicitly included by "everything that I have commanded you" or "all that Jesus commanded," and thus the Great Commission does not exclude them from its list. I agree with this suggestion with the condition that we should not centralize a cluster of listed verbs while marginalizing the unlisted ones. In such a case, the church's various works of rhizomatic politics will be sent to the back seat again while evangelism and mission continue to take the front seat.

In reinterpreting the theological meaning of Matthew 28:16–20, especially the much loaded yet unspecified phrase "all that Jesus commanded," we should critically recall and reappropriate Girard's innovative reinterpretation of Jesus's crucifixion. One of Girard's significant contributions to Christianity is his aid in helping the church overcome the sacrificial reading of the passion narratives that have made it possible for Christendom to exist for fifteen or twenty centuries.[36] As we have discussed in the previous chapter, according to Girard, although the phenomenon of scapegoating occurred on the cross, its occurrence was not for the sake of ancient theories of mythical sacrifice but for the sake of the termination and annihilation of the unjust practices of scapegoating violence. Let me reiterate Girard's statement: "First of all, it is important to insist that Christ's death was not a sacrificial one. To say that Jesus dies, not as a sacrifice, but in order that there may be no more sacrifices, is to recognize in him the Word of God: 'I wish for mercy and not sacrifice.'"[37] It is evident that Girard clearly distinguishes the church from Christendom. As Nathan Colborne points out, for Girard, Christendom is "an ironic reversal of criticism of sacrifice found in the Passion narratives."[38] Unlike Christendom, in the church, the mythical reading of Jesus's passion is no longer normalized and thus opposed.

The reason we need to recall and bring Girard in reinterpreting Matthew 28:16–20 is clear now. It is for hermeneutically differentiating the mythical-religious interpretation of the Great Commission espoused by Christendom from its authentic-truthful interpretation by the church established by the

---

36. Nathan Colborne, "Violence and Resistance: Towards a Politics without a Scapegoat," *Toronto Journal of Theology* 29, no. 1 (2013): 111–24, here 115.

37. Girard, *Things Hidden*, 210.

38. Colborne, "Violence and Resistance," 115.

Christ of resistance and liberation. Girard helps us realize that ending any form of mimetic violence and the scapegoat mechanism is acknowledged to be one of "everything" that Jesus commanded his followers. Since teaching this previously hidden yet newly unearthed commandment becomes a part of the Great Commission, whose theological significance is as equal as those of evangelism and mission, the church's rhizomatic politics becomes an essential and integral component of the Great Commission. The church thus should renew its traditional understanding by adopting a more holistic-comprehensive view while letting go of its age-old narrow and reductionist stance.

We should not underestimate the problem of a narrow and reductionist interpretation of its traditional understanding. Under the guise of the Great Commission, the Western church during the colonial period played the role of "contributing to issues of inequality, traumatic experience, and injustice as well as the influence of these factors on the indigenous African people." While acknowledging the positive impact of the missionary work (education, general health care, etc.), the South African religious ethicist Beatrice Okyere-Manu argues that the narrow and reductionist view of the Great Commission (elevating the agenda of teaching and making disciples while ignoring issues of social justice) is to blame for the "greatest tragedies" for a period of nearly five hundred years, from 1400 to 1900.[39] What we should not overlook is that such tragic history and culture have also been transmitted to the churches of the former colonies. Yonghan Chung illustrates this by writing, "When Korean churches started to missionize other countries, they went to the mission fields without critically analyzing the Great Commission and their own historical experiences. They have missionized others in the same way that Koreans had been missionized."[40] Much belated, though, the global church should seriously engage in the work of reinterpreting the Great Commission lest the tragic and deplorable history should play back in the future.

What changes could this theological reinterpretation of the Great Commission and the church's proactive appropriation of it bring to the church and

---

39. Beatrice Okyere-Manu, "Colonial Mission and the Great Commission in Africa," in *Teaching All Nations: Interrogating the Matthean Great Commission*, ed. Mitzi J. Smith and Jayachitra Lalitha (Minneapolis: Fortress, 2014): 15–31, here 16, 26.

40. Chung, "Postcolonial Reading," 277.

society? Perhaps the immediate and observable changes we can expect from the church's proactive appropriation of a new understanding of the Great Commission will be its more visible and unabashed presence and leadership within the community and the public. We should remember that according to Girard, in contrast to ancient myths that take sides with persecutors in their sacrificial ceremonies, Jesus's gospel stands with victims by defending them. Under a renewed understanding of the Great Commission, henceforth, the church begins to be more proactive and responsive to the problems of structural injustice by specifically taking sides with the victims rather than persecutors while representing the voices of the unheard within the community and the larger society. This, of course, does not mean that the church no longer pays attention to the calls of evangelism and mission. But if a local church has a mission or evangelism committee, it should also have a social justice committee. If a community church supports a mission project, it should also support community organizations or institutions that address social, economic, or political injustices. If a church plans to have a mission trip to overseas countries, it should also organize cohort groups to visit the poorest communities within its city or town. If a pastor invites a missionary to the church, the pastor should also invite community organizers or policy makers.

Under a renewed understanding of the Great Commission, the church should also renew its theological pedagogy and reform its educational programs, from children's Sunday school to Bible classes for adults. One of the purposes of this theological reorientation of congregational education is to help congregants grow out of the unholy and harmful influence of the bad theologies of Christendom. In doing so, a local pastor's in-depth knowledge and continual self-teaching of critical hermeneutics are indispensable. For instance, pastors who would commit themselves to the renewed understanding of the Great Commission should seriously consider how they would be able to critically appropriate Paulo Freire's following statement into their congregational education: "No pedagogy which is truly liberating can remain distant from the oppressed by treating them as unfortunates and by presenting for their emulation models from among the oppressors."[41] Under the renewed

---

41. Paulo Freire, *Pedagogy of the Oppressed* (New York: Continuum, 2007), 54.

understanding of the Great Commission, pastors should also reidentify their public roles and responsibilities as public pastoral leaders. Members of the church as well should renovate their social and political responsibility from a renewed theological stance. As Jeffrey Stout points out, "Members of the church, by virtue of their multiple memberships, are also *in* the world and *responsible for* worldly arrangements." It is right for him to say, "The church must hold the people and their rulers responsible for the injustices they have perpetrated and permitted. At times, it is a pastor's responsibility to speak prophetically on the church's behalf."[42]

We have investigated the theological significance of the Great Commission and a possible renewal of its interpretation with the purpose of the further development of the church's rhizomatic politics. We also have explored how the church appropriates the renewed theological meaning of this reinterpretation for itself and the community. Before concluding this section, we cannot help but ask a critical question to ourselves: What does it mean that there is a church in this troubled world where we are living now? I contend that it is the task of each generation to answer this perennial question, and the answer may vary depending on the historical context and situation. I attempt to answer this question after all these investigations and explorations by presenting a simple statement: the church today should strive to become the public church. I lay out a more detailed idea of the public church in the following section.

Before embarking on a theological construction of the idea of the public church, we need to define "the public." Recall that during the colonial period, the European church rarely discussed suffering.[43] There was another critical-theological theme the European church seldom discussed: the idea of the public. As the church began to separate itself from the state and the world of secular politics, it became estranged from the domain of the public, resulting in the intended or unintended privatization of religious faith and ecclesial life. This loss has been compensated by the theologically blind yet literally

---

42. Jeffrey Stout, "Pastors and Flocks," in Day, McIntosh, and Storrar, *Yours the Power*, 121–32, here 126 (emphasis added).

43. James F. Keenan, "Vatican II and Theological Ethics," *Theological Studies* 74, no. 1 (2013): 162–90, here 180.

meaningful appropriation of two keywords that provided the church with the needed space and time for its existence: the end of the age (Matt 28:20) and the ends of the earth (Acts 1:8). The church adopted these words not only chronologically but also geographically. Regrettably, as a result of this mythologization, it has since lost "now time" and "this space," giving birth to the so-called otherworldly gospel and Christianity. The task unearthed is, then, clear; we are to convert this mythologized space and time into "now time" and "this space," in which the church is called to become the mimetic community of Christ. I find the demythologized space and time in the idea of the "public," which becomes the church's new missional frontier toward the "ends of the earth" and the "end of the age." I develop the idea of the public church in the following section.

THE COLLAPSE OF CHRISTENDOM AND DIETRICH BONHOEFFER'S RELIGIONLESS CHRISTIANITY

Since the American Christian historian Martin Marty coined the term *public church*, Christian scholars have engaged in developing its concept further, especially among practical and political theologians. Reinhard Hütter proposes an alternative way to conceive an idea of the public church after the collapse of its dominant Christendom model.[44] It is worth summarizing his

---

44. Reinhard Hütter offers us a concise and clear description of what the "public" is. According-ing to him, the concept of the public has a long and complex history, and its contemporary use only refers to the one "public" of political liberalism composed as "society." Following the Reformed theologian William Placher, Hütter summarizes the three usages by distinguishing between three different semantic directions attaching to church or theology as public. He writes, "A theology or church is 'public' insofar as '(1) it appeals to warrants available to any intelligent, reasonable, responsible person; (2) it understands a religion as fundamentally a public, communal activity, not a matter of the individual's experience; (3) it effectively addresses political and social issues'" (Reinhard Hütter, *Suffering Divine Things: Theology as Church Practice* [Grand Rapids, MI: Eerdmans, 2000], 159).
   According to this understanding, the concept of the public church can be then generally identified as a church in a liberal society. Martin Marty, from a religious historian perspective, defines the idea of the public church as follows: "The public church is a family of apostolic churches with Jesus Christ at the center, churches which are especially sensitive to the *res publica*, the public order that surrounds and includes people of faith. The public church is a communion of communions, each of which lives its life partly in

constructive effort. Hütter's starting point is that the privatization of the church cannot be the alternative solution to the collapse of the Christendom model. The "forces of modernity," he claims, resulted in a situation in which "the church as a genuine 'public' is eclipsed." Hütter interprets the eclipse of a "public" as a critical ecclesial problem by blaming the rise of modernity or secularism. He writes, "As a political project, modernity is constituted by a particular way of organizing the 'private' and the 'public' that entails the dichotomizing—and thereby the effective taming—of religion."[45]

How does he, then, reconstruct the public character of the church? To break out of the iron cage of privatism set up by modernity as well as to revive "the church as public," Hütter suggests that the church should take dogma seriously while critically integrating Barth's constructive pneumatology. So he

response to its separate tradition and partly to the calls for a common Christian vocation. In America the constituency of this convergence of churches comes from elements within the old mainline, the newer evangelicalism, and Catholicism" (Martin Marty, *The Public Church: Mainline-Evangelical-Catholic* [New York: Crossroad, 1981], 3).

James Fowler, a late practical theologian, offers a more comprehensive definition of the practical church. He writes,

"Public church" points to a vision of ecclesial *praxis*, a proposal in practical theology. It seeks to be faithful to a biblical grounding in its claim that ecclesial community, formed by the presence and fellowship of Christ, points beyond itself to the *praxis* of God in the processes of history. It tries to point to and embody a transforming presence in human relations, in societies, and in care for embattled nature. That God's *praxis* transforms toward wholeness, justice, and peace finds witness in ecclesial community as congregations practice their principles of equality, partnership, and inclusiveness, as they welcome and extend hospitality to the stranger, and as they give their lives for transformed human community in particular contexts. (James Fowler, *Weaving the New Creation: Stages of Faith and the Public Church* [New York: HarperSanFrancisco, 1991], 151)

The political theologian Mary Doak gives us the most succinct yet clearest notion of a public church. She writes, "A public church, by which I mean one that engages the current political processes in order to develop policies and structures that decrease suffering, that preserve the earth, and that support human dignity, equality, and inclusion" (Mary Doak, *A Prophetic, Public Church: Witness to Hope amid the Global Crises of the Twenty-First Century* [Collegeville, MN: Liturgical Press Academic, 2020], xiv–xv).

45. Reinhard Hütter, "The Church as Public: Dogma, Practice, and the Holy Spirit," *Pro Ecclesia: A Journal of Catholic and Evangelical Theology* 3, no. 3 (August 1994): 334–61, here 334, 336.

attempts to reconstruct the church's public character by focusing on two theological terms: *dogma* and *pneuma*. First, referring to the intrinsic connection between dogma and a public church, Hütter claims that "the church as public necessarily requires dogma, and that dogma has a public church as its necessary consequence."[46] What does dogma have to do with the notion of a public church? Hütter draws on Hannah Arendt's insights to answer the question. According to him, Arendt's interpretation of classic Western thinkers, such as Plato and Aristotle, is critical because it offers us a crucial insight that just as the ancient polis had surrounding walls and its laws were what made its public possible, dogma becomes the defining walls that establish a public for the church.[47] This is the reason, he says, "we have to understand dogma as constituting and defining the very space that is the church's unique public."[48] Ultimately, the church becomes public in its own right.

Along with dogma, there is another element that makes the church possible as a public in its own right—that is, the Holy Spirit. Hütter asserts that "it is precisely the Holy Spirit who creates—as *Spiritus Creator*—that which makes the church possible as a public in its own right." As Hütter emphasizes, the Spirit's teaching does not remain disembodied because the Holy Spirit creates procedures—dogma and the key practices—through which the teaching occurs. He goes further, saying, "The church is nothing less than the Spirit's creature in time, the Spirit's 'announcer' and interpreter, then the Spirit's activity can easily be seen and claimed everywhere." Hütter also emphasizes that "the Holy Spirit's publicity goes beyond the church's limits, in that the Spirit creates new things and can act as a critic of the church from both within and without."[49] Whether or not one agrees with Hütter, his most significant contribution to public theology is his argument that the collapse of Christendom does not necessarily result in the annihilation of the public character of the church. But Hütter's dogma-centered ecclesial model of the public is inadequate to the idea of a "public church" that I am proposing here.

---

46. Hütter, 347.
47. Hütter, 347.
48. Hütter, 348.
49. Hütter, 357, 358, 359.

There are several reasons for that. First, instead of critically investigating and probing what went wrong with Christendom, he not only blames modernity or the project of modernity for the loss of the church as public but also attacks liberationist theologies, such as Letty Russell's feminist anti-Christendom paradigm in line with it.[50] John G. Flett argues that although Hütter carefully observes the problem of Christendom by shadowing an argument made fifty years before by the Dutch missiologist Johannes C. Hoekendijk, he exemplifies the problem rather than solving it. Hoekendijk begins his anti-Christendom thesis by saying, "The call to evangelism is often little else than a call to restore 'Christendom,' the *Corpus Christianum*, as a solid, well-integrated cultural complex, directed and dominated by the Church." He then points out that "the sense of urgency [the church's drive for evangelism, or what Hütter calls 'key practices'] is often nothing but a nervous feeling of insecurity, with the established Church endangered; a flurried activity to save the remnants of a time now irrevocably past."[51]

Hoekendijk not only calls attention to the Christendom culture of the church, especially concerning evangelizing mission, but also analyzes its historical origin. He writes, "This was natural. The Reformers presupposed the existence of Christendom. This is one of the reasons, no doubt, why they have not developed a full doctrine of the Church. Their purpose was not to create new communities but to reform those already in existence. They have therefore reduced the number of distinctive marks of the true Church to one: the proclamation of the Word in its double form: the verbal and sacramental Word."[52] Out of this unreflective presupposition evolves the culture of Christendom, which then shapes the evangelistic missionary movement. Appropriating Hoekendijk's critical missiological stance, Flett writes, "The problem is not that of cross-cultural movement [of mission]—the movement reveals the problem." Flett captures the essence of this problem by calling the

---

50. The lack of a critical assessment of Christendom can be found in his other works on ecclesiology, such as his book *Suffering Divine Things* and his article "Ecclesial Ethics, the Church's Vocation, and Paraclesis," *Pro Ecclesia: A Journal of Catholic and Evangelical Theology* 2, no. 4 (November 1993): 433–50.

51. Johannes C. Hoekendijk, "The Call to Evangelism," *International Review of Mission* 39, no. 154 (April 1950): 162–75, here 163.

52. Hoekendijk, 164.

mission of Christendom the propagation of Christian benefits: "Missionary proclamation reduced to propaganda because the form of the sending church was itself the missionary end, and this church assumed a particular cultural form."[53] Indeed, there is an undeniable link between this culture and evangelistic outreach, and this link is a "consequence of the assumed nature of the church as it developed within the political conditions of Christendom."[54] Hoekendijk's theological indictment of the Christendom model of Western missiology, Flett holds, is eventually applicable to Hütter's vision of a public church.

By turning a deaf ear to such an anti-Christendom theological reflection as Hoekendijk's missiological critique, Hütter can only develop a neodogmatist version of a public church, which then divides an "inner circle" and "outer circle" of ecclesial practices that are constitutive of the church. Unfortunately, though, Hütter's dogmatic public circle is not wide and inclusive enough to embrace such feminist constitutive voices as Letty Russell. Hütter criticizes Russell's theological works by saying,

> She points out creative new ways of continuing those practices that are faithful to God's *oikonomia* becoming "public" in the church. Yet her account remains disturbingly ambiguous since it is also deeply immersed in modernist assumptions. The normative horizon of her project does not seem to be God's *oikonomia* in Christ but rather modernity's meta-narrative of total human emancipation and liberation which is interpreted to be God's *oikonomia*. In other words, the fact that the project of human emancipation is done in a feminist paradigm (i.e., rightly exploding the middle- and upper-class self-definition of white men) does not catapult it out of the overarching modernist project.[55]

---

53. John G. Flett, "Communion as Propaganda: Reinhard Hütter and the Missionary Witness of the 'Church as Public,'" *Scottish Journal of Theology* 62, no. 4 (2009): 457–76, here 469.
54. Flett, 470.
55. Hütter, "Church as Public," 353.

Hütter's critique of Russell demonstrates what it would look like if we would adopt his version of a public church. Instead of criticizing her liberative theological exploration in the name of a "modernist project," he should focus more on investigating what went wrong with Christendom and how it affected the church's loss of the public character.

In her 2012 book, *The Church for the World: A Theology of Public Witness*, Jennifer M. McBride offers us a new way of helping the post-Christendom church become a public church with her theology of public witness. According to McBride, the church's public witness is enabled not by the reconstruction of dogma but by "confession of sin unto repentance." The word *repentance* becomes a central foundation on which she establishes her theology of public witness. She writes, "By 'repentance' I mean the church's concrete activity in social and political life that arises from its accepting responsibility and acknowledging its complicity in such sin. By granting 'repentance' social and political character, I follow Bonhoeffer, who, in those lightning flashes of theological insight, uses the concept to refer to more than the activity of the individual Christian." She emphasizes that repentance refers to "an ecclesial mode of being in the world, encompassing both act and speech, that provides the church with an ethical framework for social and political engagement and a description of particularly Christian disposition in public life."[56]

How does repentance lead the church to get involved with the public life of social and political engagement? According to McBride, the church's belongingness and relevance to the world originate in Christ's solidarity with sinners. Following Bonhoeffer's theological footsteps, she goes on and makes a key theological statement that "Christ not only dies for humanity's sin but publicly lives with our sin."[57] It is her theological mantra that Jesus was in solidarity with sinners. McBride argues that there are at least three ways in which Jesus builds up solidarity with sinners:

First, as God incarnate, he assumed sinful flesh, as Paul says in Romans 8:3. He took on human nature's damaged state and through his body

---

56. Jennifer M. McBride, *The Church for the World: A Theology of Public Witness* (New York: Oxford University Press, 2012), 17.

57. McBride, 58.

became intimately acquainted with the complexity and messiness of fallen existence. Second, he begins his public ministry by being baptized with sinners in response to John the Baptist's call to repent and in this way "numbers himself with the transgressors" (to use Isaiah's language about the suffering servant). Third, and finally, refusing to be called good (Mark 10:18), he instead accepts responsibility for sin as a convicted criminal on the cross. Throughout his ministry, Jesus denies any claim about his own moral righteousness and instead actively accepts responsibility for the world's sin and suffering on the cross out of love for fellow human beings.[58]

Christ's this-worldly existence culminates on the cross, which discloses his ultimate solidarity with sinners. McBride writes, "The cross, then, is not as much the pivotal moment for Christian witness as the remarkable disclosure and logical culmination of what Christ's public existence already reveals: God in Christ draws human guilt into the divine life, where it is then overcome."[59]

As the body of Christ, the church's role and responsibility become evident. In a quintessentially Bonhoefferian manner, McBride lays out ecclesiological tasks and responsibility as a corollary of Christology. If this is what Christ does, then the church, as the body of Christ, must do the same. She summarizes her christological ecclesiology as follows: "The church witnesses to the incarnate, crucified, and risen Christ and participates in the redemptive powerlessness of God in the world when it takes responsibility for sin through concrete acts of repentance." McBride's theological insight, especially her Bonhoefferian theological reflection on the importance of "confession unto repentance," helps us see that there is an alternative and theologically more sensible paradigm that helps the church become a "public church" in a post-Christendom pluralistic society. She rightly emphasizes, "Repentance is not the private, self-focused aim of the individual before God but is participation in the Christ event and thus existence for others and a sharing in God's

---

58. David Heim and Jennifer M. McBride, "The Witness of Sinners: Theologian Jennifer McBride on the Nontriumphal Church," *Christian Century*, November 27, 2013, https://www.christiancentury.org/article/2013-11/witness-sinners.

59. McBride, *Church for the World*, 58.

kingdom come."[60] The church's repentance not only transforms its public role and responsibility but also reconfigures the type of Christianity from the "religious" (defined and confined by Christendom) to the "religionless," as Bonhoeffer outlines it in his prison letters.

I recognize a kindred spirit in McBride's Bonhoefferian endeavor to develop a theology of public witness. But despite my overall agreement and approval of her theological vision, I also find that it has some notable limitations, which I attempt to overcome by laying out a theological direction to help the church become a public church. The first limitation has to do with her Bonhoefferian appropriation of christological repentance. McBride's central christological thesis is that Jesus was in solidarity with sinners, but this does not seem to take seriously that though the church may live up to her Bonhoefferian ecclesiological call to repentance, many perpetrators would not. With repentance alone, the church will not address the real issues—the problem of structural injustice and the suffering of the victimized by structural injustice and systemic violence. I contend that for the church's public witness to be real and meaningful, it is almost necessary for it to get engaged in rhizomatic politics, whatever form or type it may be.

Without a doubt, the church is called to walk on the path of confession unto repentance, fulfilling its responsibility to witness publicly. McBride points out the pervasive problem of mainline Christian churches as follows: "The public engagement of mainline Christians rarely gets beyond ethical religion and its innocuous volunteerism, which introduces a minority of Christians in a local body to the sufferings of the world without penetrating the comfortable lifestyle and self-interest of the church as a whole."[61] The focus on repentance, however, may miss a bigger picture. In my view, what should matter more for the church is not its responsibility to live up to a call to repent but its responsibility to address the sufferings of those who are victimized by structural injustice and systemic violence. It also worries me that as McBride develops her theology of public witness, the word *sinners* is used in a non-discriminatory manner. From a christological perspective, of course, all are

---

60. McBride, 58, 147.
61. McBride, 51.

sinners, but if the word *sinners* is appropriated by the church in a nondiscriminatory manner for an ecclesial purpose, such as public witness against social sin, then there may arise a problem because both perpetrators of structural injustice and its victims could be lumped together in the same theological category. A nondiscriminatory use of a certain theological language may indeed entail damaging effects to some constituents of political society. Besides, regarding repentance, McBride seems to focus too exclusively on the problem of a theological triumphalism of North American Christianity, thereby losing sight of other serious issues, such as the church's neutrality or benign complacency to structural injustice and ideological captivity (neoliberalism) in a post-Christendom era.

What appears to be the most lacking aspect of her theology of public witness is that she does not go far enough to fully advance Bonhoeffer's seminal notion of "religionless Christianity." To a certain level, of course, McBride addresses its theological significance, especially regarding her critique of ecclesiological triumphalism within North American Christianity. For instance, she writes, "In his first letter introducing the idea of a religionless Christianity, Bonhoeffer asks a question that provides a helpful frame for thinking about public witness in the United States. His inquiry, although arising out of his own historical context of a world come of age, parallels the driving concern for our pluralistic context, namely, how the church may witness to the lordship of Christ in a nontriumphal manner."[62] McBride, however, stops short of uncovering a more daring and transformative role of the idea of religionless Christianity as she develops a theology of public witness beyond the supportive role of witnessing the shortcomings of American Christendom.[63]

---

62. McBride, 23–24. Bonhoeffer writes in his prison letters, "How do we talk about God—without religion, that is, without the temporally conditioned presuppositions of metaphysics, the inner life, and so on? How do we speak (or perhaps we can no longer even 'speak' the way we used to) in a 'worldly' way about 'God'? How do we go about being 'religionless-worldly' Christians, how can we be ἐκ-κλησία, those who are called out, without understanding ourselves religiously as privileged, but instead seeing ourselves as belonging wholly to the world?" (Dietrich Bonhoeffer, *Letters and Papers from Prison* [Minneapolis: Fortress, 2010], 364).

63. We should note that although Bonhoeffer was on his way toward the full theological development of this seminal notion of "religionless Christianity," he was not able to finish the

How does Bonhoeffer's religionless Christianity help the post-Christendom church to reestablish itself as a public church? In two parts, the idea of religionless Christianity contributes to the establishment of a public church in the post-Christendom world. McBride shows us only the first half of its full picture by emphasizing the role of dismantling theological triumphalism. What is, then, the other half of this full picture? How could we get the whole picture of it? I contend that the other half of the full theological significance of Bonhoeffer's religionless Christianity is that it ultimately refers to the early church of the apostolic age. The word *religion* was not even a relevant category during the apostolic age. It was an invention of a later generation that came to know Jesus's movement indirectly through the eyes of others and their framework. This is the reason I argue that to have a whole picture of religionless Christianity, we should go back to the early church of the apostolic age.

What theological insights does the early church of the apostolic age offer to us as we reconstruct the post-Christendom church as a public church? The Christian historian Gerald L. Sittser argues that there is a certain similarity between our post-Christendom era and the early church's pagan era, and there is an important lesson we are to learn from the early church. This lesson is about how the church becomes itself in a pluralistic non-Christendom (either pre- or post-Christendom) social context. Sittser identifies the early church's Christian movement as the Third Way by distinguishing it from the first and the second way. By the first, he means the "Roman way, which organized life around Greco-Roman civil religion." It would not be wrong to say that the Roman way is a secular version of Christendom. By the second, he refers to the "Jewish way." Although "Jews were far more integrated into Roman society than it might at first appear," they were also separated from Roman society because they observed a way of life that set them culturally apart (the rite of circumcision, Jewish kosher laws, etc.).[64]

---

project due to his shortened life. It does not seem to be McBride's priority, though, to advance further the political theological significance of religionless Christianity, although she appropriates its concept.

64. Sittser, *Resilient Faith*, 2, 3.

What, then, is the Third Way? Early Christians appeared to live like everyone else. For instance, "they spoke the local language, lived in local neighborhoods, wore local styles of clothing, ate local food, shopped in local markets, and followed local customs." Yet, according to Sittser, "they were different, too, embodying not simply a different religion but a different—and new—way of life."[65] How specifically different was their way of life? Sittser answers this question as follows: "Christians believed in the reality of another and greater kingdom over which God ruled. It was a spiritual kingdom—not *of* this world, but certainly *over* this world as superior and supreme, *for* this world's redemption, and *in* this world as a force for ultimate and eternal good. Far from being 'resident aliens,' Christians thus viewed themselves as 'alien residents,' members of the true and universal commonwealth, but still living within the Roman commonwealth."[66] The most significant aspect of the Third Way of the early church lies in two elements: first, the genuine and compassionate care of the "least of these," and second, early Christians' presence and active participation in the public space. We should note that early Christians were known as the people who genuinely cared for the "least of these." This was contrasted with the Roman social system, especially Rome's patronage system and culture of honor and shame.[67] For instance, early Christians' practice of hospitality was distinguished from that of Greeks and Romans, in that early Christians "offer[ed] a generous welcome to the 'least' without concern for advantage or benefit to the host."[68] Paul fleshes out Jesus's subversive call for the "least of these" with his radical theological catchphrase in Galatians 3:28: "There is no longer Jew or Greek, there is no longer slave or free, there is no longer male and female; for all of you are one in Christ Jesus." Without a doubt, these words are already impregnated with certain political-theological visions that I elaborate in this book by introducing such ideas as nomadic thinking, rhizomatic politics, rhizome organizers, the public church, and so on. It is my contention that the reality of this vision may be

---

65. Sittser, 3, 4.

66. Sittser, 4.

67. Sittser, 176.

68. Christine D. Pohl, *Making Room: Recovering Hospitality as a Christian Tradition* (Grand Rapids, MI: Eerdmans, 1999), 16.

fully carried out only when "the last will be first, and the first will be last" (Matt 20:16).

Early Christians' active presence and participation in the public space is best exemplified by their involvement in "communal reading and recitation events." According to Brian J. Wright, "Communal reading events were a widespread phenomenon in the Roman Empire during the first century CE."[69] The author of 1 Timothy instructs the recipient of his letter to prioritize the communal reading of Scripture: "Devote yourself to the public reading of Scripture" (1 Tim 4:13 NIV).[70] Where did communal reading events take place? Wright holds that there were many locations throughout the Roman Empire, and some possible locations include "a village market place, an assembly hall, a reception hall, a synagogue, a theater, the house of a poor person, the house of an elite person, an urban tenement building, or out in an open space between villages."[71] Perhaps we can interpret early Christians' active participation in the public space as the early church's central mission to become the public body of Christ, where the event of the "Word becoming flesh" is to be continually renewed. Indeed, early Christians' active participation in the social setting, such as communal reading events, shows us that early Christians expressed their faith in a public space. Why does this matter? The fact that the early church of the apostolic age practiced the Third Way by showing special care to the least members of society as well as by actively participating in the public space signifies that we find an original archetype of the idea of the public church in the early church of the apostolic age.

CONCLUSION

We have not only examined the importance of community organizing for the church's rhizomatic politics but also explored the historical-theological foundation of a public church. In doing so, I attempt to finish the unfinished project of Bonhoeffer's "religionless Christianity." The idea of religionless

---

69. Brian J. Wright, *Communal Reading in the Time of Jesus: A Window into Early Christian Reading Practices* (Minneapolis: Fortress, 2017), 207.

70. Wright, 1.

71. Wright, 47.

Christianity, as McBride demonstrates, calls for the dismantlement of the theological triumphalism of an ecclesial Christendom. The idea of religionless Christianity, as I have uncovered, also calls for the church to become a public church in a post-Christendom era by modeling after the public ministry of the early church of the apostolic age. As Gerald L. Sittser points out, "We learned church history from a Christendom perspective. . . . We studied it as a kind of history of the Christian family, which was *our* family."[72] It is our task, then, to unlearn the old lessons of a Christendom perspective. Of course, the purpose of unlearning is to replace the old lessons with the new ones. I argued at the beginning of this book that the Western church should first reckon with its historical sin of colonial complicity. When the church finishes this belated work in full, it may reestablish itself as a public church whose origin goes back to the early church of the apostolic age. The future of the Western church lies in becoming a public church, and the church's rhizomatic politics is a vital aspect of this transformation.

---

72. Sittser, *Resilient Faith*, 15.

CONCLUSION

In this book, I formulate the argument that for a church to become the church it is called to be in an age of rising structural injustice and systemic violence, it should become a public church by practicing its distinctive type of ecclesial politics—rhizomatic politics. The purpose of this politics is not for seeking hegemony but for addressing the structural injustice and systemic violence of this world. There are numerous types of politics, and the church's "rhizomatic politics" is distinguished from other types, such as the state's power politics or biopolitics, that can be categorized as "arborescent." It is not accidental that the Western church seems largely quiet about, unresponsive to, and even indifferent to the various kinds of structural injustice and systemic violence in this world. As seen above, there is a much deeper historical and theological reason behind its apparent ecclesial quiescence to such issues. I discovered that this endemic symptom of the Western church has intrinsically to do with its agelong habitual thinking mechanism, which I call its "territorial thinking." The birth of the church's territorial thinking and its swift propagation during the colonial period were never incidental; they were, rather, inevitable outcomes of the Western church's decontextual approach to political theology, especially Augustinian political theology. Combined with the rise of Western secularization, the Western church during the colonial period settled itself by having recourse to a new defensive mechanism—territorial thinking. The church's territorial thinking has become a convenient yet self-destructive sickening habit to the church itself, and this paralytic thinking mechanism has become even more deadly as the twenty-first century global society is increasingly affected, reshaped, and even colonized by rising neoliberalism, from the economy to politics, from culture to technology.

The Western church has long overlooked its overdue homework. History teaches us that without finishing it, the church may not move on because it cannot become itself for failing to fulfill its intrinsic mission to become the body of Christ in this world. During my research for this book project, I realized that there is a deep-rooted correlation between the European church's complicity in colonialism and the contemporary church's ineptitude regarding the problems of structural injustice and systemic violence. I also came to the sense that the church's historical sin of colonial complicity must be named and reckoned with no matter how long it takes to finish the entire process. Indeed, it may take the whole village for the church to finish this deferred work. One of the goals of this book is to show how the church can dismantle its agelong habitual way of looking at the world and itself (territorial thinking) by introducing a new way of thinking (nomadic thinking). Nomadic thinking is designed for the fundamental and structural change of the church's engagement in the world, especially its response to the structural injustice and systemic violence of this world. From the perspective of nomadic thinking, the basic paradigm of the church's political theology is reformatted from the traditional "church and state" approach to a new formality of the "church versus structural injustice" approach. Additionally, from the perspective of nomadic thinking, the space called "public" becomes indispensable because we can only verify the church's genuine work of reckoning with its historical sin in that public place rather than within the church. The public ought to be a space where people anticipate the coming of the kingdom of God with hope and patience. In this respect, it is not too much to say that the public is a new sacred space for the church's ministry of justice and peace.

For the church to become a rightful agency of the kingdom of God in the public, its political engagement is inevitable (because structural injustice and systemic violence seem endemic in this world), and I illustrate the distinctive type of this politics as a rhizomatic politics by appropriating the biological (botanical) notion of a rhizome. It is one of this book's fundamental contentions that the church's distinctive politics should be rhizomatic rather than arborescent. This positioning is not arbitrary; it is, rather, theological at the core. One needs to be reminded that I adopted the term *nomadic* not in the sense of being random or wayward but in the sense of nomos and deterritorial movement, whose origins I discover in Scripture. The idea of the church's rhizomatic politics is nothing new at all because it originates in the early church of the apostolic age. The early church of the apostolic age was truly deterritorial from its beginning, as it was deeply rooted in Jesus's words and acts. With numerous myth-busting parables and wondrous acts of healings, Jesus not only exemplified the life of a nomad but also practiced the archetypical rhizomatic politics with his disciples and followers. By mirroring and transmitting Jesus's words and acts, the early church of the apostolic age practiced its distinctive politics for the lost and the "least of these."

One of the essential aspects that composes the church's rhizomatic politics is none other than particular types of leaders whom I identify as rhizome organizers or community organizers. To illustrate who they are and how they practice their rhizomatic politics, I conducted in-depth conversations with selected church leaders whom I identify as rhizome organizers. In my interviews, I realized once again the importance of theology. These rhizome organizers were certainly able to lay out and articulate their theologies; what struck me the most, however, lay in the fact that they were able to live out their theologies without losing hope for justice and faith in humanity despite systemic obstacles and political challenges. It is not a cliché to say that theology matters, and in this regard, the church must teach theology and practice it. What does it mean for the church to teach theology? It means that the church becomes the good news itself for those who are desperately in need of it in this broken world. It is the church's main business to live out this sacred call because it is the body of Christ.

INDEX